Driving Down Russia's Spine

DRIVING DOWN RUSSIA'S SPINE

Tracking the Russian soul from the Arctic to the Black Sea

Paul E. Richardson

Russian Life
BOOKS

Contents

PART TWO

From St. Petersburg to Moscow

PART THREE

Russia's Belly

PART FOUR
The South

Barents Sea
Kirkenes
Murmansk
Nikel
258
NORWAY
Kirovsk
Monchegorsk
Apatity
Kandalaksha
White Sea
RUS
Medvezhegorsk
Povenets
SWEDEN
1825
Lake Onega
FINLAND
Kinerma
Petrozavodsk
Novaya Ladoga
Lake Ladoga
Staraya Ladoga
2445
St. Petersburg
Krasniye Sta
Veliky Novgorod
Valdai
2720
Krestsy
Torzho
ESTONIA
LATVIA
Baltic Sea
LITHUANIA
BELARUS
POLAND
GERMANY

The Spine of Russia
Map of the route, with towns visited
and trip odometer distances (kilometers)
Scale: 1 inch equals approximately 500km
KAZAKHSTAN
Caspian Sea
ow
Yelets
Voronezh
Livny
4620
Taganrog
Sea of
Azov
Krymsk
Krasnodar
Anapa
5641
Sochi
Novorossiysk
GEORGIA
ARMENIA
CRIMEA
Black Sea
TURKEY

In art, just as in life, nothing happens by chance.

– Anton Chekhov

Introduction

Nadya and I wait in the car as Mikhail disappears out of sight down the side of the hill, camera in hand.

We are in the middle of nowhere and, in the eerie silence surrounded by the opaline Arctic landscape, Nadya makes an unexpected observation from the back seat.

"This is just like the beginning of a horror movie," she says.

I laugh nervously.

"But I'm not worried," she continues, "because the pretty girl always survives in the end."

It was not the beginning of a horror movie, but the start of a 6,000-kilometer road trip from Russia's northernmost border with Norway to its southern tip on the Black Sea.

Our month-long trip, dubbed "The Spine of Russia," took us straight through the Russian heartland, home to more than half of the country's residents. The itinerary was ludicrously ambitious:

travel across the full breadth of Russia in 30 days, doing quality photography and in-depth interviews along the way, aiming to collect human stories that showed a more subtle, complex picture of Russia – the country that is fast again becoming the United States' main global adversary – to be published in an eponymous, bilingual 200-page coffee table book, *The Spine of Russia*.

How hard could that be?

Not hard enough. Let's kick it up a notch.

The trip must cost nothing out of pocket, sponsors must be found to provide in-kind donations, and you must travel in close quarters for a month with someone you have never before met in person.

And it must be done during the worst downturn in East-West relations since the end of the Cold War.

Check, check, and double check!

THE IDEA FOR The Spine of Russia project began to gel in January 2015. I had been toying with the concept of an epic journey through Russia for over a year, but nothing quite grabbed me. Then, while editing a story by Nicky Gardner for *Russian Life* about the Murman coast, I learned about the E105. It is a single, continuous road that runs from Russia's northernmost border to the shores of the Black Sea, in Crimea. I had found what I was looking for. The project proposal almost wrote itself:

> Everyone knows about the Trans-Siberian, the 9300-kilometer, east-west vein of steel that transects Russia and Siberia, binding the multi-national, multi-temporal Russian Federation into a more or less governable whole.

Yet there is another significant Russian artery (this one running north-south) that has yet to be explored as such: the unglamorously named E105.

Next, I had to find someone crazy enough to make the trip with me, yet sane enough that I could feel safe with them behind the wheel or sleeping in the next bunk. I asked our editor in Moscow, Maria Antonova, about this fellow Mikhail Mordasov, whose excellent photo features we had run in *Russian Life*. He seemed to get around quite a bit to rather exotic places (crazy), yet he was educated as a lawyer and had worked for reputable media outlets (sane). She recommended Mikhail highly and thought he would be just fine to travel with. So I fired off an email.

> I have what may be a crazy idea, but also a very interesting one. The idea is to travel by car the entire length of the E105 through Russia… it is a route with very interesting historical points, from Murmansk to Klin, Novgorod, Kursk, etc., and of course Moscow and St. Petersburg. It is also very interesting from a modern perspective.
>
> It would be a fascinating look at modern Russia for our readers, but it would be even more interesting to our readers if the trip was done by a Russian and American photojournalist together. I really like your photojournalism work, and Maria highly recommends you.

Mikhail was as taken with the idea as I was, and in the months that followed, we got acquainted over email, fleshed out the idea in greater detail, and began researching the cities and towns along the way.

The financing piece came together through Kickstarter. Our company had done crowdfunding before, in fact just as this idea was taking shape, *Russian Life* was successfully completing a Kickstarter to fund *Red Star Tales*, the translation of a 400-page volume of 100 years worth of Russian and Soviet science fiction (published in November 2015).

The Spine of Russia funding campaign ran through the month of July 2015 and surprised both of us by not only reaching its target, but also surpassing a stretch goal that required us to make the book bilingual. The excitement of our successful funding, however, was immediately tempered by the reality of the calendar.

Since the trip began in the Arctic, and we didn't want to do it in snow and ice, we needed to begin in late summer or early fall. That was just weeks away. We had been preparing and researching things since January, but now all of a sudden time was horrifically compressed. In early August we gritted our teeth and tentatively set a start date of September 15, unclear how we would get everything done that needed doing in just five or six weeks.

Mikhail got to work rounding up sponsors and, before long, was able to secure key support from Volkswagen, Nikon and Azimut Hotels. Our pre-trip checklist was all but finished.

Then, in mid-August, Mikhail was offered a contract photography job he could not pass up. The problem was, it would occupy 110 percent of his time through early October. I could feel the Arctic chills of late fall enter my bones, yet I advised him to take the job. Bird in the hand and all that. We reset our start date to early October.

PART ONE

The North

The Road to Kirkenes

October 7, 2015, was the 63rd birthday of Russian President Vladimir Putin. But, for Mikhail and me, that was neither here nor there, because while the president was busy celebrating by playing an exhibition hockey match pitting Russian hockey stars against bureaucrats, we were working on getting ourselves to our journey's starting point: Kirkenes, Norway, the start of the E105.

Just a dozen kilometers from the border with Russia, Kirkenes is the top of the inhabited world, and getting there was a journey in and of itself. On October 7, Mikhail and I were almost on opposite sides of the globe – I was in Vermont, and he was on Lake Baikal. That put each of us about 4,000 kilometers from Kirkenes as the crow flies.

But there was no crow-flying for Mikhail. First there was a train to Krasnoyarsk, then a jet to Moscow. There, he picked up our official Spine of Russia vehicle, a golden Volkswagen Polo, which he and his wife Nadya then drove the 2,000 kilometers north to Murmansk.

I had it a bit easier. I flew from Boston via Reykjavik to Oslo, where I hung out for two days, trying not to feel guilty about all the driving Mikhail and Nadya were doing.

On October 8, I spent most of the day walking the city, forcing myself onto the local time zone, oblivious to the fact that Belarusan writer Svetlana Alexievich had on this day, in this very city, been announced the winner of the 2015 Nobel Prize for Literature. Notably, exactly 45 years earlier, on October 8, 1970, in Oslo, Aleksandr Solzhenitsyn was announced as the winner of that year's Nobel Prize for Literature.

OSLO, I AM told, is the sort of city where everyone you meet is from somewhere else. It can be very hard, they say, to find a native of Oslo. Yet apparently everyone in Norway wants to live here, making it the fastest-growing city in Europe, about a quarter of which is immigrant.

Perhaps it is because the city has a friendly multiculturalism. Mosques and Protestant churches stand near one another; Pakistani bakeries perch across the way from Indian restaurants; exotic communes are parked a stone's throw from posh apartment complexes ("we have no ghettos here," asserts my host Marcy, herself an expat from the Netherlands); crime seems low, and there is no significant police presence on the streets.

Even my short stay, allowed me to pick up on the profound civility of this city of 600,000 (closer to a million, or about a fifth of the country's population, when one includes the suburbs). What few cars there are on the wide, clean streets stop for pedestrians at un-signaled crosswalks. Everyone seems eager to help a tourist who is directionally challenged by the fact that no street seems to go straight for more than 100 yards. Even the beggars are uncommonly polite.

Oslo is not a beautiful city in the same sense that Paris or San Francisco are beautiful. But it is tidier than Paris and better-organized and less crowded than San Francisco (and more expensive in the bargain). There is ample green space and little tolerance, so it seems, for trashiness. Unlike, say, Naples or Rome, there is only modest tagging and graffiti, which is well drowned out by whimsical flourishes of street art and attractive murals that cover entire sides of buildings. Nothing lightens up a kid's playground like a huge mural with ravenous piranhas!

DESPITE NORWAY'S PROXIMITY to Russia, there is no evidence of any Russian influence here. Well, except the fact that Russia had invaded and occupied the country three days before my arrival, and average Norwegians were being forced to choose between collaboration and resistance.

Oh, right, that was just the TV show, *Occupied*, based on a novel by Jo Nesbo, which debuted here a few days before my arrival. Its premise was that a Green government had come to power in Norway and turned off the oil and gas taps to Europe, so Europe had no other option but to ask Russia to invade.

As a Russian friend likes to say, "Logical, but harmful…"

Television notwithstanding, Norway has a rather complex recent history with Russia.

Tsarist Russia was one of the first countries to recognize Norway in 1905, after the Scandinavian nation had finally gained its independence from Sweden (a longtime rival with Russia in the Baltic). Yet the Norwegian monarchy was certainly no friend to the Bolsheviks, and in 1920 about 1,000 White Russians escaped to Norway from northern Russia aboard an icebreaker, eventually settling in Lillehammer and Oslo. A little over a decade later, Leon Trotsky wrote *The Revolution Betrayed* while in exile in Norway.

The country's northern regions were liberated from Nazi occupation by Soviet troops in World War II, yet Norway became a front line

NATO nation for the entirety of the Cold War, one of only two of that bloc's nations (the other being Turkey) that shared a border with the USSR. Border and environmental disputes between the two countries simmered through the remainder of the twentieth century.

Meanwhile, what Russian émigré presence there was in the capital dissipated (there are only about 3,000 Russians left in Oslo). There is a Russian Orthodox church on the outskirts that, reports indicate, has struggled in recent decades to maintain its "Russianness." And an advertised Russian restaurant in the city center turned out to have either gone out of business or never existed.

Today, Norwegian public opinion as a whole is staunchly anti-Russian. A 2014 Gallup survey of 41 countries found that Norwegians were the nation most negatively disposed toward the Russian leadership, with 89 percent disapproving.[1] The key factor influencing this disposition has been events in Ukraine, before which, experts said, Norwegians actually tended to be a moderately well-disposed toward Russia.

As a graphic reflection of this trend, in September Norway took delivery of the first of 52 US-made F-35 fighters that it sees as critical for ensuring the state's future security in a world where, according to Norwegian Defense Minister Ine Marie Eriksen Søreide, "Russia has shown both the ability and willingness to use military force to achieve its strategic objectives."[2]

DESPITE ALL THIS, often when walking down random side streets, I encountered blocks of buildings that seemed lifted directly from St. Petersburg: stolid, pastel-colored neoclassical buildings of granite or other stone, with three or four stories of large windows (and *fortochkas*, little ventilation windows typical of Russia). But of course these were merely samples of a style of architecture that took root throughout the Scandinavian region in the eighteenth century.

In Petersburg it is probably more characteristic, since the city was built from scratch at that time. Here, there is a more eclectic collection of styles, both old and new, including of course some very modern buildings that make great use of the city's waterfront (e.g., the Opera House and hip Tjuvholmen district).

Maybe it is the architectural echoes, but I can't help having the sense that Norway is what northern bits of Russia might be like if it had (a) taken part in the Renaissance and Reformation, and (b) skipped the Revolution. Those are three pretty big Rs, but their absence or presence have shaped the face of Modern Russia, even down to its architecture.

The fact is, Norwegians and Russians are both northern peoples. And the ancient Russian chronicles have it that Rurik, who was asked to come rule over the disputatious Rus – Finnic and Slavic tribes – in 862, was Varangian, i.e., Scandinavian.

But of course a lot has happened (or not) since 862.

Quirkiness

It is a drizzly Sunday morning when Mikhail and I finally meet face-to-face in downtown Kirkenes. He has taken the bus over from Murmansk, and we stash his stuff at our AirBnB lodging before exploring the town together. We walk much of it in about an hour and, after a bite of lunch, return to our house, where I dig in to writing a blog post.

Paul: I'm not really forming a distinct impression of Kirkenes.

Mikhail: I have an impression. A *very distinct* impression.

Paul: Yes?

Mikhail: Empty! Kirkenes is an *absolutely empty* town.

Now, to be fair to Kirkenes (which, for some reason, spell-check keeps wanting to change to Quirkiness), it *was* Sunday, and, like much of Europe, shops, restaurants and bars here are shuttered on the Christian Sabbath.

On the other hand, few people were working in gardens, or strolling with their dogs or children. It was eerily quiet, even for a northern European town in October. On Saturday, there had been a bit more bustle, but even so, by late in the day the streets emptied out as if in anticipation of something. Sunday, apparently.

NORTHERN IS CERTAINLY an impression this quirky town leaves you with. The rocky, extra-planetary Arctic landscape, and the inlets, bays, fjords and lakes surrounding the town are stunning. And the light here – there is no light like the light in the Far North. The Golden Hour before sunset seems to last three or four hours. And two nights of brilliant off-season Northern Lights were an unexpected bonus.

But in all honesty, Kirkenes is not in any way attractive in the normal sense of the word. Yet it is appealing in its profound utilitarianism, its orderliness and compactness. ~~Quirkiness~~ Kirkenes is stolid.

And no wonder on any of these points. Aside from the fact that this is a Norwegian working town (mining, shipbuilding), it was raised from the ground up 70 years ago, having been obliterated during World War II.

Kirkenes, says Thomas Nilsen, editor of *The Independent Barents Observer*, endured the largest deployment of German troops in Norway during the war – 100,000 in all. They were part of the Operation Silver Fox forces that were to take Murmansk (which never happened, though Murmansk was, as a result, destroyed on a scale only exceeded by Stalingrad). This turned the town into a major Allied target and made Kirkenes, Nilsen says, "the second most bombed city in Europe during the war… just eight buildings survived the bombing and the Germans' scorched earth policy when they evacuated."

Soviet troops finally entered the devastated town on October 25, 1944. Because of the brutal fighting to liberate the region, Nilsen says, "more Russians died on Norwegian soil during the War than did Norwegians – this is something people should be reminded about."

A monument to the liberating Soviet troops stands on a hill overlooking the town, and that liberation is certainly part of the reason there are such warm feelings toward Russia here. Also the fact that this is one of the few places in Europe that Soviet troops de-occupied voluntarily after the war.

Another reason? The shopping. Or more properly, the shopping that went on before the 2014-15 ruble implosion (set off by falling oil prices and sanctions). Nilsen lists off four pillars that he says support the local economy: the local iron mine, marine repair works, winter tourism, and Russian shoppers. Since the 1990s there has been a thriving cross-border shopping trade from as far away as Murmansk (225 kilometers). But, again, that has dropped off over the past year and, Nilsen notes, is one reason that things were so quiet, even on Saturday. "Normally, before the crash," he says, "the downtown and the two malls would be very busy." Retail trade in Kirkenes in the good times was 3-4 times what one would normally see in a town of 10,000.

THE RUSSIAN-NORWEGIAN BORDER is just 196 kilometers long. Formed in 1826, it is one of the youngest borders in Europe, but also one of the few that has not changed in nearly 200 years of otherwise tumultuous history.

It may be Russia's most peaceful border, but not as you'd know it. "No place else in the world," says Nilsen, "has more deployed strategic nuclear weapons." Nilsen is something of an expert on the subject. He asserts that Russia, limited by the START treaty, has been swapping land-based nuclear capacity for sub-based weaponry in the region – part of Russia's turn to the Arctic.

Still, the "New Cold War" has not touched this town that is nearly as northerly as Point Barrow, Alaska, and as easterly as Istanbul. Strong pro-Russian feelings remain (counter to the trend in Norway as a whole); local street signs are often in both Norwegian and Russian; any shopkeeper or waitress worth their salt can speak some Russian; many Russians live here as expats, and many others work here long-term; there is plenty of cross-border travel (350,000+ crossings in 2014), albeit mostly in the Westerly direction (a Norwegian-Russian compact allows anyone living within 30 kilometers of the border on either side to travel visa-free to and from the other country). It is estimated that 5-10 percent of the locals are Russians or of Russian extraction.

What is more, this trend seems to have colored the future. "The first generation of Russian-Norwegians [the children of marriages made in the 1990s] is just coming of age," Nilsen says. "They have grown up bilingual and travel there frequently. This is good for our region, for future trade and business."

On the eve of our entry into Russia, we visit one of the few Kirkenes restaurants open on Sunday night and order a large pizza. It is a pie of truly massive proportions, and we are torn between prudence (eating only our fill) and economy (this being Norway, it is a very expensive pizza, and we don't want any of it to go to waste). Thankfully, prudence wins out. Mostly.

Russia's Arctic Back Door

We had been planning our trip for months, yet we were not certain until 12 hours beforehand how, exactly, we were going to get into Russia.

Volkswagen generously donated to our expedition the use of a new Polo. The only problem was that the car's papers did not allow it to make the short jaunt over the border into Norway to pick up its passengers.

So, we thought, perhaps we can take a Norwegian cab the 12 kilometers from Kirkenes to the border, then walk across to the other side, where our Polo will be waiting for us?

Nyet.

The Norwegian and Russian border checkpoints (Storskog and Borisoglebsky, respectively) on the E105 are separated by about 200 meters of "no man's land." Regulations specify that one cannot traverse this 200 meters on foot. One must be in a vehicle. Even if one had a vehicle, say a bike, to ride across this short stretch, it is another 10 kilometers from the eastern, Russian checkpoint to the Russian side of the "exclusion zone," (and still further to the edge of the Greater Exclusion Zone) inside of which it is forbidden to go on foot or stop a car.

The solution, it turns out, is Russian-simple. We put in a call to a recommended cab service based in Nikel, the Russian town nearest the border, and agree to pay $40 for a taxi (which has the proper papers) to drive to Kirkenes and shuttle us over the border. There, Mikhail's long-suffering wife Nadya will be waiting for us just outside the exclusion zone, at a makeshift Russian park-n-ride, having driven the Polo up that morning from Murmansk.

Truth be told, we did consider riding bicycles across the 200-meter stretch from Norway to Russia. Heaven knows, there were plenty of bikes at the border, left behind by the Syrian tide flowing through this newly-discovered, frigid back door into Europe's Schengen Zone. In the month or so leading up to our trip, war refugees from the Middle East began flying or training from Moscow to Murmansk, then paying traffickers to get them up to the Russo-Norwegian border.

In fact, our cab driver, Alexander, says that the entire Murmansk region has been emptied of bikes in this new human trafficking slash emigration crisis. Fixers bring the bikes – still in their shipping boxes – to the afore-mentioned park-n-ride, where shuttle buses wait for Syrians driving up from Murmansk to pair them with.

The current going rate for a "package deal" of transport from Murmansk to the border, bike included? About $1200 per person.

Our driver laughs as he recounts the story of how one young Syrian boy was so happy with his new bike that he didn't just ride straight through the 200-meter transit zone, but started zipping around in circles, evading frustrated guards and causing a general ruckus. Good for him.

We think of how our 200-meter ride could be a sign of solidarity with the 100-200 Syrians who are crossing the border in the other direction each day. But our idea goes nowhere, because the bikes are not available for our use. They are collected on the Norwegian side and loaded into a truck for transport to a demolition site (much to the consternation of Norwegian locals, who wonder why they can't be donated to a worthy cause). The bikes, it turns out, do not meet Norwegian safety standards and it is cheaper to simply destroy them than, say, bring them up to standards and donate them to a local charity.

WE PASS OVER the border more or less quickly. Well, Mikhail does, anyway. My appearance sticks a wrench in the spokes.

The almost genial border guard seems a bit thrown that an American has shown up at an outpost only accustomed to Norwegians, Russians and Syrians.

I remind myself what a helpful soul in a Position of Knowing intimated a month prior to our departure: that I should not use the word "journalist" when it was not necessary. Which it rarely is.

"You neglected to fill out the 'places to be visited' section on the migration form," my new friend notes, handing the form back to me.

I had done this on purpose, because the space provided on the form was about twice the width of my pencil nub. We will be visiting at least a dozen cities and even more small towns, so I didn't know what to put down. Also, my handwriting is atrocious.

"Where will you be staying tonight?" he asks helpfully.

"In a hotel."

I receive the blank stare taught to border guards the world over for dealing with foreign morons. His raised eyebrow communicates volumes.

I write down Murmansk. Then, for good measure, I squeeze in Moscow. Sochi spills over to the right-hand sheet.

"So, you will be going to Murmansk, Moscow and Sochi?" he asks, a faintly mocking tone slip-sliding between his words.

"Those are the beginning, mid- and end-point cities of our trip, yes."

No reply. I watch as he leafs through my passport page by page, or at least that's what it sounds like he is doing, because of course I cannot see his hands.

He calls over what I assume to be a supervisor. They speak quietly and there is nodding in my general direction. The supervisor, just in from outside and still wearing his overcoat and hat, rushes off. The leafing through pages resumes.

I turn to the line of truck drivers piling up behind me and apologize for gumming up the wheels of commerce. They reply with stares that are pale, Norwegian reflections of the border guard's.

All of a sudden, the supervisor returns, rushing at me with the urgency of an arresting officer, having discarded his coat and combed his hat hair. He is about 5' 3", dressed in black from his tie to his boots, but wears no uniform. He might be 22.

"As I understand it, you speak Russian," he says. A statement, not a question.

I have indeed been speaking to my buddy the border guard entirely in Russian, given that it is the mother tongue here, even though years of experience have demonstrated to me that speaking only English and playing dumb often gets things like this solved more easily.

"Да." (Yes.)

"And what is the purpose of your visit?"

"We're making a book. Traveling the length of Russia, collecting images and stories about Russia to share with the world" (I am careful to avoid The Word Which Shall Not Be Spoken).

"And where will you be stopping?"

I almost blurt out, "in hotels," but think better of it. "In many places. We start in Murmansk and end in Sochi a month later."

"And which car is yours?"

I describe our cab driver Alexander's Toyota, but the border guard talks over me and describes it better.

The black knight nods knowingly and strides back to his office.

I turn back to the border guard, who is now comparing me carefully with my passport picture and – this is the first time I have seen this in my 20+ years of traveling here – he squinches an ocular magnifying glass into his eye socket and holds the other end flat up against the security imprint on my visa.

Seriously? Is Russian visa forgery a thing?

I look out the windows, glance to the left and right, pretending to read this or that, so as not to leave a guilt-ridden impression on whatever is or is not recording me at that moment.

Then, suddenly, I hear the longed-for *ka-chunk* of the entry stamp. I step outside, half expecting several black-clad inspectors to have the contents of our bags strewn about on the pavement around our car, asking about the varieties of embargoed cheeses that Mikhail picked up at the Kirkenes supermarket early this morning. But there is only Mikhail and Alexander in the car, wondering what took me so long.

"Well?" Mikhail asks as I get in the car.

"No problem, I say. I was careful not to mention that we are journalists."

"Oh," Mikhail replies. "When they asked, I told them we were journalists and we were making a book."

Nikel for Your Thoughts

To say Nikel is dirty or ugly would be an insult to the words. We could also insult grubby, dilapidated, run-down and sad.

Nikel is not a pleasant place.

On our way into town we stop alongside a small lake with some unclassifiable, live birds floating on the surface. From this distance, there is nothing even remotely attractive about Nikel, set as it is into the blackened hills, surrounded by massive, toxic tailing piles, the towers of the nickel refining plant spewing sulfur dioxide into the atmosphere.

OFFICIALLY DESIGNATED AS a "settlement of the municipal variety" (посёлок городского типа), Nikel and its 12,000 residents are located just seven kilometers from the border with Norway, in Russia's Pechenga region. This area originally began to be incorporated into Russia in 1533, after the Novgorod monk Tryphon (now revered as a saint) established a monastery on the Barents Sea. His goal was to evangelize the local Sami Skolts tribe, to show that Christianity could flourish even in the harshest of conditions. And flourish the monastery did. By the time of Tryphon's death, some 250 monks and lay followers were living an ascetic existence along these frigid shores.

Six years later, at the start of the Swedish-Russian War, Finnish troops under Swedish command (Finland then being part of Sweden) decimated the monastery and murdered 116 monks and lay followers. The monastery was moved east and would not be restored in its original location until 1886.

Over the next two centuries, the region remained sparsely settled, largely by Sami and by Pomors who emigrated here from the South. The border began to be established in the first part of the nineteenth century when, in 1809, as the result of the Finnish War between Sweden and Russia, Finland became a principality of the Russian empire. Just over a decade later, in 1826, the 196-kilometer border with Norway was also established.

When the First World War ended and the Russian Empire crumbled, Finland declared its independence, codified in the 1920 Treaty of Tartu, in which Bolshevik Russia ceded much of the Pechenga region (which the Finns called Petsamo) in exchange for two regions in Eastern Karelia.

The following year, prospectors discovered huge deposits of nickel in the Petsamo region, and by the mid-1930s foreign firms were laying plans to mine here, building a railway between the ice-free Finnish harbor of Liinahamari and Kolosjoki (the original, Finnish name for Nikel). Before mining could get underway, however, the Winter War between Russia and Finland (1939-40) intervened, during which Petsamo was occupied by Soviet troops.

After the Winter War, Petsamo was returned to Finland and the first mining began in and around Kolosjoki. For the next four years, the mines supplied the German war machine, until Petsamo was retaken by Soviet Russia. In November 1945, as peace treaties began to codify border changes, the Soviet Union asserted its control over the Pechenga region, with Nikel as its administrative center. Because the industrial base was devastated by the war, mining and refining did not resume until 1946.

Over the past 70 years, the mining complex comprised of the "settlement" of Nikel and the nearby city of Zapolyarny has grown to one of the world's largest copper-nickel mining operations, extracting over 7 million tons of ore per year from four mines. The refining is done at the massive plant in Nikel, which also processes ore shipped in from Norilsk, an even more dismally polluted city in Siberia's Far North. The industrial activity at what is today known as the Kola Mining Metallurgical Company (part of the company Norilsk Nikel) comes at a significant environmental cost, however, spewing an estimated 100,000 tons of sulfur dioxide into the atmosphere each year, according to the company's own data and that of environmental watchdog Bellona.

Throughout 2015, Russia's state environmental agency, Rosprirodnadzor, repeatedly found KMMC to be releasing sulfur dioxide at levels six or even ten times the allowable standard. In April, the pollution level in one day was measured at 12.6 times the maximum allowed SO_2 concentration. For this, KMMC was fined R25,000 rubles, or less than $500.

WE ARE IN Nikel to meet the deputy head of the regional administration for economic development, Alexander Molodtsov, who has what the reality-based among us might call a wild dream. He wants to transform an obscure, Soviet era scientific facility into a tourist attraction.

Fit, compact and sporting a crewnecked sweater and the neatly trimmed beard of a hipster, Molodtsov speaks like a lottery ad disclaimer on speed. Earnest and intelligent, he was born in Grozny (yes, that Grozny, capital of Chechnya), lived in Moscow, worked as a consultant, and about a year ago was recruited to serve in this hardship outpost. He is a new breed of consultant cum apparatchik, young and flush with hard-nosed enthusiasm to make his country a better place.

His idea is at once simple and ludicrous. He wants to turn the Kola Super Deep Borehole (Кольская сверхглубокая скважина) into something people will travel from all over the world to see.

"This place is comparable to what CERN might be in 30 years," Molodtsov says, referring to the laboratory outside Geneva, Switzerland where 2500 employees oversee the Large Hadron Collider and other physics laboratories. "We expect to sign an agreement in the coming days and turn it into a tourist complex… In principle, it will not take that much investment. As you will see when you go there, one building is in very good condition. We just need to slap in some windows and we can have an information center, a museum about the Borehole, etc… The former head engineer has an excellent collection of historical materials."

When asked if it is realistic to think that people will travel hundreds of miles to breathe toxic air and contemplate a seven-mile foot hole in the ground (admittedly, the question was stated more diplomatically), Molodtsov seems to not recognize the challenge. "There is lots of international interest," he says. "Recently a German artist came all the way over here especially to see just this."

"It's also the source of lots of urban legends," Molodtsov says, for the first time cracking a smile. "Surely you have heard about the myth how they dropped a microphone down the well and heard the sounds of screaming in Hell?"

Okay, now we are interested.

DRILLING OF THE Kola Super Deep Borehole was begun in 1970 on the 100th anniversary of Lenin's birth (because nothing says "we love you" like a borehole). It reached a maximum depth of 12,262 meters (7.6 miles) in 1990 and soon thereafter funding ran out. The purpose of the hole was entirely scientific, and the project was launched at this location because it represented the shortest distance to the point where the Earth's mantle and crust were separated by the Mohorovicic discontinuity. Translated into lay language, the goal was to drill as deeply as possible into the Earth's crust.

As it turns out, drilling also had to stop in 1990 because the temperature at the bottom of the well was almost twice as high as expected, and the drill bits stopped working.

The site delivered much useful scientific information for geologists and physicists (little beyond the four kilometer drilling mark was as expected) but if anyone in the non-scientific world knows about the Borehole it is likely because of the urban legend known as The Well to Hell.

It began life as the sort of harmlessly bogus story one might expect to read in an obscure Finnish evangelical newspaper, because that is exactly where it began (its editors claiming they sourced it from a newsletter of messianic Jews in California). For some reason, the tale was then picked up by the Trinity Broadcast Network (see Pat Robertson) in the US, whence it bounced to mainstream media and the ever credulous internet.

The story goes like this: A group of Russians, led by a Mr. Azzacov [sic] drilled a 9-mile-deep [sic] well somewhere in Siberia [sic], whence the hole broke through to a cavity of some sort where the temperature was 2,000° F [sic]. So, of course their first thought was to drop a heat-tolerant microphone into the Borehole. Lo and behold, what did they hear but the tormented screams of the damned [sic?]. A recording subsequently circulated that was later found to be a loop track for a 1970s horror flick.

But the best part is that a Norwegian teacher, Åge Rendalen, saw the story when visiting the US and decided to have a bit of fun at the expense of mass gullibility (those crazy Norge). He wrote to TBN, claiming that he had additional information about the story, confabulating a tale about a bat-like apparition that escaped from the mine just before the microphone was lowered down the hole.

TBN re-reported the story with Rendalen's colorful addition, not bothering to follow up and check on the false sources he provided.

In reality, as disclosed by David Guberman, the Borehole's last director, in 1995, the year the operation was closed down, there was an inexplicable incident of a strange explosion after hearing sounds of unknown provenance.

"When, at UNESCO, they asked me about that curious event, I didn't know how to answer," Guberman reported to the Russian edition of *Popular Mechanics*. "On the one hand, it was damn nonsense. On the other, as an honest scientist, I could not say that I did not have any idea what happened in our facility. A very strange sound was recorded, then there was an explosion... nothing was discovered about it over the next several days."[3]

MOLODTSOV HAS ANOTHER meeting, so he can't accompany us to the Borehole, but his wife Liza is kind enough to provide us with detailed instructions, given the fact that the roads are not on any map, not even Google Maps.

Liza begins inscribing directions in my notepad. They begin with a turn down a nameless road just before a "rather disturbing" billboard and end with a "sharp right turn when you are surrounded by massive tailing mountains." She notes down several interchanges, separated by the estimated time to travel between them.

"How long to get there?" the intrepid adventurers ask.

"About 20 minutes," Liza says, "40 for non-locals."

Her estimate proves to be wildly optimistic on either count. And, in any event, we need to first visit a hairdresser.

The Hairdresser

Lena Kolesnik is the proprietor of a bright, cheery hairdressing salon on Nikel's main drag, just down the street from the central square and its requisite Lenin monument. Easy going with a ready smile, she bounces between very delicate, close work on an elderly woman's manicure, answering the phone to set appointments, and upselling a second client on her solarium's new lamps.

Kolesnik has been running her salon for 12 years. She started it simply as a small business, but then it turned out she liked the people side of things, getting to know her clients, gossiping and talking to them about local news. When asked about the greatest difficulties of running a small business in Russia, she does not decry red tape, corruption or government oversight.

"There are simply not enough specialists," she complains with a sunny smile. "I can't find a hairdresser or a masseuse. You see that 'Help Wanted' sign in the window? It's been there four months, and I have had exactly one person walk through the door."

No one wants to take the time to get good training, Kolesnik says, and then put their new talents to use in Nikel. All the young people leave town for Murmansk or points south. She's had employees in the past, she says, but lately she can't get anyone who is qualified, so she seems resigned to running a one-woman shop.

Not that she doesn't love her work. Her caring and interest in her clients is evident as she gently caresses an elderly client's palm while simultaneously trimming her nails and chatting cheerily with a couple of journalists who have dropped in without notice, claiming to be writing some sort of book about Russia.

We stuck our heads in here as a bit of fact-checking, because Alexander Molodtsov asserted that Norwegians were not just slipping over the border to fill up their SUVs with cheap Nikel gasoline ("Nikel has the cheapest gas in Norway," a Norwegian had joked). Apparently they also come for the inexpensive but quality dentists and hairdressers, and to party in the city's cafes, where the drinks and food are far less expensive.

Kolesnik offers a more sobering picture. For her, the Norge are just a small percent of her business, she says – low single digits. "It used to be more. I used to have a banner hanging up outside, advertising the salon's services in Norwegian, but someone vandalized it, so now we don't get so many Norge."

Why stay? Clearly her skills are transferable, in demand, and Kolesnik could set up shop anywhere.

"Oh, we do think about leaving all the time," she says. "My husband is online every night, looking at homes in Belgorod, where he grew up. It's so beautiful, but they say it's hard to start a business there, more expensive." And, despite the pull to stay put – friends, community and a successful business – they want to leave.

"I want to breathe fresh air, and for my children to do the same," Kolesnik says, smiling.

Hunting the Borehole

We drive past Nikel's belching, mile-long nickel refining plant (why would you need to drill seven miles down to find Hell when it has such a suitable replica right here on the surface?) and climb long roads of blackened earth, met only occasionally by an oncoming semi. Finally, a few kilometers out of town we reach the noted billboard (it is an ad to encourage seatbelt use: a man reaches around and across a woman from behind, as if his arm were a seatbelt, although he could just as easily be assaulting her from behind), and head higher still into the hills.

The first wrong turn takes us to the top of a hill (constructed of massive tailing boulders) where there are stunning views out over the Pasvik Valley (a nature preserve inconceivably located just a few kilometers downwind from the town, along the border with Norway). The smoke from the refinery settles over the valley like a toxic meteorological blanket.

We stop for a few pictures after realizing our error, then backtrack to the Y in the road we missed.

Soon after we climbed out of the town, the road conditions changed significantly. The smooth, crushed-stone secondary road was covered with a crusty, slippery snow that hid potholes and pointed tailing shards alike. Plus of course it was bitterly cold. So we traversed the empty miles in anxious anticipation of a blowout, joking about Liza's overly optimistic directions.

This dampened our enthusiasm somewhat for the starkly beautiful terrain surrounding us, yet when we arrived at the massive tailing mountains (sharp right turn) the human imprint on this desolate, deserted landscape was thrown into mind-blowing relief.

Countless ten-story skyscrapers of boulders loom about us as far as the eye can see in every direction, castoffs from seven decades of digging and hauling from the mine at Zapolyarny. It is difficult to imagine the thousands of massive trucks that delivered their tens of thousands of payloads here, because the valley is silent but for the grind of our little car's engine. There are other tire tracks in the snow, but we do not see another living soul during our long drive in and out of the area, even though we are never more than 15 kilometers as the soot-covered-crow flies from Nikel.

Finally, just as we are beginning to think we will never find the Borehole and are negotiating over how much longer would be considered a "good faith effort" to find it before we turn back, we crest yet another long hill over rutted roads and see a complex of abandoned buildings nestled in the valley below. We cheer, never having expected to be so excited to see a site of industrial and scientific ruin. Then, of course, we stop for photos.

Nadya and I wait in the car as Mikhail disappears out of sight down the side of the hill, camera in hand.

We are in the middle of nowhere and, in the eerie silence surrounded by the opaline Arctic landscape, Nadya makes an unexpected observation from the back seat.

"This is just like the beginning of a horror movie," she says.

I laugh nervously.

"But I'm not worried," she continues, "because the pretty girl always survives in the end."

WE BRAVE THE damp, blowing wind and explore the site. Yes, one main building is more or less standing, as Molodtsov suggested. But to think that all you need to do is slap in a few windows and you have a welcome center seems something many levels of magnitude beyond optimistic. We dodge heaps of twisted metal, disemboweled electronic devices of unknown significance, and a huge porcelain bathtub. The buildings are eerily quiet and empty. There is not even the usual startled fluttering of pigeons, the denizens of every other abandoned and hopeless building the world over.

We spend some time on post-apocalyptic art-photography and root around, trying to locate the site of the actual Borehole. We know it has been covered over and Molodtsov had said it would undetectable, since the tower encasing it was torn down. Still, we search until our fingers are numb and the depressingly shabby surroundings take a toll on our psyches. The place has not gotten to this state by simply falling down for 20 years; scavengers, looters and vandals have clearly been legion.

The journey ends with a cup of hot tea near a small pond adjoining the complex – we don't dare think what sort of heavy metals might have settled into its silt. Then we hastily hop back into our chariot for a sunset drive back to civilization, past gargantuan, man-made mountains, geological reject piles doomed to erode over the centuries in the cold back of nowhere.

Just past the ten-story tailing piles we see a large, black crow soar overhead. It is the only living thing we have seen since leaving Nikel hours before.

BACK ON THE E105, we pass Zapolyarny, Sputnik and other depressingly desolate and remote settlements, all separated by the beautifully stark, Nordic landscape, now lit by an eerie blue and yellow sky.

Several military garrisons are also located along this stretch of the Barents Sea. From 1957 to 1960, Yuri Gagarin, who, on April 12, 1961, became the first human being in space, served in nearby Korzunovo, flying a MiG-15 and defending the Soviet Northern Fleet. Today, Korzunovo is largely deserted, the inscription on the side of one abandoned building reportedly proclaiming that "The Victory of Communism is Inevitable."

By the time we come to the other end of the wider Border Exclusion Zone, darkness has settled in irretrievably. Technically, it should take only about half an hour to drive here from the border, but our stopover in Nikel and the visit to the Borehole lengthened our stay to more like eight hours.

I am in the driver's seat and the guard asks to see our passports. He does not seem surprised to see a blue, American booklet and does not ask any questions, but hands it back and asks – in Russian of course – what my last name is. I tell him. He does not reply to me, but says something I cannot fully hear through the half-closed window to his partner, whose job it is to manually raise the *schlagbaum*. But I do hear my name voiced in a manner of recognition. So I imagine the exchange as:

"That Richardson guy they called about is finally leaving the Exclusion Zone."

"Took him long enough."

"Yeah, they said there was something not quite right about him."

"Probably a journalist."

Murmansk

As far back as the 1860s, Russia's military and political leaders expressed concern that Russian ships would be bottled up in the Baltic and Black Seas by England in the event of war. Indeed, this was the main reason Tsar Alexander II dispatched Russia's fleets to San Francisco and New York harbors during the American Civil War (that it also demonstrated support for the North and staved off British intervention on the side of the South were added bonuses).

In 1894, Tsar Alexander III sent his Minister of Finance, Sergei Witte, to survey the Murman coast ("murman" being a linguistic alteration of "Norman," as the Norge were called) as a possible location for an ice-free port. He sent Witte because other advisers were arguing for expansion of port facilities at Libau (modern Liepaja, Latvia), and he knew they would not give an objective report on the Arctic option. Witte traveled to Catherine's Harbor (Екатеринская гавань), a Russian fishing and whaling port on the Barents Sea that had been active since the early 1700s, and came back with a glowing assessment:

> It is an excellent harbor – large, deep, ice-free because of the Gulf Stream, well protected. I had never before seen such a magnificent harbor. It was even more impressive than the port and harbor of Vladivostok.

> Also several features of this region made a powerful impression on me as a newcomer. I was impressed by the fact that the sun never sets here during the summer, making it possible to light a cigarette [at night] by use of a magnifying class. I was impressed too by the whaling I was able to observe…[4]

Witte proposed expanding Catherine's Harbor into a naval port, extending a railway line there, and building an electrical station to support it.

Unfortunately, Alexander III died that same year, before action could be taken, and his son, Nicholas II, rejected the idea, a decision Witte later called "ill-fated." Meanwhile, Libau was expanded and outfitted for naval service, at considerable cost. And, since it was on the Baltic, it really did not solve the problem of offering Russia unfettered access to the open seas.

Not one to be easily deterred, Witte proposed to the State Council in 1896 that Russia, "with a view toward the development of commerce in the North and to weaken its dependence upon foreign merchants… urgently set about building a commercial port on the Murman coast… which could at the same time serve as an administrative center."

The proposal was accepted in early 1896 and thus was founded Alexandrovsk-on-Murman (today Polyarny), a port on the tip of the peninsula that juts into Kola Bay, on the site of Catherine's Harbor. It developed into a vital commercial port and later, from the 1930s on, was transformed into a naval base (even today, it is part of a closed military zone).

THE OUTBREAK OF World War in 1914 lent new urgency to the task of connecting the Murman coast via railroad with Petrozavodsk (and thus Petersburg), a project that had been repeatedly discussed and delayed since the 1870s, well before Witte's proposal. The plan was hastily approved in January 1915, and some 170,000 laborers set to work on the 1,053-kilometer rail line, among them 40,000 Austro-Hungarian and German prisoners of war.

Since the location of Alexandrovsk-on-Murman on the left side of the Kola Bay inlet was not ideal for the railway's termination point on the Murman coast, another end point was sought. In 1915, the port village of Semyonovsky was established about 20 miles south of Alexandrovsk, on the right, eastern side of the bay. Within a year, the village was renamed Romanov-on-Murman, and on September 21, 1916, its establishment was made official with the laying of a foundation stone for the church named for Nikolai Mirlikysky, a patron saint of sailors. It was to be the last city founded by the Romanovs.

Just over a month later, the railway connecting Romanov-on-Murman and Petrozavodsk was completed, but it came too late to help Russia's war effort. In fact, six months later, after the February Revolution swept the Romanovs from power, the town's name was simplified to Murmansk. Soon thereafter, the town was occupied by British and American forces. Ironically, the newly finished railway greatly facilitated the Western intervention.

IN JULY 1918, two days after he decided to send US troops to intervene in the Russian Civil War, President Woodrow Wilson offered a telling prediction of the course of US policy toward Russia over the next two (and indeed the next 100) years: "I have been sweating blood over the question what is right and feasible to do in Russia. It goes to pieces like quicksilver under my touch."[5]

The purpose of the intervention (alongside British, French, Japanese, Greek and other allied forces) was to resurrect the Eastern Front against Germany by rescuing stranded Czech Legion forces and overthrowing the Soviet government. But the US commitment was insufficient to the task, poorly managed, and ill-advised.

In August 1918, some 5,000 US troops were sent to Arkhangelsk to protect allied munitions and supplies sent to that city, and to connect up with Czech forces stranded along the route of the Trans-Siberian. The first goal turned out to be moot, because the Bolsheviks had already acquired the munitions, and so US forces focused on the second, battling their way south until their supply lines became over-extended and winter set in.

Then, in November 1918, an Armistice was signed with Germany and the sole remaining reason for the intervention evaporated. US forces found themselves stranded, fighting a rear-guard action against the Bolsheviks, with the frozen Arctic Ocean at their backs.

It is in this context that, on February 12, 1919, President Wilson ordered an additional 720 men to Murmansk (yet, strangely, four days later he decided to evacuate all troops from Russia). This was the North Russia Transportation Corps Expedition, and their mission was to safeguard the Petrograd-Murmansk Railway so as to allow possible overland evacuation of US troops stranded in Arkhangelsk. They were from the 167th and 168th Railroad Companies stationed in France, and while they were only sent to maintain the railway, their "eagerness to join in the fighting led them into skirmishes with the Bolsheviks, sometimes with fatal results."[6]

The troops arrived in Murmansk in April, and Major Edward MacMorland, who was in charge of the operation, described the city of 2,500 at that time as "an unsightly collection of unpainted warehouses and dwellings, sprawled in the snow on the sides of the hills. We saw wharves, railroad yards crowded with decrepit rolling stock, and piles of supplies."[7]

For the next four months, the construction forces supported (often with fire) British forces seeking to drive south to Petrozavodsk, with the intent of overthrowing the Bolsheviks. The Americans got as far as Kyappeselga, some 575 kilometers south of Murmansk, before being ordered to retreat at the end of July 1919. The infantry they had been sent to "rescue" had left Arkhangelsk in April.

Three American soldiers died in skirmishes with the Bolsheviks during the four-month deployment. One man wrote: "If war was hell for Sherman, marching through a southern State in time of abundant harvest, then it was hell frozen over for this battalion marching through the tundras and snows of Russia."[8]

THE 1920s AND 1930s saw phenomenal population growth in the region, following on discoveries of important mineral deposits and a dedicated effort to build Murmansk's shipping facilities. On the eve of war in 1939, the city was far from "an unsightly collection of unpainted warehouses and dwellings"; it had raised several dozen brick and stone buildings, and grown to a population of 120,000.

While the city was never captured by the Germans in the Great Patriotic War, it was bombed with a ferocity that surpassed every other Soviet city save Stalingrad. By the end of the war, three-quarters of the city lay in ruins.

Not surprisingly, therefore, after the war Murmansk was one of 15 Soviet cities prioritized for rebuilding. By 1952 its housing stocks had rebounded to pre-war levels. By 1970, the city was flourishing and the population had grown to over 300,000 (to peak at 489,000 in 1989), driven by shipbuilding, the navy (which after the war moved its main northern base from Polyarny to neighboring Severomorsk), and fishing.

In 1969, Georgi Vladimov, one of the finest Soviet-era writers, published a novel based in Murmansk, *Three Minutes' Silence*. It is a tense, character-rich novel about life in the city, life at sea, and the corruption of those in power. Toward the end, the feckless protagonist ruminates in a very non-Soviet way about the meaning of life, in the process putting a pin in the map to mark Murmansk, the world's largest city above the Arctic Circle, as a place where people think for themselves.

…one thought wouldn't give me any peace: why were we all such strangers to each other, why were we always each other's enemies? No doubt this is to someone's advantage; sad to say, we are all simply blind and we can't see where it's taking us. What disasters we need to bring us to our senses, for us to recognize our fellow-men as our brothers! But we are good people, that's what we have to understand – I couldn't bear to think we were worthless – yet we put up with pigs; like sheep, we obey people who are stupider than we are, and we torment each other for no reason… And so it will be – until we learn to think of our own neighbor. But not to think about how to stop him from getting one up on us, or how to outflank him: no, that way none of us will ever save ourselves. What's more, life will never set itself to rights on its own.

We, each of us, if only for three minutes a day, ought to shut up and listen out to hear if someone's in trouble, because that means you're in trouble too! – in the way that all Marconis at sea observe radio silence and listen out, in the way that we get concerned about some distant people on the other side of the Earth… Or is all that just useless day-dreaming? Yet it's not much – just three minutes! And then, you see, you gradually turn into a human being…[9]

THE 1991 COLLAPSE of the Soviet Union precipitated a demographic crisis for Murmansk. Since 1995, the city's population has fallen by 25 percent, primarily from the ranks of the young, most of whom seem to be leaving for opportunities below the Arctic Circle. As a result, the birthrate has plummeted and port industries are having trouble filling jobs. Add to this the economic challenges of the fishing industry

– which has been sending increasing proportions of its catch to more profitable foreign ports for processing, instead of through domestic fish canneries – and the city faces serious economic challenges.

In 2010, Murmansk was officially declared a Special Economic Zone in order to attract foreign investment and reinvigorate the port. But by 2014 not a single foreign company had expressed interest in investment, and the Ministry of Economic Development argued that the Economic Zone should be shuttered.

The Fisherman

Eight minutes.

Above the Arctic Circle in October, with each setting of the sun, each day is eight minutes shorter than the one before it. Eight minutes may not sound like much, but it adds up quickly, like compound interest. On October 1, there are about 11 hours of daylight here. By October 31, daylight has decreased to just six hours and 53 minutes.

By early December the sun will give up entirely on Murmansk and its environs, retreating below the horizon for the 40-day spell known as Polar Night, when the sun never gets higher than a few degrees below the horizon, giving the overcast (and often snowy) sky a cool, twilight glow for most of what counts as day here.

If that doesn't put gloom in your shoes, even when the sun is up in October, it's generally pretty grey out. Statistically, in October it's mostly cloudy or overcast for about 85 percent of the daylight hours in the Murmansk region. Nice soft light for photography, perhaps. But one does long for a bit of contrast.

Our time in Murmansk fell solidly into the 85 percent. It was persistently grey and drizzly, yet slightly warmer than expected, so we took that as an upside and threw on raincoats.

Our first day in the city began with a 9:30 meeting with Nikolai Petrovich Kalinikhin, a private fisherman who works out of Murmansk. At 10, the boat he owns is coming back from three days at sea and he is taking us with him to meet it on the wharf.

We meet Kalinikhin by the side of the road, so that he can guide us the last kilometer. "You won't find the road on your GPS," he says.

Indeed. We trundle down a narrow track sprayed with potholes that winds past a truck graveyard, a ramshackle wooden building or two, then turns onto tarmac that leads toward fish warehouses and a wharf.

Three small, 15-20 meter fishing boats sit tied up at the dock. Kalinikhin hops out of his black Toyota Landcruiser and comes over to greet us. He is short, compact, and fit from years at sea, with greying red hair and a brush mustache. He carries a leather man purse from which he quickly extracts a cigarette pack after exchanging handshakes.

"Before you is the Gift of Medvedev," he quips as we walk the short distance to the dock.

Kalinikhin explains that one of Dmitry Medvedev's last acts as president before vacating the throne for Vladimir Putin's third term in 2012 was to decree that all small ships (those under 20 meters in length) be re-registered under new, more onerous regulations. The precipitating cause was the July 2011 sinking of the *Bulgaria* on the Volga River, killing 122 – the worst Russian maritime disaster since the *Admiral Nakhimov* disaster of 1986.

"We have far too many old ships sailing our waters," Medvedev said the day after the *Bulgaria* sank. "Shipowners will either have to give their vessels a full and complete overhaul, or stop operating them if they are no longer fit for this kind of transport. This should be carried out across the whole country, because the fleet of ships is very old now, and it is partially in private hands. Only a small part of the fleet is still state-owned, but this does not mean that the state can stop ensuring proper oversight of the situation."[10]

Rather than deal with the revealed safety issues in a focused, measured way, Kalinikhin avers, the decree was sweeping and uncompromising. And it crippled Russia's private fishing fleet.

"We sat in dock for 18 months, reacting to this change, re-equipping our ship and meeting the new regulations," Kalinikhin says. "All these other ships," he continues, pointing to three small ships tied up nearby, "sit here unable to work."

There used to be about 40 private fishing vessels in these waters, Kalinikhin says, but the new decree forced most of them out of business. Those that were not chopped up for scrap were repurposed as tourist vessels or small ferries.

KALINIKHIN'S SHIP, THE *Ladoga*, has returned with three tons of cod and halibut on board, and his captain and two crewmates are unloading it from the hold. The compact ship is a model of simplicity and efficiency. A hand-cranked crane lifts each of the 50-kilo boxes of cleaned fish from the hold and swings it around over the dock. These fish are all line-caught, whereas the big factory ships that head out from Murmansk are trawlers whose massive nets vacuum fish up indiscriminately from outside the 12-mile nautical line, beyond which Kalinikhin's crew cannot venture.

"We lay down 10 kilometers of line, over 6,000 hooks," Kalinikhin explains, pointing to the neatly folded and hung lines on the large rack amidships. "The hooks are automatically baited with chum as the line unfurls, and after about six hours we reel the line back in slowly, ungigging the caught fish one by one." Later, the three crew members clean the catch and head back to port. Typically, weather permitting, they will make four or five outings per month. "This is a much more ecologically clean way of fishing than what the trawlers do," he adds. "They pull up whatever their vast nets capture."

"No government, no banks gave us money for this boat," Kalinikhin says matter-of-factly. "We did it all ourselves." Kalinikhin is on a pension now, and only oversees the general operation of the fishing ship, but holds an interest in another boat and, one guesses, several other ventures besides. Indeed, his ship, which he designed in partnership with a shipyard near St. Petersburg, was to be the prototype for production of several dozen small shipping boats to be sold to private fishermen in the North. Since the 2012 decree, however, those plans have been put on hold.

"We paid off the *Ladoga* in seven years," Kalinikhin says. "When it was built, it was just an empty shell. We would take it out fishing for three days, come back and rest in port. While we rested, the carpenters would come in and finish the interior and make it habitable. Today, such a boat would cost $1 million to build and outfit to the new specifications. It would take 10 years to pay that off. Who is going to give you money for that?"

What Kalinikhin and crew can catch is strictly determined by a state quota system. They presently have a multi-year license to bring in 3,000 tons of fish per year, with allowances for different types, from cod to halibut. Their quota runs through 2018, and Kalinikhin has no idea what they will be allowed to fish after their term runs out.

KALINIKHIN'S CAPTAIN, Konstantin Tretyakov, is a wiry, plain-spoken man who has served on ships all over the world, from Chile and UAR to Norway. "Those require long periods away, six to nine months or more. And I recently had a kid, so I decided I needed to stay closer to home," he explains.

In Russia, crews like this typically move together. Kalinikhin hires the captain, and the captain picks his crew. "It's much better working for just one boss," Tretyakov says, comparing his work now, for Kalinikhin, with work on larger ships. "If you have a problem, you just work it out one on one."

Kalinikhin notes it is not easy to find good captains like Tretyakov. "Kids today don't want to go out to sea," he says. "They want to work with their minds. Everyone wants to be a lawyer. It's nice, stable work. Thankfully, my son is interested. I'm on pension now and training him to take over the business. He's finishing training at the institute and my wife does the books. It's so much easier, everything in one family."

The Foreign Agent

Natalia Viktorovna Kolesnik hardly looks like a foreign agent.

She is young (26), attractive and energetic, with thick, dark hair and hip glasses. A creative type, yes. But surely nothing treasonous.

Then again, perhaps she is putting us on. After all, how can you really know? Perhaps she is a master of deceit, a wolf in sheep's clothing.

In her own telling, Kolesnik is just a filmmaker (though she says her family would have preferred she pursued something more stable, like become a lawyer). We visit her in her "studio," which is the converted bedroom of a large apartment near the center of Murmansk. It is strewn with cameras, light stands, computers and a neon green mountain bike. She offers us tea in the break room, otherwise known as the apartment's kitchen.

We are here to talk about Mr. Pink,* which is something Kolesnik started along with Yevgeny ("Genya") Gorman, and worked at for five years. It was, in her words, a space "to give kids a place to realize their ideas, to get off the streets, to do productive work."

Mr. Pink was patterned on a similar youth center in Tromsø, Norway, which had a philosophy that was both simple and radical, Kolesnik says: "You don't need to tell people what to do or how. They already know. If they ask a question, then you should help them. You should not impose on them your own ideas of how something should be done."

It was a safe place for young adults 14-30 to gather, work together, and test out their ideas about art, theater or business and to find ways to turn them into business-related, profit-bearing activities. It occupied the 350 square meter ground floor of a large apartment building on the city's northern outskirts, and the kids decorated the interior and repainted the exterior to their whimsical, colorful tastes.

Born in the fall of 2011, "free of politics, religion and grown-ups," Mr. Pink was the city's first true center for youth. Kids came here to make films, rehearse with choir and musical groups, or do art and design projects.

One successful project, Cave, created and sold branded clothing and other items that have become very popular among young people in the city: "For those who love Kolsky region."

Mr. Pink also gave birth to the Barents Youth Film Academy and a popular local singing group, The Choir (Хор).

"We tried to do what we loved, what we wanted, and we were an authority among kids…" Kolesnik says. "We constantly compared the success rates of projects we completed and those completed by state

---

organizations… and they were completely incomparable figures, a huge difference."

Despite that, in May 2015 Mr. Pink was shuttered. Not for lack of funding, but because it had the wrong kind of funding.

When the center was started, the city of Murmansk donated a printer and about R13,000 ($215 today). The region was more generous, granting about R2.5 million ($40,000), but that could only be used on programs, not overhead, staff or services. The center earned a bit from putting on films and other activities, but it was not enough to cover their costs. And, given the difficulty of convincing local businesses to donate to nonprofits, the founders decided to look to neighboring Norway – after all, Mr. Pink had been inspired by a Norwegian youth center. Remarkably, they got a grant. A few years later, that grant would be their downfall.

In November 2012, Russia's "Foreign Agent Law" went into effect. It stipulated that any nonprofit organization that receives foreign funding and engages in political activity will be subject to branding as a foreign agent. Such organizations must undergo additional audits and preface all of their written and oral public statements with a warning that they are coming from a foreign agent. The state can also intervene at will in the activities of the organization and suspend its operations for six months.

In December 2014 Mr. Pink had just passed through a very trying audit with the Ministry of Justice, but came away without being branded as a foreign agent. Shortly thereafter, however, they received information that the Information Bureau Council of Ministers of Northern Countries was to be designated a foreign agent. Mr. Pink had recently completed a project with this organization and merely had to do a final report to receive from it their final piece of grant funding. "It was a rather big sum of money," she says, "and we were counting on it." But they were told that, if they had dealings with a foreign agent, they too would need to declare themselves a foreign agent.

"We realized that we could not handle this financially," she says. They estimated it would cost them an additional R200,000 per year ($3,000) to deal with the additional audits, to say nothing of the bureaucracy and paperwork. This would have crippled their work, she says, forcing them to be constantly on the defensive. Their tiny staff, "already buried in paperwork," would have spent all their time hustling for money and filling out reports, and no time running useful programs. So, because of this, and what Kolesnik called an "ever broadening scope of laws that limited our activities," Mr. Pink made the difficult decision to shut down. "Unfortunately," Kolesnik says, "many NGOs find themselves caught in this vicious circle."

And many get trapped by the law. As of the end of 2015, just in Murmansk and Murmansk Oblast,* at least three NGOs had been identified as foreign agents (Humanist Youth Movement, the Bellona-Murmansk Regional Social Environmental Organization, and the Maximum Center, which provides social, psychological and legal help to victims of discrimination and homophobia) and another five had been warned that they were to be labeled agents (Nature and Youth, The Sami's Civic Association of Murmansk Oblast, Kola Environmental Center, Apatity Environmental Center, Kola Center for the Defense of Wild Nature).

"I can't yet accept, emotionally, as Genya says, that we succeeded," Kolesnik says. "But the methodology we used worked, it was unique... We worked at it 24 hours a day without vacations... It was very hard, but we loved what we did... But one doesn't always have the strength to keep fighting."

---

* Oblast is the Russian word for an administrative province.

Did she ever think of working within the city administration?

"Yes, there were proposals," she replies, "but nothing came of it… I would never work in a state structure… These people have very limited views. They are people who live in a case," she says, making reference to the Chekhov story, "Man in a Case."

In fact, working closely with the state would have contradicted much of what Mr. Pink had been trying to achieve over the past five years. "We tried to remove all sorts of bureaucratic red tape so that kids could do what they wanted to do," Kolesnik says.

And they were not interested in politics. Yes, they did have a film festival about human rights that got them into some hot water. But Mr. Pink was primarily focused on the arts. "Politics is the ability to influence people's minds and change their opinions…" Kolesnik says. "If we show people works of art and have discussions, of course we are going to be having an influence on people's ideas, so is that politics? We were never part of any political party… one of our basic founding ideas was to be outside politics… To have refused to do that film festival would also have been a political decision…"

In today's Russia, very little is outside politics.

That said, Kolesnik has a deep affection for Murmansk. "I consider myself a patriot because I have spent so much energy doing everything I can to help my city," she says. "I love it. I want it to be an amazing place, where people can live in comfort. Lots of people are leaving. Everyone is going to Petersburg, Moscow, to other countries. We have an expression here, *'pora valit'* (time to head out)… people are always surprised by what we are doing [in the city]… it's so sad, they just work and sit at home and watch TV… They don't try to do anything new, to participate in the city. They don't do anything to make the city theirs, comfortable, interesting, classy. Although, thank God, now I do see that changing; there is more activism…"

The city would do well to learn from the efforts of Mr. Pink, she adds. "The city needs people who don't move away. The government needs to understand its city… while they are just concerned with training workers. Government is a place for profit, not a place for doing good."

Kolesnik is clearly dejected by her experience, by talking about it, by visiting the now empty building that once housed Mr. Pink. It has all been exhausting for her.

"I have had many proposals to leave…" she says, "and unfortunately I am leaving, for personal, family reasons, entirely. It's really hard for me, I've struggled with it for six months. For a long time I thought I would never leave…" She will be working with a group in Tromsø, Norway, and, for now, must turn her back on her city, on her dreams.

"Maybe I will return," she says. "I would not exclude the possibility. Ever."

Espionage

Several scenes in Georgi Vladimov's novel about Murmansk, *Three Minutes' Silence*, take place in the Arctic, the hotel that was the city's social hub. Built in 1933, it was, at the time the novel takes place, a run-down four-story hotel with just 100 rooms. Then it was turned into a typical Soviet-era *dolgostroy* (long-term construction) project: from 1972 to 1984, the hotel was torn down and a new 18-story Arctic Hotel was built in its place. Through the 1990s and aughts, the hotel went through ownership and management shifts reflective of the turbulent times. Finally, in 2009, it was closed again for reconstruction and in 2014 it reopened as a complex including the four-star Azimut Hotel, with offices and retail space.

This is where we find the offices of the local bureau of the newspaper *Komsomolskaya Pravda*. The editor, Veronika Seliverstova, wanted to interview Mikhail about his photography and our trip. After that, she takes us to the hotel's top floor to enjoy the view. The Arctic is the tallest building above the Arctic Circle, so we are, quite literally, standing at the top of the world. That, however, is not enough, and Veronika insists that they take us over to Abram-Mys; the view of the city lights is amazing from there, she says. We are tired after two days tromping about the city and want to retire to our hotel, yet we also feel an obligation to see and absorb all that we can during every waking hour. We can sleep when we are dead, we admit, and so we relent.

Yet on the way we must make a stop. Because eighteen stories below us, in the shadow of the hotel, is a rather utilitarian looking white monument. It is about 20 meters wide, with steps leading up either side to a second-story balcony. Unveiled on the tenth anniversary of the October Revolution, in 1927, it was to be used as a place for delivering speeches, for ceremonial meetings with guests. It is in fact the monument "To the Victims of the 1918-20 Foreign Intervention," and beneath it are interred the remains of 24 Bolshevik prisoners who escaped a White (as in anti-Bolshevik) war prisoner camp on the Barents Sea, but died while being transported to freedom and Murmansk.

There is no sense of gravity to the 90-year-old monument. It feels like a forgotten relic that happens to adjoin an alley of trees and a short promenade. We walk around it, considering whether there is an interesting way to photograph it in the fading light. There is not.

BY THE TIME we head out of the downtown, five of us stuffed into a Subaru sedan, it is pitch dark, Polar dark. We drive south of the city center, along the embankment, and then across the 2.5 kilometer bridge that spans the Kola Bay. When it opened in 2005, this was the world's longest bridge above the Arctic Circle. But it relinquished the title in 2009, when a four-kilometer span was built over the swampy surrounds of the Yuribey River, on the Yamal Peninsula.*

Never mind. The Kola Bridge is plenty long. It seems to take ten minutes to cross, and there is little traffic going either way at nine o'clock on a Tuesday evening.

Interestingly, two days after we left Murmansk, the Kola Bridge became the sudden focus of a national scandal. It turns out that Oberega, the firm with a contract to protect this important strategic object, was cheating the state. Oberega was supposed to man four bridge posts around the clock, yet from March 1 to July 30, 2015, only three of the posts were being manned; the other was being, well, mannequined. That is, there was a dummy in the post, pretending to be a human. Over the five months that it was on duty, the mannequin drew a salary of 321,000 rubles (about $1,000 a month at the current rate of exchange).

AS WE REACH the far end of the bridge, Veronika warns, "Don't speak any English, and for God's sake, don't smile, it gives you away as an American."

Abram-Mys, a rocky cape that towers above Kola Bay opposite Murmansk, is supposedly off limits to foreigners (there is some sort of sign somewhere indicating this, but we don't see it). Veronika assures us this is a silly technicality.

We park in a makeshift parking spot and walk through a memorial alley where airplanes, rockets and anti-aircraft guns are mounted on soaring pedestals, aimed skyward, eerily lit by the glow of the city from across the bay.

---

* For the record, Russia's longest bridge is far below the Arctic Circle. Also opened in 2009, it stretches near six kilometers across the Volga River at Ulyanovsk. It is called, of course, the Presidential Bridge.

We climb a dark, slippery trail to a lookout that opens toward the glittering lights of Murmansk, the shipyards, and the occasional ship floating past. The view is indeed breathtaking.

"We came out here on New Year's Eve," Veronika says. "It was excellent. We had a generator, food, drink, and then there were fireworks."

Tonight, the drizzle that dogged us all day is gone, the wind dies down, and the cold, for the first time on our trip, is non-Arctic. It's just a plain, ordinary cold.

We have no fireworks, but the lights are brilliant, and I feel a bit surreptitious being here. When no one is looking, I sneak a smile.

Pomorye

Russians in these parts are different from those in the rest of Russia.

There are those who will claim this is because they have a unique "ethnos" – they are Pomors, meaning people who live by the sea. Other than the indigenous Sami, the first settlers in the White Sea region were emigrants from the Novgorod region – traders, fishermen, boat builders. And because Russia did not generally suffer security threats from the North, Pomorye – which originally just referred to the lands along the White Sea coast – was never brought under the thumb of Novgorod or, later, Moscow.

Pomorye was also different because there was never any significant serfdom here, but there were many monasteries, and there was significant trade with the West (England and Holland) at a time when the rest of Rus was largely isolated. This has led some, including Aleksandr Solzhenitsyn, to conclude that the Pomors were Russia's only truly indigenous, democratic subculture:

The Russian character developed naturally in Pomorye, uninhibited by Moscow's rule and without inclination to maraud, a tendency notably adopted by the Cossacks of the southern rivers. (That the light of Lomonosov came to us precisely from Pomorye was no accident.)"[11]

Another thing the Pomors had going for them, other than a sea-going history and an absence of slavery, was their storytelling. In the pre-Soviet era the region apparently had a particularly rich heritage of long-form oral storytelling – part and parcel of what, as one expert noted, gave the region "a higher level of cultural development compared with residents of other Russian regions."[12]

There was also a practical tendency toward "peaceful coexistence." Many different peoples lived in the region of Pomorye – Karelians, Sami, Nenets, Norwegians – and they had a long history of exchanging knowledge, collaboration and cross-cultural influences.[13]

By the early 1700s, the definition of what Pomorye encompassed had expanded to include the Arkhangelsk region, Kola and Karelia – an area comprising some 60 percent of the territory of the Russian empire at the time, according to one scholar, and this "Greater Pomorye" had a very significant influence on the economy, particularly in foreign trade.[14]

With the arrival of the twentieth century, however, discovery of the region's wealth in natural resources, particularly rare metals, brought a new reality to Pomorye: the arrival of Soviet mining, hyper-development, and Gulags, all of which combined to inject toxic industrial cities into an otherwise pristine and healthy northern landscape.

MONCHEGORSK IS ONE of the most polluted cities in Russia. Its Severonikel Factory processes nickel and copper ore as part of the sprawling Norilsk Nikel Company, belching tons of contaminants into the surrounding countryside. It is also home to an air force base. Ironically, the name Monchegorsk derives from the Sami and means "beautiful mountain."

Founded in 1935 as a worker's town for nearby mining operations, from January 1940 to June 1941 there was a Gulag based here with nearly 15,000 prisoners who were tasked with building the metals processing factory. Legend has it that the town was founded on this spot because surveys by the noted Academician Alexander Fersman* predicted a mineral motherlode that never panned out, so to speak. Since the beginning, most of the nickel and copper refined here has come from the east, from Norilsk.

On our approach to Monchegorsk, we spy beautiful snow-capped mountains and stunning lakes. The setting would be breathtaking, if industrial excess had not made it, well, breathtaking. As we close in on the town we pass through several miles of deforested tundra littered with twisted, bare tree trunks. Large tailing mountains tower along the road.

The town of 45,000 (which, we later learn, is 54 percent female) is mostly a one-street, one-company affair with few amenities or commercial flourishes. Yet at the far end of Monchegorsk on this cold, October afternoon, the cheerful sounds of young people making music – a piano tinkling slightly off-key, a soprano warming up with scales, a shy bayan player tuning her instrument – escape through the double-paned windows of the Monchegorsk Music School, filling the caustic outside air with hope and life.

---

* Two chemical elements and a crater on the moon, to say nothing of roads in several northern towns, including Monchegorsk, plus a research ship, are named for him.

The music school is a shining gem amid environmental depravity. The dedication and creativity of its 29 teachers is beyond admirable. Yes, there is no escaping the scolding Soviet pedagogical method, yet it is loving, and the mood here is welcoming and determined.

We sit in on several one-on-one classes and on a delightful folk ensemble practice (guitars, bayans, domras, bass domra, drums) in the 200-seat auditorium (which some consider the best in the oblast) rimmed with large portraits of classical composers, mostly Russian. Conductor Yevgeny Grigoryevich Barilo, a 40-year veteran of teaching, is so focused on his work that when he notices us a few minutes after we have slipped in the side door, he becomes flustered, apologizing profusely for not greeting us when we first arrived.

The students are fidgety, but Barilo knows how to rein them in and focus their efforts.

Fourth-year student Lyosha Zibinsky is tagged for a solo performance of *Kak pri luzhke, pri luzhke* ("Oh, by the meadow, the meadow") on bayan.

"This is my favorite song," says the school's director, Svetlana Sulim, an intense, engaging, 40-something woman who fixes you with 110 percent of her attention when you ask a question or engage her in conversation.

Young Lyosha smirks and grimaces every time he hits a wrong note.

"The great thing about an orchestra," Sulim says, "is that it is a way of communicating. Kids these days sit at home on their computers and don't even go out into their courtyards to play or mess around. But these kids get together a couple of times each week and play together, to communicate and work with each other, and they are the better for it."

FOUNDED IN 1948, the Monchegorsk Music School offers free lessons and ensemble training to over 300 students aged 5-17. However, if parents want their kids to start before age five, that is possible for a fee. "There's a rising birthrate now," Sulim says, "and parents are taking a greater interest in their kids' education."

While the after-school program is free, it's not for everyone. Sulim explains how entry is based on a competitive assessment of each child's musical potential – rhythm, the ability to carry a tune and distinguish tones. Still, Sulim estimates that seven percent of all the city's kids pass through her school, and she says they are a healthy mixture of socio-economic classes.

Those that get in are doted on and pressured to practice and improve. While this is not a place for training professional musicians, some do go on to receive high honors and awards at both national and international competitions. Yet the main role of the school is to urge the young to embrace a life enriched by music – "it improves the emotional side of us, making us more empathetic," Sulim says. And the teachers we witness are enthusiastic and serious about their charges.

"All our teachers are actors," Svetlana Sulim says. "Sometimes we will even get up and dance with the students, if that will help."

There is greenery throughout the building – mini-jungles in the waiting areas, vines sprawling down pianos, large potted plants on windowsills. I can't help wondering how the greenery fares through the long, sunless winter months, but surely it is a source of comfort in this bleak, toxic environment.

We sit in on a piano lesson in a room that is, of course, filled with plants. A cute, chipmunk-cheeked student gets a charge out of performing for visitors and seems to thrive on her teacher's brisk alternation between overly-affectionate hugs (and cheek-squeezes), and reproach-filled drills.

By contrast, down the hall, Darina, a slightly older girl taking a bayan lesson, is shy and withdrawn and not enamored with the idea of being photographed or watched during her private lesson. It is clear she would prefer we left now, please.

We wander the bright green, spotless hallways of the school (this is its third home since its founding nearly 70 years ago) and, as one would expect, wherever Sulim pops in, we witness the unique Russian cocktail of deference and regard that is evoked by the first name plus patronymic form of address. In other places, the cocktail may include doses of fear, loathing, or even irony. But here we sense only respect and admiration, a warm affection between the teachers and their headmaster. Perhaps it helps that Sulim, a Monchegorsk native, is herself an alumna of the school. In addition to her administrative duties, she teaches guitar and bayan. As a student, she says, she took up the domra because all the other instruments were taken by the time she got to choose what she wanted. The teachers were in a quandary, she says. Here was this student who clearly had talent and interest and they didn't want her to slip away.

"So, let it be the domra," she says. "The main thing was to be studying music."

WE CONTINUE OUR drive southward after a pleasant meal in a town cafe and some depression-inducing photography of the industrial plant at sunset.

Our stop for the night is the city of Apatity, where we will cadge a couple of beds, get stuffed to the gills on fine home cooking, and drop off Nadya, Mikhail's wife, at her mother's place.

But before dinner we make a long side trip to neighboring Kirovsk, to sit in on another sort of class: Mark Ivanovich Smirnov is training teens (about a dozen boys and two girls) to box.

He's been doing it for 16 years and can't stop.

Forty-two, crew-cut, 5'9" and every inch a muscular, loud, pushy drill sergeant, Smirnov is in reality a softy.

He loves these kids. He loves shouting at them, upbraiding them, nailing them with a cutting insult about their punches ("This is not a Vychegodsk scuffle. Don't be Russians. Jab like you mean it!"). And they love giving it back as good as they get. They respect and fear him, but stand up to his barbs. They are, after all, being trained to box.

The basketball gym has been divided up by crisscrossed ropes into eight sparring rings. Smirnov stands, hands clasped behind his back, glaring at one set of sparring partners and then another, calling them out for weak technique, swearing like a sailor when they show signs of fatigue or laziness. "They say a fog has settled in over Kirovsk. Has this somehow affected your brains?"

"What the hell are you up to?" he yells at one scrawny, twelve-year-old kid. "Get over here," he shouts, cursing someone's grandma. The kid approaches sheepishly, expecting to get chewed out. Smirnov instead bends down to tie the kid's loose shoelaces and sends him back into the ring.

Then he turns to watch Lena (one of two girls in the class) and Alyosha, two 10-year-olds not doing a very good job of moving about the ring. "Remember," he barks, "one step back is defense, two steps back is flight."

"We have Azeris, Ukrainians…" Smirnov shouts, "not a single Russian here."

He seems to be picking up a running joke here. Since there are no "Russian" kids in this boxing class in a northern Russian town, Russians become an object of mirth, and Smirnov repeatedly tells kids to stop fighting like Russians. Sloppily, is what one gathers he is saying.

AFTERWARD, WE HAVE a long chat with Smirnov, and he tells us how boxing has changed his kids' lives, how it is keeping them off the streets, teaching them discipline, making them fit. Just in the last year, he has trained some 90 kids.

There is suddenly the sound of a drummer coming from next door and it drowns out our conversation. It feels like we are suddenly on the set of the film *Birdman*, and I half expect Michael Keaton to come walking through the gym's back door, over which a large cartoon rabbit has been painted.

"Did you see Ilya?" Smirnov asks, raising his voice. We did. Even though we are far from boxing aficionados, we immediately recognized Ilya as the quickest, most able boxer in the group. He is thin and wiry, very agile, and has a fast jab. "He was hugely overweight when he started," Smirnov says. "And now look at him."

Smirnov tells stories of other students who literally had to be dragged to class but now can't be kept away. Yet, he admits, "training kids is for rich people..." After 16 years he finally had to take another job. The classes don't pay enough for him to live on, even though he does it every night of the week, to say nothing of traveling to tournaments. But he can't give it up.

He's addicted to transforming these kid's lives and, partly as a result of that, he's on his third marriage.

Smirnov mentions that he does a lot of reading when taking the kids to tournaments, that he thinks it is important, as their role model, for them to see him reading. We ask what he reads and he reveals that his favorite story is Chekhov's "Vanka," about a young, poor, forgotten boy and his longing for the lost comforts of family life.

As the kids finish changing into their street clothes, they return to the gym one by one to give Smirnov a hug or a prolonged hand-grasp. When they do, every last one says something they have clearly been taught by this energetic teacher with a telling sense of humor: "Thank you Mark Ivanovich for our happy childhood."*

ON THE WAY back from Kirovsk, I point out to Mikhail that our chariot needs a name.

Ostap Bender had the Antelope-Gnu. William Least Heat Moon had Ghost Dancing. Duke and Gonzo had the Great Red Shark and the White Whale. Quixote had Rocinante.

Any great, legendary road trip, even one that is epic merely in the minds of its participants, must have a named chariot. But the name must fit the vehicle, it must properly express its character and temperament, and that may be difficult to sort out so early in these proceedings.

Polo, with all its preppy or equine connotations, just seems wrong for our tough, gritty little Volkswagen. And too generic.

While inching though the fog to our rendezvous with Smirnov in Kirovsk, we moot the idea of "Yozhik" (Hedgehog), in memory of Yuri Norshtein's classic animated film *Hedgehog in the Fog*. Then, suddenly, like one of the apparitions that materialized in Norshtein's film, we see a sign for the ski resort Kukisvumchorr. (It is, we later learn, Sami for "the spine of a mountain with a flat crest and a long valley.")

Now *that's* a name.

We decide to try it on for a few days and see if it fits.

---

* The reference, for those not familiar with that period in Russian history, is to Josef Stalin. In the later, cult-building years of his rule, it became an established trope for Young Pioneers to proclaim, "Thank you Comrade Stalin for our happy childhood."

Potatoes and Kulaks

The price for our overnight in Apatity is that we must lend our backs to the family's annual fall tradition of putting up potatoes. Dug up at the dacha, washed in the city, they have been dried and laid out in large, stackable wooden trays. Now they must be transported a few miles away to the family's garage, which acts as cold storage, supplying Nadya's family with tubers through the long, polar winter.

Introduced by Peter the Great in the early 1700s, the potato had a rather inauspicious Russian debut. First, people ate the wrong bits of it (the foliage that grows above ground), then the peasants, being a conservative lot, dug in their heels and refused to grow them.

It was not until the iron hand of Tsar Nicholas I forced cultivation on state farms over a century after Peter's death that the potato began to, ahem, take root. Its main proponent, Count Pavel Kiselyov, argued that it was a protection against the relentless tides of famine. Yet even the aristocracy was against the humble crop. Countess Eudoxie Golitsyn, immortalized in verse by Pushkin, launched a vehement counter attack against Kiselyov, calling the potato a threat to Russian national traditions.[15]

There were massive potato riots in the 1830s and 1840s, and in one of his reports, the tsar's secret police chief wrote:

> Ignorant allegations to the effect that the potato is a cursed fruit whose cultivation brought about God's refusal to bless the Russian land with fertility have provoked disobedience by Moscow Province's peasants, who, in some villages, destroyed entire potato fields.[16]

But the real fear may not have had more to do with economics than superstition. State peasants feared that potato cultivation would further impoverish them or, just as bad, lead to their transformation into state-owned *udelnye* peasants. In the recent past, peasants had been forced to grow beetroot and then work in sugar factories to process the plants – taking them away from the land they loved.

Yet, by the turn of the twentieth century, Russians had come around and accepted the potato, even boasting of "native" varieties of the South American tuber. In the first half of the twentieth century, the proliferation of potatoes surely saved many Soviets from starvation and became a vital dacha crop that helped city dwellers make it through long, cold winters.

Yet, even after industrialization of the economy, the potato had a tough time sloughing off its association with compulsion. In the late Soviet era, it was a common practice to require students at institutions of higher learning to spend a month or longer on "potato missions" – helping dig potatoes on understaffed collective farms.

We undertook our potato mission out of gratitude and familial obligation rather than compulsion. In the frigid morning air, we emptied Kukisvumchorr's trunk of sleeping bags and suitcases and filled it with crates of potatoes, then made the short drive across town as Nadya's mother reminisced about how many potatoes they used to put up for the winter when the kids were living at home. They can hardly believe, it seems, that we are only hauling six crates – probably about 100-120 pounds – this year.

POST-POTATOES, WE HAD a significant drive ahead of us. Our goal was Medvezhegorsk, on the shores of Lake Onega, about 500 kilometers south of Apatity.

En route we had to visit our second sea, the White Sea. So, about 100 kilometers down the road, we pull into Kandalaksha, a small working town nestled on the shores of a deep bay at the northernmost point of the White Sea, in reach of over 350 picturesque islands, most all of which comprise a nature preserve founded in the 1930s to protect the common eider, prized for its fine down feathers.

The rocky Niva River (site of the Kola Peninsula's first hydroelectric plant, which we do not visit) runs down to the bay from the steep mountains surrounding the town. We drive up one of these mountains with our local guide, Ilona Isayeva, a 25-year-old kindergarten art teacher. She leads us past a downhill ski area popular with the locals to a rocky overlook. The view out onto the bay is stunning, even on this grey, overcast day.

Reportedly, humans have lived on this spot for thousands of years – evidence of settlements dating to 2500 BC have been found on the coast. The copious fishing and shorebirds, coupled with the wealth of the forests (bear and moose are still plentiful) surely made this place hospitable. The climate is generally colder and drier than in Murmansk, more continental. Yet it is still polar, and while it is far enough south not to suffer from the 40 days of Polar Night, its days do get excruciatingly short in winter (approximately 1 hour and 13 minutes on December 22, but who's counting).

The town was first mentioned in chronicles in 1517 and was home to a monastery for about half a century before the area was repeatedly overrun by the Swedes and Finns in the sixteenth and seventeenth centuries. The monastery was shuttered in 1742. As the threats from Scandinavia ebbed (in a bizarre side note, in July 1855 British troops tried, unsuccessfully, to take the town during the Crimean War), the town grew. In the Soviet era, an aluminum factory was opened here, and the town was both a source for electricity (thanks to its hydroelectric plant) and an important station on the Petersburg-Murmansk railway line.

Isayeva says her family ended up in Kandalaksha because her great grandparents were exiled here as *kulaks* (rich peasants who were "liquidated as a class" during collectivization in the 1930s; an estimated 60,000 families were sent to labor camps, another 150,000 were resettled in Siberia, the Urals and Central Asia); her large family has stayed here ever since. While she enjoys traveling, Isayeva says she loves how close she is to nature in this town of 35,000, how she can be off skiing or kayaking in 15 minutes.

But of course Isayeva is unusual. Most Russians her age don't want to live in a town this size, and she says it took her about a year after returning from college to find a group of friends to hang out with. "Everyone is going to St. Petersburg," she says, echoing what we heard at points farther north. But Isayeva has no interest in moving away. Not yet, anyway. "My family is so big," she says, wistfully. "And I want to take as much as I can from here first, before I would move away. I want to visit all of the Kola Peninsula, and there is so much to see there."

TWO HOURS LATER, at 5:09 PM local time, we exit the Arctic Circle.

We stop at a fading blue monument surrounded by stacked rocks. The roadside trees 50 meters in either direction are tied with ribbons and strings, as a sign of "I have been here," or for good luck, or because everyone else seems to be doing it.

Soon thereafter, we cross into Karelia, the northern Russian republic that borders Finland, and with which Vermont has a sister state relationship. It is a long drive through sparsely inhabited wilderness. For hundreds of miles there is no cell service nor a single radio station. Just miles of the smoothly paved E105, lined by an endless row of towering birch trees.

Clearings open up every few miles to views of shallow, marshy lakes, surrounded by rust-colored turf and birch, pine, and spruce trees. Occasionally, there is a small stand of larch, their golden needles shimmering amid the evergreens and denuded birch.

Sunset lasts a full two hours, with long periods of glowing blues and reds. We have been passing stunning lake scenes all day, but just as the sky turns a brilliant red, it becomes impossible to find any body of water where we can capture a powerful sunset photo. We seem to be on some sort of geological highland where there are no lakes. When we do finally find something satisfactory, the red has faded and we are less than satisfied with the results.

It is nine in the evening by the time we finally arrive in Medvezhegorsk, and Mikhail doesn't even want to check in. He is bordering on "hangry" and must be physically restrained from charging into the dining room of the cozy lakeside resort where we are staying, Malaya Medvezhka.

We take five minutes to check in and drop our bags in our rooms, and dinner tastes the better for the waiting. Determined to eat and drink local, we order up entrees of bear and moose, as well as two portions of a local Karelian liqueur. Mikhail takes one sip and decides it tastes like medicine, sliding it over to my side of the table.

Waste not, want not.

We each sample both entrees and agree that they taste rather similar. For all we know, they could both be beef, even though the young waitress offered to show us some sort of certificate proving that the bear was harvested humanely and in keeping with all Russian decrees and precepts.

We are almost alone in the restaurant, but for a couple of tables with thick-necked *biznessmen* and their scantily-dressed dates. Appropriately, they pay no attention to us, speaking in low whispers, periodically filling their vodka glasses, and practicing their blank, intimidating stares into the middle distance.

After dinner, we step outside into a stunning nightscape. Stars carpet the sky down to the horizon. We spend an hour or so doing night photography and stumbling on the undergrowth before calling it a night.

Lake Onega

In the daylight I see that the Malaya Medvezhka actually looks a lot like an Adirondack lodge, except that the waitresses are more surly, until you ply them with sufficient smiles and compliments to show them you are harmless. It also helps if you don't wear your coat in the dining room…

After a nice breakfast, I am writing in my room when Mikhail charges in with a handful of *chernika* (bilberries) and cranberries he netted from the forest. He insists that I eat them in the Russian style (i.e., without rinsing them). I, for my part, insist on making the treat a cross-cultural adventure and so I rinse and de-stem them in the bathroom before tossing them back.

They are good.

IT IS DIFFICULT to imagine, as I sit looking out over Lake Onega, that just under a century ago American warships attacked and took this town.

During the US-British occupation of the Murmansk region in 1918-19, American forces, which were supposed to be merely guarding the vital railway line, hatched a plan to attack Medvezhegorsk, then held by the Bolsheviks, from the water. Up the road a bit, they unloaded two 50-foot US Navy patrol boats and then cut through two miles of forest, laying track as they went (pulling the rails up behind them, like some sort of Hanna-Barbera cartoon) to get to Lake Onega. Miraculously, they succeeded. It was the first Allied flotilla in the lake (and presumably the last); the Americans captured the town and 11 more British ships soon arrived.

Indeed, this little town, lying as it does halfway between Murmansk and St. Petersburg, has seen its fair share of history. During most of the period of construction of the notorious White Sea Canal, excavation and Gulag operations were managed from Medvezhegorsk. There is still a prison in town, just to the west of where we are staying.

When we exit the Malaya Medvezhka Resort a few hours later, we turn east.

White Sea Canal

About 15 kilometers from Medvezhegorsk is Povenets, a small town on the shores of Lake Onega that happens to be the starting point of the White Sea Canal – a monument to much of the best and worst that the Soviet Union was capable of. Okay, mostly the worst.

The White Sea Canal "was the first, last, and only Gulag project ever exposed to the full light of Soviet propaganda, both at home and abroad."[17] Its goal was to connect the White Sea with St. Petersburg and the Baltic, replacing a longer international shipping route (over 3,000 nautical miles through the Baltic Sea, and up and around Finland and Norway) with a protected internal route less than one-tenth as long. Given the drift toward war in Europe in the early 1930s, and the Soviet drive to rapid industrialization, it could be argued that such a canal made sense. Yet the reality was that the flow of traffic between the White and Baltic Seas hardly justified the effort, especially since a canal already existed (the 64-kilometer Northern Dvina Canal, finished in 1828) that connected the White Sea with the immense Volga-Baltic Waterway.

But Stalin wanted an industrial triumph with which to cap his first Five Year Plan (1928-1932). So, in February 1931, the official decision was taken to build the 227-kilometer (141-mile) canal. Seven months of engineering work followed (even so, the full route was never properly surveyed).

Interestingly, the idea to build a canal between Lake Onega and the White Sea was not new. It first arose under Peter the Great, but was not seriously considered until the nineteenth century, over the course of which at least four proposals were developed on government orders, none of them accepted (however the last one, in 1900, won a gold medal at the Paris World's Fair). Thus, in the larger scheme of things, the canal was potentially a worthwhile infrastructural project, but because it was turned into a political object and rushed to completion, it ended up slaughtering tens of thousands of workers and falling far short of its potential economic worth.

The slaughter part resulted from the White Sea Canal being the first major Soviet industrial project created with forced labor – a scheme attributed to the advocacy of former Solovetsky Prison Camp inmate turned Gulag administrator Naftaly Frenkel. It was Frenkel who first asserted the economic value of using Soviet prison labor for large industrial projects, with prisoners fed in accordance with how well they worked. Through implementation of his plans, some 250,000 prisoners were sent to the canal Gulag during 1931-33, with about 100,000 working on the canal at any one time. Official figures state that 12,800 died during construction (two-thirds of them in the final, all-hands-on work of the last year), but other estimates at least double those casualties.

Workers suffered from extreme malnutrition (500 grams of bread per day the average ration), the bitter northern cold, and the brutality of un-mechanized construction. Virtually all of the nearly 100 major project components (including 19 locks), the laying of over 2,500 kilometers of rail line, and the movement of 21 million cubic meters of earth, was done by hand using crude implements, including wooden wheelbarrows, wooden spades, pickaxes and metal prybars. Very little was brought in from the outside, and the majority of the canal was built using the readily available local ingredients: wood, stone, soil and turf.

The economic fiasco came about because Stalin had decreed – for no apparently rational reason – that the massive project be completed in 20 months, over the objections of multiple, brave advisers. As a result, compromises had to be made on design. Most importantly, the canal was only dug 12 feet deep (3.5 meters), making it unsuitable for many sea-going vessels. And it was often narrow. When Stalin cruised the canal upon its completion in the summer of 1933, he is said to have remarked, in what is certainly one of history's most trenchant project reviews, that it was "shallow and narrow, pointless, and unnecessary."

Nonetheless, the canal bore Stalin's name and its opening in August of 1933 was kicked off with a Potemkin village boat trip by 120 artists and writers, with Maxim Gorky at their head. Some 36 of these writers later collaborated on a 600-page book glorifying the project. It was a natural extension of the canal's role as propaganda vehicle, in which construction work by prisoners was heralded as reforming them from enemies of the people into honest workers, while serving society through the creation of projects vital to industrialization. In one camp newspaper, *Perekovka* ("Reforging"), there was a telling quote from a speech made by Lazar Kogan, a camp boss:

We cannot judge whether someone was rightly or wrongly imprisoned. That's the business of the prosecutor... You are obliged to create something valuable to the state with your work, and we are obliged to make of you someone who is valuable to the state.[18]

Among other things, the canal project bequeathed the Russian language the term *zek*, shorthand for political prisoner. It was reputedly derived from Kogan's proposal to call the prisoners working on the project "canal soldiers" (каналоармейцы), based on the word for Red Army soldiers (красноармейцы). Thus, *zaklyuchyony kanaloarmeyets* ("imprisoned canal soldier") was abbreviated to z/k, which morphed into *zek* and was later used to refer to all prisoners throughout the Gulag system.

Unique to this project, given its high propaganda profile, was the early discharge of prisoners upon the successful opening of the canal in August 1933. Reportedly, over 12,000 prisoners had their terms shortened and over 59,000 were freed (though of course there are no statistics on how many were re-arrested in later sweeps, something gruesomely common). Yet others stayed on. In the late 1930s, the Gulag that built the canal was transformed into a vast canal zone network of prison camps utilizing slave labor – an estimated 100,000 workers – to develop Karelia in other ways (hydro plants, forestry and associated industries).

Then, just over eight years after the canal was completed, all of its locks were exploded to stem the advancing Nazi-Finnish attack in December 1941, inundating and destroying the town of Povenets, among other side effects. The strategy worked, and the canal became a front line in the war until the region was liberated by Soviet troops in June 1944.

The canal was reopened in the middle of 1946, and Stalin's "shallow, narrow, pointless and unnecessary" channel soldiered on until the 1970s, when its minimum depth was increased along its entire length from 3.5 to 4 meters. Still shallow, but less so. Ship traffic peaked in 1985, when 7.3 million tons of cargo transited the canal. Today, at best half a million tons per year ply its waters, and it is typical to see only four or five ships a day pass by.

WE DRIVE INTO Povenets from the north and find the city's monument to canal victims just along the main road, at the intersection with – wait for it – Lenin Street. Its inscription reads: "To the innocents who died in construction of the White Sea Canal, 1931-1933." But apparently it can't be left at that. At the bottom of the stone is a second inscription, "In commemoration of the 500th anniversary of the founding of the village of Povenets."

Further down the road, near a pull off by the canal, there is a sad looking field gun, perhaps a mortar that once targeted Nazis, and a sign indicating that this was the front line in World War II. On the opposite side of the parking lot is a large, new church with a small playground and swimming pool behind it. It too stands as a memorial to those who built and served the canal, as well as a testimony to the rising authority of the church here.

Up the canal, about a kilometer away, we can see the impressive lock mechanisms. Over a span of twelve kilometers from here to the east there are seven short locks ("the Povenets Stairway") that lift ships 69 meters to the highest level along the canal, then another twelve locks that provide a descent of 103 meters to sea level at the White Sea.*

---

* By way of comparison, the 12 locks in the 77-kilometer Panama Canal lift and lower ships just 26 meters.

We drive over the canal and weave our way to the shore of the lake. The wind picks up and the sky begins to look forbidding. We take a few photos then dive back into the car to head back to the Canal Museum. When we stopped by earlier, a pensioner appeared out of nowhere, folded his arms in front of his chest, and announced that the museum was closed for lunch until 1:30.

At 1:45 I enter the building, looking for the museum, and a door-woman announces that "the museum is closed, she's on vacation." I wonder who *she* could be and don't dare ask if there could only be one employee for a museum to commemorate one of the most murderous construction projects of the Soviet era. I play the foreigner card, joking that I have come "all the way from America" to see this museum, couldn't they please let me in to just look around a bit?

I already know the answer, but maintain my bluff, just to see what happens. The door-woman runs off to the deputy head of administration, who clearly can't just open the door and let some strange person in a Finnish cap look around however he likes. She puts in a call to the museum curator, to see if she will pop in to the museum and open up the exhibits for a foreigner.

I wander back out to the lobby and stare at a huge, wooden, wall-sized map of the White Sea Canal. A few moments later the deputy director sticks her head out of the dark hallway and informs me that, "She can't come in. She's gone off to the forest."

WE SPEND A bit of time wandering around Povenets. There is a bright, colorful grocery shop, a drugstore, and some decently constructed, Soviet-era cement housing blocks at the edge of the village, where canal workers live. There are also the usual ramshackle, need a coat of paint and considerable nipping and tucking at the eaves, maybe a new roof, and certainly a new gate, homes. And there is the Center for

Culture, painted a jarring pink and blue. Someone clearly got a deal on brightly colored paint and devil take him who objects to the hot pink and neon blue color combination. A neglected band shell crumbles in the weeds, and a playing field surrounded by half-submerged truck tires lies overgrown and unused.

We encounter a pair of friendly babushkas in red scarves – Tamara and Galina – who delight in having their picture taken. Both worked on the canal for over 40 years and have spent their lives in this little town. They walk off with the hobble of retirees with aching hips and ankles, their grandson in tow.

School let out a few hours ago and the town is now crawling with kids making their way home, dawdling with friends, hanging out in the run-down town park.

Mikhail talks to a little boy of about seven, Vadim, at the White Sea Canal monument, asking him if he knows why the monument is here.

"I don't know what it is for, but I'm made of iron," he says. "I don't let anyone push me around or make fun of me. If they do, I whomp them. Today, someone made fun of me and I punched him in the stomach."

THE ROAD BETWEEN Povenets and Medvezhegorsk is recently paved and blissfully smooth. Beautiful, thick pine forests crowd the shoulder of this quiet, winding road set back from the flat shoreline of Lake Onega. Yet in a few places workers are trimming the roadside woods back several dozen meters, as if there were plans to expand the two-lane road into four.

Little did we know at the time, because there were no obvious road markers or historical indicators for the turnoff, but just a few miles north of Povenets we drove past Sandarmokh – one of Russia's largest mass grave sites for victims of the Stalinist purges.

On October 27, 1937, over 1,000 prisoners from the Solovetsky Prison Camp were loaded onto barges and shipped out. For 60 years, their fate was unknown; it had been thought they drowned in the White Sea. As it turned out, they were brought here and shot in a mass execution that lasted several days. But it did not stop there. Through 1938, nearly 10,000 victims of some 58 nationalities were shot and buried here in over 200 mass graves. Many were workers on the White Sea Canal, but there were also members of the Ukrainian intelligentsia, and idealist Finnish-Americans and Finnish-Canadians who had emigrated to Soviet Russia. The graves were discovered in 1997 by Memorial, the Russian NGO that is devoted to preserving the memory of those who perished in the Stalinist purges. Today there is a chapel and many somber grave markers.

But there is not, as one might expect, a prominent sign on the main road, pointing passersby to the solemn site that lies just beyond the tree line of this prosaic lakeside community, a region that has been the site of incalculable human suffering.

ON THE WAY back through Medvezhegorsk to the E105, we search the main road for some food to keep us going. The roads, as everywhere in Russia, are steeped in history. The main drag, along which we pass our resort and its neighboring detention center, is Dzerzhinsky Street, named for the founder of the NKVD, Felix Dzerzhinsky. Just past a large shopping complex, once the headquarters of the White Sea Canal Camp Administration, the road is lined with low, yellow stone buildings. We turn off onto Solunin Street, named for Vasily Petrovich Solunin, a leader of the Communist forces resisting foreign intervention who was killed in a forest not far from here in 1919.

Three small walk-in kiosks huddle along the pock-marked side road. One sells flowers, the other "Euro Mix Stock and Second Hand" clothing, and the third pizza, Georgian *khachapuri* and Caucasian meat pies. We have arrived just as they are taking the cheesy *khachapuri* out of the oven and so our choice is obvious – we take a little of everything. Some of it will travel with us for two days before we finally give in and throw it away at the other end of Lake Ladoga.

From Medvezhegorsk we have just 150 kilometers left to cover to reach Petrozavodsk, and we travel down miles and miles of smooth Karelian roads lined by towering birch trees. Mikhail naps most of the way. At one point, as I crest a sun-kissed hill, the iPod cues up Van Morrison's *Brand New Day*. It is a fitting epilogue to a day spent in some of recent history's darker pages.

> When all the dark clouds roll away
> And the sun begins to shine
> I see my freedom from across the way
> And it comes right in on time
> Well it shines so bright and it gives so much light
> And it comes from the sky above
> Makes me feel so free makes me feel like me
> And lights my life with love

Petrozavodsk

In September 1703, as Russia's Great Northern War with Sweden raged, Peter the Great ordered his trusted aide, Prince Alexander Menshikov, to found Petrovskaya Sloboda as an iron foundry to manufacture cannons and anchors for his young Baltic Fleet. In the beginning, the works used the name Shuysky Zavod (literally, "factory on the Shuysky River"), but within a decade it had become Petrovsky Zavod (Peter's Factory).

After Peter's death, the town declined, its foundry silenced for half a century. Then, in the 1770s, it was revived when Catherine the Great needed cannons for her wars with Turkey. In 1777 the town was re-named Petrozavodsk and incorporated. During Catherine's municipal reforms a new city center was built, radiating out in a circular pattern.

Today, Petrozavodsk is the pulsing capital of the Republic of Karelia, with a quarter million residents. Compared to the behemoth that is Murmansk and the smaller mono-factory towns we visited in the North, this is a clean, pleasant city with a reasonably compact center and a very pleasant waterfront.

We pull into the city around five in the evening and hit some spots of traffic and construction. Mikhail directs me to the hotel, which, is named 13 Chairs (13 Стульев), a riff on Ilya Ilf and Evgeny Petrov's classic novel, *The 12 Chairs*. This is appropriate, given that we have been joking about us being Ilf and Petrov, not sure who is who.

We made our reservations at this boutique hotel (two comfortable rooms, breakfast included, for $98 a night) – as we will for much of our trip – from the road just a day or so in advance, using the travel site booking.com. It is a sign of how much things have changed in Russia, that one can now easily book accommodations on the fly, based on visitor ratings, price, and location, without special permits, approvals or red tape. Later, south of Moscow, we will find things to be a bit neo-Soviet, but here, up in the North, there is a refreshingly relaxed attitude toward travel.

After settling in, we decide to let Kukisvumchorr rest in the parking lot and we walk to our meeting, since the light is so good, though we don't take any pictures, as the route we take is along ugly, traffic-plugged streets.

On the ground floor of the aging, Soviet-era Kalevala theater (named for the Finnish folk epic), we meet Valentin Svatovoy, proprietor and senior baker at Konditerskaya Valentina ("Valentine's Bakery").

Tall, broad-shouldered, with close-cropped hair and a wide Scandinavian visage, Svatovoy is an imposing presence. I worry he is going to be a close-lipped, difficult interviewee. He seems a bit offended that we don't want any tea, coffee, or sweets (we explain we have just eaten), and leads us to a corner table in his colorful, tastefully decorated bakery.

When we ask him about himself, he immediately opens up, animatedly gesturing as he speaks, his face frequently breaking into a warm, inviting grin.

"I am a product of Soviet nationality policy," he laughs. Born in Moldova, raised in Ukraine, he has lived in Karelia for most of his adult life. Trained as an agro-technologist slash veterinarian, he was the first person in Karelia to artificially inseminate pigs. It's the sort of claim to fame you just can't *not* mention.

"People ask me, 'You are so easygoing, you can talk to everybody. Where did you learn that?'" he says. "When you spend three years overseeing tens of thousands of pigs, each with its own, unique personality, it's very easy to shift to dealing with people! Only, in contrast with humans, pigs are dirtier. But each pig has its own distinct personality, as hard as it is to believe; they each have their own mind. It is a totally unique animal… I think they may survive us. It won't be a Planet of the Apes, but a Planet of the Pigs…" he laughs.

After pigs, he moved on to managing a milk factory, then a brewery, then newspapers, and finally some acquaintances asked him to open a bakery to supply their new restaurant. There, he says, he found his calling, his true passion.

"I had been baking since I was a young kid, living in a village. But there it was not accepted for a boy to bake… When my mother would take my goods to work, I asked her to say that they she had made them. And when someone would ask her for her recipe, she would have to say she didn't remember and had to bring the recipe from home."

Baking became his passion, what he lived for. "There is something magical about how flour and yeast and water all come together and make this thing called bread," he says. He invented a new sort of bread, Virma (named for a Pomor village on the coast of the White Sea) – a rye bread made with a *kvas* wort that had the shape of an overturned Pomor boat. It was hugely successful.

But there were two problems. The first was that the restaurant and bakery were opened in February 1999, on the heels of the financial crisis. The second was that he is a perfectionist, and the restaurateurs, while committed to their business, were more utilitarian. "They told me (and they tell me to this day) that I do things how they *must* be done, how they *should* be done; they do them like they *need* to be done, in order to survive."

The partnership only lasted six months before they decided to part ways. So, Svatovoy says, for the first time in his life he found himself without work, without someone needing his services. So he sat down and made a list of the things he loved and the things he was good at, and, as a result, decided that he would open a confectionary.

For the first time in his life, he was working for himself, he says, "and I decided that in our little city, it would be very important that behind a specific product there stood a specific person." So he decided to put his name on the business.

Starting with an investment of $10,000, within a year he was clearing $6,000 a month, plowing every dollar back into his business. "Those first years were so profitable," he says, "that there was no need to hide profits. You could pay your taxes, pay your employees, and there was still plenty left over to re-invest back in the business." One bakery became six during the boom years of 2003-2012 and he had 55 employees. Through it all, he insisted on doing business above board, to prove that business could be run honestly and profitably in Russia.

"We have been in business for 16 years, at one legal address, under one legal name, and have never had anything to hide," he says. "Perhaps it is again the perfectionist complex, but I wanted to prove that you could run a business honestly… perhaps I could have earned more through other means, but I live peacefully."

In Russia, government auditors typically leave businesses alone during their first three years of operation, Svatovoy says, so it is a typical ruse to start up a business and three years later shut it down, then shift resources to a new entity and start operating for another three inspection-free years. The modern Russian business landscape, Svatovoy says, is littered with such "dead souls" of commerce.

Yet, if you haven't got any of those dead souls, he says, you've got nothing to hide. "Every time we've been audited (and now it is only once a year, versus five or six times a year at the start), we have come out clean and have never been asked to pay any kind of bribe at all," he says. "Especially since auditors have a far more positive attitude toward me than to those who have entered the market more recently. Because they know what I started with, what I overcame, and how I work… they know if they find some shortcoming, I will fix it."

People also know who they are dealing with when they deal with him, Svatovoy says. That's part of the upside that comes with his decision to identify his business with himself personally, to put his name right out there. Which, of course cuts both ways.

"I did not anticipate the extent to which I would become a public person," Svatovoy says. "When people talk about Valentin's Confectionary, they are not talking about my colleagues, my workers, but about me personally. Of course that is good and pleasant, but when there is a mistake, and people talk about it, it becomes personal, and that is very difficult." And things have been tough lately. "Baked goods are products of 'non-rational demand,'" Svatovoy explains. "So it is one of those things that one can cut back on before anything else." And since their production relies so heavily on newly embargoed imports, they have been pinched in both directions – supply and demand.

Today there is just one shop, and times are tough.

"The government does not like small business," Svatovoy says.

"I know what I am paying in taxes to various funds," he continues. "But the workers are not interested in that; they only know what they receive... In contrast to my workers, I understand that I pay a huge amount of money to the state, which it needs in order to survive. The state does not have its own money. It has only the taxpayers' money. When a worker comes and asks for a raise, I have to say, 'Listen, in order for me to pay you R1,000 more, I have to pay the government almost R600.' Imagine if I gave my workers their entire salary, and they had to pay the government themselves for medical insurance, for pension and insurance. They would say, 'Excuse me government, why am I paying you so much money? And why do I receive such a small pension?' That's not good for the state. I now have 20 employees, and if these 20 knew how much they were paying the state, it would not be good. And just try to subdue 20 people… Therefore, if there were more people who understood how much they are paying in taxes to the state where they live, that they respect, that they hope will be there to protect them if something goes wrong, well, such people are not needed…"

That Svatovoy's shop is different from cookie-cutter cafes and coffee bars is apparent the moment you walk through the door. It is pristine and painted in bright, primary colors. There is no dust even in the tight corners. It comes from taking care of things in a consistent, persistent way, not opening a shiny new store, raking off profits and letting it deteriorate before shuttering it and opening a new branch. The decor is simple and inviting, not gaudy or over the top, as is so common in many Russian retail outlets aping Western chains.

We ask how the stores came to look like this, to have a reputation as a safe, family place. He visibly darkens for the first time in our conversation as he talks about how, when he was a child, his father would take him to beer dives – noisy, smoke-filled establishments that reeked of salted fish. "You didn't want to not be with your father, because you got so little time with him," Svatovoy says. Yet there were also better memories, like when his father would take him and his brother to a bright, pleasant ice cream shop.

He recalls all this and then notes how, back in the heady, boom times, everyone was opening up cafes where you could get alcohol, beer, even take-away spirits. But he set a different course. He declared that his confectionary cafes would be alcohol- and smoke-free. "I wanted to create a safe place," he says, "where you don't meet with boorishness or drunks, where young people can hang out worry free... It's very difficult, when you are 13 or 14, and you get together with your girl and some guy is in the corner leering at her. A guy has to go up to him and say 'What are you looking at?' Ours is a place where no one is leering at your girl, and no one is going to be waiting for you outside, to show you who's boss. That's important. To be secure and comfortable."

The Barbell Maker

Since we find ourselves in Peter's cannon-forging city, it is natural we would want to meet Vadim Markelov, 52, who is giving Petrozavodsk's cannon-making heritage a new twist by producing barbells.

Also, we were intrigued by his project to install weight-lifting equipment along the Petrozavodsk embankment. These are not the sort of Nautilus or body-weight machines you meet at your local gym. They are all-weather devices designed down to the last nut to be safe from the elements, as well as from vandals and thieves.

On a cool autumn day on Petrozavodsk's bustling waterfront (opened in 1994 on the 50th anniversary of the city's liberation), we watch several users – most pensioners – easily adjust the brilliantly-designed weighting system, then work their quads, delts and abs before continuing their stroll along the waterfront.

WE TRACKED DOWN Markelov at a high-walled compound along the river, outside the city center. We meet him at the front door of his showroom and offices, and he takes us on a short drive to the company's sprawling production complex, which is several large, industrial buildings set amid a metal scrap yard.

Trim, with short-cropped dark hair and a serious demeanor, he wears darks slacks, a pastel blue floral shirt and a lightweight fall jacket, and he sports a Bluetooth earbud so that he can call and communicate with various guards and assistants en route.

Markelov got his start in business a few years before perestroika, as a grey market production line manager, shifting state resources to satisfy private needs. By 1986 he started making his first weights – combining his experience in iron works and his interest in sport and weightlifting. When cooperative enterprises were legalized in 1987, he and others took the venture private, and by 1988 had 600 workers, even making weightlifting machines for Western brands.

In the early 1990s, the cooperative movement fell apart when the state enterprises many of them worked under were sold off for kopeks. Markelov had to start from scratch. But this time he decided to completely verticalize his business. "The only things we buy," Markelov says, "are water, gas, scrap metal, and black rubber. From that we make everything we do."

"This is a technology park," he continues, showing us a spare parts storage room off the line where they forge the weights, which adjoins a building where they do galvanizing, another for repairs, and still another where welding and painting takes place. "If we want a particular nut, it is much easier to just make it ourselves, instead of finding a supplier." A spin-off benefit of that, Markelov says, is that, "because we do all of this ourselves, it gives birth to new ideas and product lines."

Like a new line of body-weight and weight-based rehab machinery that has zero electronics, making them far more affordable for small clinics or small towns.

Thankfully, we are visiting Markelov's factory on a Saturday and little is working. There are so many machines here, the din must be deafening when work is at full steam.

While about half of Markelov's lines are new, business is brisk and machinery, raw materials and half-finished equipment is stacked and boxed every which way in the sprawling, labyrinthine sheds. This is not a neatly ordered, painted-floor, OSHA regulated factory like you might visit in Bonn or Sunnyvale. This is a gritty metal works where dust, grease, input and output mix in a particular post-Soviet efficiency.

Yet it works.

By Markelov's reckoning, each month he sells nearly 300 tons of barbells and 2,000 weightlifting machines. Customers include construction developers, the military, prisons, as well as plenty of foreigners. But the real market is domestic.

"The sanctions are good for a business like ours," he explains. "It makes the country open to us but closed to outsiders, so we have no competition. If the crisis lasts another five years, it will be good for us."

After the tour of his extensive facilities, including demonstration halls where we sling some kettlebells and test out the various exercise machines, we retreat to Markelov's office for tea and preserves.

While the tea is steeping, Markelov steps into a storage area adjoining his office and returns with a massive, three-liter glass jar full of glistening, golden cloudberry preserves. But these are not just any cloudberry preserves – they are Markelov's own homemade cloudberry preserves.

"Women don't know how to make preserves," he says, proudly setting the huge container down on the table, then proceeding to fill a large bowl with about a pint of the shimmering essence. "They overcook it and dump in too much sugar. The key is to just bring the fruit barely to the boiling point and then stop."

We taste the preserves with our tea and immediately conclude that the pint Markelov has served up will probably not be enough, what with us having skipped lunch and all…

The preserves carry all of the tangy freshness of the cloudberries, with none of the sugary sweet overtones that often characterize homemade jam. Tiny cloudberry seeds crunch in our teeth and we savor each mouthful, washed down with a light black tea.

"Preserves is kind of a hobby for me," Markelov says. He retreats again to the back room, coming out this time with two smaller jars, one that glows red, the other purple – gooseberry and black currant, he says. These too are fine, but, honestly they cannot measure up to the masterpiece that is the cloudberries. Markelov dispenses another pint and the talk continues, bouncing from politics to history to business. And back to preserves again.

I mention that Vermont is famous for its maple syrup. This has Markelov up from his chair and off to a different storeroom.

"Okay," he says on his way out the door, "you want to taste something different? I'll give you some and you have to try to guess what it is. It is preserves from a local forest."

We readily agree.

He returns cradling a small bowl protectively, as if it contains the very essence of his being. It looks to hold about half a cup of thick honey, with bits of some organic material floating in it. Mikhail dips in a spoon and takes a taste. I do the same.

It has a fragrant sweetness. Earthy and fruity all at once, with the texture of honey or molasses.

"Guess!" Markelov says, smiling.

"It's not from berries, is it?" Mikhail asks.

"No."

I am at a loss and guess apples. Which is wrong.

Mikhail guesses pinecones. He is correct, and rewards himself with another big spoonful.

Apparently, you can make rather amazing preserves from young pinecones, distilling them into an earthy, sweet concoction that is not only tasty, but also good for you. "This has all sorts of helpful bacteria for your digestive tract," Markelov says.

This leads into a discussion of health care and Markelov shows us a few medical devices he has designed and put into production, and for which he holds the patents (he claims to have over 60 patents). He is proudest of an electro-muscular stimulation device that he insists is built on a breakthrough in this 200-year-old technology. It works, he says, in an entirely different way, by introducing feedback mechanisms that actually make the therapy effective.

It reminds me of a Russian inventor I met two decades ago who claimed to have discovered a method for revolutionizing plastic injection molding – a multibillion dollar industry – that had somehow been overlooked by generations of plastic makers in the West.

That Russian engineers are among the best in the world is without question. But some of them also share with the broader Russian population an irrational faith in the quasi-miraculous, in parascience and folk healers, so long as they are rooted in Russian soil. The tendency reached new heights in the 1990s, when the nation was cut loose from its 70-year-old ideological and cultural straight-jacket and began groping for answers to life's questions, yet had not (given the tenets of Marxism-Leninism) been taught to think critically. This tendency has been tempered in recent years, but, alloyed by the sense that Russia is somehow different – more soulful, mystical or spiritual – from other nations, that things can happen here (or be invented or designed here) that could not happen anywhere else. It still colors world views and plunders the state budget. Indeed, in late 2015 the Russian Academy of Sciences set up a Commission on Pseudoscience and Research Fraud to combat pseudosciences such as homeopathy.[19]

AT SOME POINT, because we are engaged in a marathon tea drinking session, and because this is Russia, talk turns to history and to the current situation in Crimea.

"History is full of paradoxes, and it is hard to tell what those in power have in mind," Markelov says, after noting he is a huge history buff. "Stalin may have been a tyrant, but he may also have been a genius. Take the Winter War with Finland [1939-40]. It is generally seen as a complete failure, and showed the weakness of the Russian military, but it added the Karelian Isthmus to Russia. If that had not happened, in the Great Patriotic War, Hitler and the Finns would have taken Leningrad in a day." So, Markelov posits, perhaps there is more going on regarding Crimea than anyone outside the Kremlin has any idea about.

Perhaps too much, I offer. Wouldn't Russia be better off with a greater measure of accountability and democracy?

"What kind of democracy can you have when 60 years ago they were shooting us at will?..." Markelov answers. "We are all the children of slaves... What kind of democracy can we have when we still have streets named after terrorists like Pestel?"*

Such pessimism – his company's economic success notwithstanding – also colors Markelov's take on the economy. It is not a certainty, he says, that the government will survive a prolonged recession. "Russians will withstand much," he says, recounting a story of an employee who lived on bouillon for two years after the difficult factory closures of the 1990s. "Russia is absolutely unpredictable. You can't tell when people like this worker might come out into the streets, or what they will put up with. Russia is a completely irrational place. You can't figure it out with math."

The Petrozavodsk Phenomenon

On September 20, 1977, something strange happened over Petrozavodsk that also could not be figured out with math.

Sightings of unidentified luminous objects began around 1 AM in the skies over Karelia, and over the next four hours independent sightings were reported over a vast region stretching from the Baltics to the White Sea and beyond (including from planes landing in Moscow).

Descriptions included "bright, luminous bodies surrounded by extended shells and emitting light rays or jets of quaint shapes...,"

---

* Pavel Pestel (1793-1826), a Russian revolutionary and leader of the Decembrist revolt who advocated violent overthrow of the monarchy and regicide. He was hung along with four other members of the Decembrists.

"a spinning object similar to a buoy, 10 meters in diameter…," "a dim, translucent ring, with the color of a dark amethyst, with intense light radiating from within…"

Remarkably, the "unexplained phenomenon" was widely reported in the official Soviet media. Correspondent Nikolai Milov described it as a "huge star in the dark sky" that spread out over Petrozavodsk in the form of a jellyfish, "showering the city with a multitude of very fine rays which created an image of pouring rain." He wrote that, "after some time the luminescent rays ceased" and "the jellyfish turned into a bright semicircle," which resumed its movement towards Lake Onega.

Government reports were inconclusive and eyewitnesses who underwent psychological testing were pronounced sane.

Over the years, various explanations, from aurora borealis (too high and not bright enough), a satellite launch (wrong direction), and "chemiluminescence" (not realistic), have all come up short, and the mystery remains just that. As Ukrainian scientist Oleh Pruss wrote, after discounting the idea that the glow was the result of a satellite launch that took place that day: "there was something completely different over Petrozavodsk."

ALMOST THIRTY-SIX YEARS to the day after what has since come to be called The Petrozavodsk Phenomenon, on September 11, 2013, something nearly as strange happened in Karelia's capital city. Russians showed up to the polls and voted to toss out incumbent mayor Nikolai Levin, an influential member of the pro-Kremlin United Russia party. In his place, they voted in Galina Shirshina, a 34-year-old psychology PhD and member of the opposition party Yabloko. She became the city's first woman mayor and practically the only truly independent municipal leader in all Russia.

"We were very happy when we elected our mayor," says Natalya Sevets-Yermolina, "but then it turned out she was subjected to serious pressure from the governor's team."

Sevets-Yermolina, a former journalist who heads up the cultural initiative Agri-Culture, says that what sets Petrozavodsk and Karelia apart is that "Karelia never had slavery… The best people were exiled here by the tsars: oppositionists."

Sevets-Yermolina has wild dark hair and an unprepossessing style. She is gregarious and engaging, announcing proudly over marinated mushrooms (we are meeting during dinner) that she is a "double-agent," by which she means she graduated from two institutions that have since been declared foreign agents under Russian law: the Institute for Regional Press and the Moscow School for Political Investigations.

"Here in Karelia, the proximity of Finland and the West can be felt in everything," she says. "Even in the Soviet era, people here dressed more stylishly than in Moscow and St. Petersburg. They used to trade berries for jeans. What makes Petrozavodsk different is that fashion begins here. They say that fashion begins in Moscow, but often intellectual fashion in Petrozavodsk overtakes Moscow… for example books. I see what my friends here are reading and then later it takes off in Moscow. I am certain that we have a very progressive community here."

The election of Shirshina was surely a sign of this progressiveness: an independent-minded city at the periphery stands up against the wishes of the imperial center. Yet history teaches that such "revolts" rarely end well, and even though Shirshina won by a plurality of over 13 percent, as an outsider she faced immense pressure from the ruling party. Finally, on December 25, 2015, two months after our visit to the city, she was voted out of office by the City Council for "non-fulfillment of her duties." She vowed to fight the decision, but the odds are stacked against her. As Irina Khakamada, a longtime

Yabloko activist said, "the conclusion is that the people's mandate is not worth anything, it can be violated at any moment. It is a clear example of the imitation of democracy."

Cultivating Civility

Creating a democracy is hard. Maintaining it is even harder.

And the reality is that it does not begin at the ballot box, but in schools and homes, with how children are brought up.

Nadezhda Pykhonina teaches physics and math at Shuysky Middle School, 17 kilometers outside Petrozavodsk. She has been teaching physics for 30 years, but is most animated when speaking about her role as "class leader," in which she leads "class hours" (классные часы) – a required weekly time for all students, from first grade through high school, in which the teacher talks about general, non-scholarly subjects, from patriotism and morality to ethics and culture. Indeed, there are official websites* where teachers can download prepared materials to deliver lectures on everything from Lomonosov to etiquette for young girls to the occupation of Crimea.

Eschewing such staid options, in her class hours Pykhonina has developed sessions based in part on the work of an American non-profit, The Democracy Project. It has as its goal raising responsible citizens, of developing in students seven civic skills (cooperation, patience, fairness, respect, strength, self-improvement, balance) thought to contribute to the healthy development of a democratic polity.

"I have these seven skills posted in my classroom," Pykhonina says, "and every skill is focused on separately in class hours." She does not

---

* For example, klassnye-chasy.ru

lecture, but orients her hours around discussion and activities, on engaging the students.

We attend a session of such a class staged for us at a Petrozavodsk hotel. The instructor, while well-intentioned, is ham-handed and resorts to lecturing, giving out "right" answers rather than provoking interesting discussions. But, in the few break-out sessions where students are asked to collaborate (say on creating a drawing of an ideal citizen), there does seem to be sincere participation and face-to-face interaction that is difficult to come by in the Age of Facebook.

Pykhonina says she is committed to this work because civic skills help "the child understand that he is a person, that he can develop himself. So that in the future no one, not his mother, not his father, will control his life, so that he will live of his own accord… so that he can find his path in life by himself and become a person. Of course, he is born as a person, but he needs to develop it…"

There are echoes here of what Natalya Sevets-Yermolina is doing across town with her Agri-Culture "anti-crisis space" (she jokes: "after the crisis is over, we will shut the doors and go home").

The project, Sevets-Yermolina says, started with no money. "We are trying various methods to earn money for culture. In our country, culture is kind of an orphan. Culture is always asking for money from the state: 'Give us something, we are a cultural country, give us something!' But culture is not an industry, it is the social sphere. Yet throughout the world culture is a huge industry and there is lots of money floating around."

"The plan," she says, "is to earn a bit of money, to teach people to earn money from culture. We want to do lots of start-ups on the basis of our project and create a support fund for various initiatives."

So they are turning their accessible space into a place where people can meet, learn together, and engage in civil discourse. Among other things, there are English language classes offered at half the going market rate, performances by foreign musicians, and knitting circles where babushkas can turn mittens and cozies into sources of side-income.

As with Pykhonina's classes, Agri-Culture focuses on interactivity. They don't like more "passive" activities like lectures. "We are striving to ensure that no one suffers from culture," Sevets-Yermolina jokes.

Indeed, Sevets-Yermolina and Pykhonina are working two sides of the same coin: helping citizens of every age to realize their potential, to engage with their community, and through it all to make that community stronger.

A true citizen, Pykhonina explains, is "a person who is not indifferent to the people and reality that surround him. A person who applies his intelligence and ability to not merely improve himself, but also the society in which he lives."

"But isn't a good citizen also someone who makes the state uncomfortable?" we ask Pykhonina.

"You are correct, in part. But a good citizen will not be one, not two, but many. And if such citizens come to power, you have to agree that the government will be transformed. But, you have to give them the chance to do this.

"We do this so that people will believe in themselves. Not just so there will be one or two citizens, but a group of active citizens who can transform the world. Of course, you understand, these are general words, and I don't know if this will happen in the near future, or if things will just keep on as they are. But we want to do something so that these children are sure that they are doing the right thing in life."

If they succeed, history may record a different Petrozavodsk Phenomenon, but one with decidedly more explicable roots.

Kinerma

Across the room an iPhone alarm rages.

I open my eyes. Or at least I think I do.

I cannot tell if I am asleep or awake, alive or dead.

An utterly absolute blackness surrounds me. Eyelids closed: pitch black. Eyelids open: pitch black. It is a very unsettling feeling, as if I could reach out and touch infinity, which I have no intention of doing.

Apparently (I later learn), the photographer I am traveling with decided to get up to shoot the stars just before dawn. He then thought better of it, shut off his alarm, and crawled back into bed.

I realize it is the middle of the night, yet it takes me a few moments to get my bearings. Gradually I remember that we are sleeping alongside a massive Russian stove in a century-old wooden house, which happens to be located about an hour's drive west of Petrozavodsk and 60 kilometers off the E105.

We are in rural Karelia, in the tiny village of Kinerma, population 5.

Four of those five are the Kalmykov family.

NADEZHDA KALMYKOVA, 48, says as a teen she would do all she could to avoid coming here. Her mother had been born in the village and the family would come back to Kinerma for vacations and weekends. And it was all work, something as a teen she obviously wanted to avoid.

But people change. Kalmykova changed. About 15 years ago, when she told someone she was from Petrozavodsk, they didn't believe her. "You are always talking about 'Kinerma, Kinerma,'" she recalls them saying. She soon realized that her future lay in the preservation of this tiny village.

In fact, Kinerma is the last extant Karelian village preserved in largely the state it was in 150 years ago. It has been saved by several historical flukes, but mainly because it does not sit on a lake or near a river, meaning it was never a highly desirable location for summer dachas. Also, Kinerma was home to "the only miracle-working icon in the Olonets region," Kalmykova says. "I am sure that is what has really protected us."

The village is arranged in a circle about its old, wooden chapel, which nestles in a tall pine copse, its grounds humpy and uneven from unmarked graves. The village has 11 buildings in various states of repair that either belong to those who live in them, or are kept in a family and passed on to descendants. Yet, unlike most Russian villages you come across in the North, only a few of the buildings are in dire condition. "People have started coming here from all over the world," Kalmykova explains, "and many heirs are living here all summer, and they have already started taking better care of their homes and yards. The village is being transformed."

Each August there are celebrations in the village on the annual name day for the church's famous icon, and there is a steady flow of tourists who come by minibus from Petrozavodsk, as part of tours that include the architectural sanctuary on Kizhi Island. Finnish organizations also provide valuable in-kind support.

THE 120-YEAR OLD Karelian house we are staying in has been ret-rofitted to hold up to 14 visitors, which it often does, with Kalmykova cooking and cleaning and giving guided tours (along with her husband and young sons).

"What makes a building Karelian is that the livestock and people lived together under one roof," Kalmykova explains. "You had the warm, heated side, where the people lived, and the cold side where the livestock lived. Above the livestock was the feed storage, with natural aeration to keep the feed dry… They were built this way because of the weather, so that you could survive for several days without having to go outside, as long as you had a supply of water."

In this building, where the feed loft would have been, Kalmykova has built a small, tastefully outfitted, trilingual museum to convey the history of the town and of Karelian architecture and life.

Meanwhile, at the center of the building's warm side is a massive Russian stove. Two, actually – one for the main room, which is both living room and kitchen, the other for the bedroom where we slept. The stove takes a day or more to stoke and get up to proper temperature. A few quarter-split logs are burned in a carefully controlled manner, so as to heat up the huge mass of masonry. Then the flues are sealed off and the stone maintains and emits its heat for hours, days even.

Why did she decide to do this? "The main reason, of course, is to preserve Kinerma," she says. "It is always on my mind…"

IN THE AFTERNOON, Mikhail convinced Kalmykova to have her sons stoke up the communal banya, so that we could "enjoy" a post-prandial steam.

That evening, after a tasty dinner of locally caught trout, potatoes and carrot salad (and a couple of shots of vodka to get us in the right frame of mind), we stumbled down the hill through the gathering darkness to the "black banya." I am told it is called a black banya because it has no chimney, so that heating up the main room with a wood fire blackens the interior of the building.

Later, after we are forced to retreat from the heated space until it can air out a bit, I decide the real reason it is called black is because this heating technique creates a huge quantity of carbon monoxide gas that can bring your life to a swift end. As in turning out all the lights.

We strip down to our birthday suits and proceed to sweat all the toxicity from the first week of our travels out through our pores. I am lashed with *veniki* (birch branches bound together into a bunch) to within an inch of my life, and then we rinse and wash in the hot, damp heat before stepping out buck naked into the blackened night – woozy in our carbon-monoxide, heat-stroke induced state – to marvel at the stars packing the Kinerma sky from one horizon to the other.

It is apparently in this lowered state of mental awareness that Mikhail decides to set his alarm to ring at an hour when, in reality, he has no intention of doing anything other than going back to bed.

The Berry Seller

Igor Drozdov is sitting next to a fire and a large baby carriage, about 30 meters from the road, when we stop several car lengths in front of five large buckets of cranberries he has displayed on the shoulder. He leaves his fire and walks slowly toward the road, waiting for us to approach.

The camera hanging from Mikhail's shoulder alerts Drozdov to the fact that this is not going to be a typical buy-and-sell operation. But he quickly seems at ease and talks freely with us about his life and business.

A trim 5' 8", he has close-cropped hair, teeth that have put in 52 good years, and wears a smart, sporting outfit of stone washed denim jeans, an Adidas windbreaker and black baseball cap. He has the vise-grip handshake of a farmer or sailor. Tattooed hands peek out of from coat sleeves.

"I just got out in August," he says after we exchange first names, explain what we are doing here, and ask him to tell us a bit about himself. "It was a 12-year stint."

What his prison term was for, we don't ask; that's his business. We are here to talk berries. The main roads through Karelia – a rich, forested republic – are sprinkled with berry sellers like Drozdov and, earlier in the season, with mushroom sellers as well. They can do a brisk business; Russians like knowing where their forest treasures come from.

"I walked 20 kilometers to pick these," Drozdov replies when asked if these are the fruits of his own labor or if he is just reselling others' pickings. "I live just there, in Matrosy," he says, thumbing over his shoulder to the road through the forest behind him. "There's no work. I've been out two months. There are no jobs in the village, so everyone picks berries to sell by the side of the road."

It's a decent business. He and two relatives take turns picking cloudberries, cranberries or bilberries all day in the forest, with one of them sitting by the road for the day. "Sunday is a slow day here," Drozdov says. But come 5 o'clock, he says, cars can line up in a matter of minutes and he may sell out his entire stock (which looks to be about 30 liters, priced at R200 per liter). He runs through the numbers and we learn he averages about R6-8,000 a day ($100-150) when traffic and picking is good.

In addition to picking berries, Drozdov is a cobbler. He has applied for work in the city – Petrozavodsk, about 15 kilometers away – but does not seem eager to move there. "It's very dirty… the bushes are filled with trash," he says.

As we are packing up to leave, Mikhail asks him the question he has been posing to every subject we meet with and photograph: "Do you consider yourself a patriot, and if so why and of what?" Drozdov is the first who refuses to answer, perhaps seeing it as a trap:

> Whattya mean? What's this about? A patriot of berries? Or a patriot in general? Depends on what you mean by patriot. There's

all sorts. I won't answer that question. I don't even know. How can I be a patriot? No, I don't even know what that means. All of the patriots have died off. All that's left are us survivors.

Two Ladogas

It is not entirely clear which first bore the name Ladoga – the river or the lake, and where the town fits into that chronology. But we do know that the town was first mentioned in the year 1010, in a Scandinavian poem. The etymology of the name Ladoga has been variably attributed to the Finns, Slavs and even Germans. But the general consensus is that it was a word meant to describe the river's low elevation.

Scandinavians appear to have shown up here, along the lake, sometime in the 750s, a couple of centuries before any Slavs. Reputedly they were what we now call Swedes, from the island of Gottland, which lies in the Baltic Sea off what we now call Latvia. The settlement was an important trading point on the north-south river route "between the Vikings and the Greeks," and coins and beads dating from the first millennium have been found here.

According to tradition (see Novgorod, below), Rurik arrived here in 862 (actually, records suggest it was 856) and made it his capital – technically speaking, the first capital of Rus. From there, he and his fellow Scandinavians moved on to Novgorod and Kiev, his descendants forming the nation of Kievan Rus.

During this period, Ladoga was the most important trading center in Eastern Europe. The Varangians ruled over the area for most of two centuries after the Rus moved south, until the twelfth century, when the town became an important outpost for the strengthening Novgorod Republic.

The town's churches of John the Baptist and St. George date from about this time, as does the first stone fortress along the waterfront. For the next several hundred years, until 1703, when Peter I more or less settled the matter conclusively, the area was alternately held by Swedes and Russians.

The town is small, with just about 2,000 souls, and there is not much other than the ancient churches and the large historical complex built around the old fortress and St. George's Church. As we enter the town, we notice the *kurgans* (burial mounds) just outside the city center, one of which reputedly holds the grave of Rurik, and another that of his successor, Oleg.

Another Rurik, this one spelled Roerich (the painter and mystic Nikolai), said this area offered the best landscapes in Russia. With the churches and fortress perched along the water, a fairly strong case could be made. After World War II, the town became something of a colony for St. Petersburg painters and writers.

We stop in at the towering John the Baptist Church and chat with the inevitable two babushkas staffing a small stall by the entrance that offers candles, icons and cards. I slip into the tiny sanctuary and capture a few images of sunbeams shining in through the windows, and then we tromp off to investigate the fortress. We are two of only a few visitors on this weekday afternoon. The only other sign of life is a suspicious looking construction worker restoring a crumbling bit of the northern wall. Suspicious in the sense that he doesn't really look like he knows what he is doing.

IN 1703, WAR was raging with Sweden, and Peter the Great ordered the residents of Ladoga to move downstream, to a settlement surrounding the Nikolo-Medvedsky Monastery, where the Volkhov River flows into the lake. He established a shipyard and named the town Novaya (New) Ladoga; the pre-existing Ladoga immediately became Staraya (Old) Ladoga. It was a very busy year for Peter; he also founded another city a bit further to the west: St. Petersburg.

Only slightly larger than Staraya Ladoga, Novaya Ladoga nonetheless has a more industrial feel. We enjoy a light lunch at a cafe with excellent service, where we meet up with local contacts and stroll a residential neighborhood. There we stumble across the statue of Yurik, unveiled here less than a month ago.

Yurik (also known to respond to Shaverma or Druzhok) was a homeless neighborhood dog, a German Shepherd. He arrived in town sometime in 2011, reputedly on board a bus from the village of Issad, which lies about halfway between Staraya and Novaya Ladoga. Yurik was a very genial dog, and many tried to adopt him, but he preferred life on the street, where he was free to roam and where he made many friends among the locals. He would show up at all sorts of town events, walk in parades, and accompany local kids to and from school. Even the mayor knew him, it turns out. Wherever a crowd formed, Yurik would show up.

In the spring of 2014, Yurik disappeared. People searched for him everywhere, to no avail. Only later was it learned that someone had shot him.

For six months, locals collected over 75,000 rubles in donations (not just from locals, but, thanks to the power of social media, from all over the country) to make a monument to the friendly Yurik. The sculpture was done by St. Petersburg artist Artyom Rychkov and now sits on a street "where he had his main office," said the organizer of the campaign, Pavel Koin, "right near the store that trades in *kolbasa* and hot dogs," so that passing students and others can pat his head or shake his raised paw for good luck.

There are plans later to add a plaque that will say, simply, "He taught us to be human."

The Blacksmith

One of the first things Leonid Baluyev tells us is that he is a Jehovah's Witness. Which is why he has been a blacksmith on someone's payroll for the past 23 years and has not opted to venture out on his own in business. He just does not have the time.

"You need to properly set your priorities," he says.

The dark, grimy shop is a photographer's dream. Light streams in from a southern window and catches dust in the air. Cast iron railings gather dust in a pile behind the forge. Electrical wires dangle menacingly from the ceiling. Sparks fly from a grinder, metal is pounded with a heavy, thudding press, and Baluyev whacks and turns a piece of metal over on an anvil in the center of the room. Four photographers elbow each other at the back of the room, angling in the tight space for the perfect shot.

Baluyev forges everything from beautiful iron roses to cast-iron fencing. It depends on what orders come through. But, since his shop is attached to a shipping yard (the same one, chance has it, where Murmansk captain Nikolai Kalinikhin had his boat made), mostly he makes anchors and the picks that ice fisherman use to chip open large holes in the ice (when augurs aren't enough).

Baluyev is easygoing and likable. He is slim and does not fit the stereotype of the hulking, sweaty blacksmith who has been swinging a sledge against an anvil for 23 years. He is dressed casually in a light sweater and what appear to be dress shoes. He is a man of few words, yet one gets the sense that he is holding back, that he wants to witness his faith every chance he gets, but recognizes it is taboo. After all, the Russian government considers the Jehovah's Witnesses a harmful foreign sect, one that is beyond the pale of accepted belief. In September 2015, a regional court in Kurgan branded several of their texts as "extremist" and most of their websites are blocked in Russia.

Perhaps this is one reason that Baluyev is adamant that things in Russia now are far worse than they have been at any time in recent memory. "Things are bad, very bad," he says, almost whispering. "With everything." He really does not want to get more specific than that, but agrees this extends to price uncertainty, inflation and of course the state of US-Russian relations.

"There will never be any peace," he says. "The US will always put its priorities first. And the other one will push for his [priorities], in reply… in his macho way…."

"Between normal people, there are no negative feelings," he continues. "We have a bunch of Ukrainian workers here, and we all get along just fine. There is no swearing or accusations. Everything is fine."

Peace is a difficult thing, I offer.

"It's easy to describe peace," Baluyev says. "It was explained long ago, in the Bible. It's all precisely written down."

The Teacher

Tatyana Churova, 48, is an energetic teacher who loves her charges, a group of 17 students who have arrived in the early afternoon for an excursion through the tower and basement off Novaya Ladoga's historic Nikolsky Cathedral, built in the latter half of the 1400s. Constructed in the Novgorod Style, the church was once part of Nikolo Medvezhsky Monastery, Rus' northernmost monastery outpost when it was built, in 1050.

The church is named for St. Nicholas, patron saint of fisherman, sailors and travelers, and perches on the banks of the Volkhov River and near the Ladoga Canal,* which was built between the Neva and Svir rivers, so that sailors could avoid the unpredictable waters of Lake Ladoga – Europe's largest lake. As many as 1,000 ships a year used to go down in the lake's turbulent storms.

Churova shows us a small donation collection box built into the church's outside wall. In the pre-revolutionary era, parishioners would routinely collect R250 a year here, she says, to aid families of sailors who perished. Two hundred and fifty rubles was a lot of money back then – equivalent to a priest's annual salary.

When the kids arrive, they rush up to Mikhail and me, eager for contact with Americans. When Mikhail explains that he is from Sochi, he is dropped like a hot stone, and suddenly every 13-year-old wants to take a selfie with the exotic foreign specimen.

Little Kirill gets right in my face, "Say something in American!" he commands. I struggle to pull an appropriate movie line from memory, but come up blank. Finally, after a bit of mimicry and back and forth, I say "I'll be back!" which seems to fly over their young heads, but they

---

* The "old" part of the canal was begun under Peter the Great.

are happy anyway, smiling at each other in the novelty of their mutual incomprehension.

Kirill asks to use my iPhone to take a selfie. Then he insists that somehow I have just gifted the phone to him, which then becomes a source for banter between us for the next hour, with him finally reminding me that next time I come I should not forget to bring his iPhone.

We climb the narrow steps to the top of the church tower and listen in on Churova's lesson. She does after-school classes like this on cultural/historical subjects, but also on photography. She is an exacting teacher, ordering the squirrelly kids back into line at the slightest infraction, repeatedly chastising the chattering girls on the edge of the group, quizzing the kids about what they remember from their previous visit, upbraiding them for being outshone by one young boy, "who was not even here on our last trip, yet he knows the answer."

Finally, we exit the musty church basement and Churova tells the students the lesson is over and they are free to ask the foreigners any question they like. More selfies ensue and Kirill resumes his attempts to wrest away my phone. Celebrity is exhausting.

We haul the class over for a picture in front of Kukisvumchorr and promise we will return one day. Then we head off to capture a few images along the pretty canals of this sleepy town during Golden Hour before making the evening drive into St. Petersburg.

Time

"The strongest of all warriors are these two — Time and Patience."
    – Lev Tolstoy, *War and Peace*

"I'll be ready in seven minutes."

The first time Mikhail said this, in Kirkenes, Norway, I believed him.

He showed up 15 minutes later.

The phrase soon became a running joke.

Yet, what is interesting is that often we would be traveling in a city, with our local contact sitting in the passenger seat, giving directions to this or that landmark, and one of us would get impatient and ask our host how long it would take to get where we were going.

Invariably the answer was seven minutes.

But that seven minutes was always more like 15 or 20.

What we were witnessing was local time versus visitor time. When you live in a place and are used to its distances, you often develop a warped sense of how long things really take in your local milieu. It is a bit like the famous but apocryphal experiment of the frog in the saucepan, only with humans in the continuum of time.

However, it is also important to note that Russians and Americans have very different relationships with time, formed by their different cultural and historical backgrounds. Time, after all, is a social construct.

To Americans, time is a linear yardstick; it is money. Being late is rude (and even abusive of the person waiting), planning is deified, and deadlines are fixed and certain.

To Russians, time is elastic and cyclical; it must always be subordinated to people and circumstances. Being late is not rude (often expected, in fact), planning is a sign of hubris, and deadlines are fungible.

Our language of time is also different.

To Americans, time is singular and immutable, ever passing, as it has been since Augustine phrased it such ("time present – if it be time – only comes into existence because it passes into time past"). To Russians, time is actually plural (a watch is часы, literally "hours").

In English, we have days, which can signify both daylight hours and the 24-hour rotation of the Earth. Russians have days too (*dni*), but their 24-hour period is the *sutki*, which also includes the night (*noch*). English does not have a translation for *sutki* that encompasses the fullness of its meaning.

In addition, our boundaries of night and day are different. To Russians, it is night until dawn, or just before dawn. To Americans, three or four AM is already morning.

To Americans, daytime is generally from sunup to sundown. For Russians, daytime (*dnyom*) is from noon to sunset.

Americans have simply "night" (though some do say "evening" without irony), while Russians have evening (вечер), which is generally thought of as from 6 PM until about 11 PM, and night (ночь), which begins where evening ends and stretches until morning, which, as previously noted, does not generally begin until five or six AM.

For Americans, the most interesting time frame is the future. The past is done and buried, and the present is already underway. The future, meanwhile, is full of potential and promise.

For Russians, the most interesting time is the present. The past is fraught with nostalgia and regret, and the future hangs in the balance between chance and fiat. The present, however, is here to be savored, for it is something that can be controlled.

In Chekhov's seminal play *The Cherry Orchard*, the action all seems to take place in an infinite present tense. The characters dither and wait, seemingly unable to accept the inevitable estate auction and the chopping down of the orchard that lies just beyond the time horizon.

A typical American watching the play will think, "Why don't they *do* something?" A typical Russian watching the play will think, "Look at what they are *doing* to live in the moment before the future comes crashing down." There is a very keen sense of time and the present in Chekhov's plays, so much so that the critic Jean-Louis Barralt once commented while discussing Chekhov that, "The Russian temperament is best prepared to perceive the present time."

To underscore that observation, we have the superb words of Tolstoy, from his morality tale, "Three Questions." In that story, a tsar is tormented by three questions:

> How can I learn to do the right thing at the right time? Who are the people I most need, and to whom should I, therefore, pay more attention than to the rest? And what affairs are the most important, and need my first attention?

The tsar goes to visit a hermit (and there is lots of action leading up to the conclusion), at which point the hermit gives the tsar a single wise answer for all three of his questions:

> Remember then: there is just one most important time: now, and it is the most important because it is the only time over which we have any power; the most necessary man is the one you are with right now, for no one knows if he will have any dealings with any other person; and the most important thing is to do good, because it is for that reason alone that man was given life.

This American-Russian temporal disparity had the greatest impact upon our trip when it came to the logistics of setting meetings. With few exceptions, none of the people with whom we wanted to meet would set an appointment any further than a day or two in advance. One could make a preliminary agreement a week or so out about the projected day for a meeting, but it always required a follow-up call the day before to set the meeting definitely.

(In practical terms, this meant that most of the time while the American was driving, the Russian was on the phone, firming up the next day's meeting plans and reconfirming those of the present day.)

This actually worked to the advantage of us itinerant journalists, because our schedule needed to be flexible, to account for travel delays and itinerary changes. But it also meant that, because people are used to working this way, it would occasionally be possible to call someone important out of the blue and find time on their schedule the next day, or even the same day. When everyone is setting his or her schedule at the last minute, it is more likely you can slide into an open slot closer to the date of meeting.

What is more, with rare exceptions the people with whom we met were generous with their time on a Tolstoyan scale, giving us their full focus and attention, allowing us to mess up the rest of their day's schedule with a prolonged portrait shoot, or willing to toss aside other plans to have a lunch or dinner with us. Or, if we were running over the time someone had originally allotted (it happened), they would just call their next appointment and say they were going to be a bit late.

Seven minutes late, to be precise.

From St. Petersburg to Moscow

Piter

Driving west from Novaya Ladoga, we traverse unreasonably flat landscapes and savor a beautiful, lingering sunset that seems to be almost southerly. St. Petersburg greets us at dusk (certainly not yet evening), via a dark, wet, four-lane road crammed with rush hour traffic.

By car, the Venice of the North has a sprawling, unkempt feel that one doesn't get arriving by train, which drops you off nicely near the city's pulsing heart, atop Nevsky Prospect. Neon lights on bulging trade outlets blink and shimmer through the rain-soaked air, while drivers jockey for position, competing for a place in line over the narrow bridge that takes us toward our hotel.

Shortly after crossing the bridge and a bit of fighting with Ira, the navigational guru that lives inside Mikhail's iPhone, we cross Nevsky. It is good to finally see Nevsky Prospect. I have been to Petersburg countless times, yet I can never navigate here without first setting my bearings on Nevsky.

We barrel down a narrow, one-way embankment that is marked for two lanes but, due to the peculiarities of Russian parking traditions, is barely one, and miss our hotel on the first pass. After considerable trial and error, we locate its nicely secured parking lot and promise Kukisvumchorr that he will have a three-day rest. In our first week we have covered well over 1,500 kilometers. We look forward to exploring on foot for a change.

The Azimut St. Petersburg is a nice, comfortable hotel.* Back in the bad old days, it was the Sovietskaya Hotel, and if there is anything this place is not, it is soviet.

At check-in, the front desk staff is exceedingly tolerant of our loopy humor, a result of two hours spent in slow traffic breathing truck exhaust. There is a well-appointed lobby bar and shops, fast elevators and superb amenities, even in our basic rooms. A feature I love, but which I have seen in no other hotel, is a peg-rack that stretches the length of the room. Before long I have all my items hanging along the wall in easy reach.

Mikhail texts and we agree to meet in the lobby in "seven minutes." The twenty minutes of leeway gives me time to upgrade my Uber app and then we take a 10-minute, $2 ride to a nice restaurant near Nevsky where we meet up with two of Mikhail's friends for dinner. They are both named Sasha and are married (to each other), but before you go jumping to any conclusions, remember that this is Russia and Sasha is short for both Alexander and Alexandra.

If you believe the stories of Gogol, Dostoyevsky and Bely (and why should we not?), Petersburg is an unreal, or surreal, city. By all rights, it really should not exist. Dredged from the swamps through the will of an intelligent, cruel emperor, and at the cost of tens (perhaps hundreds) of thousands of commoners' lives, it was a terrific drain on Russia's treasury and history. When Peter (and his armies) defeated the Swedes in 1709, Sankt-Piterburkh was barely a boatyard and a ramshackle collection of wooden houses. Surely the tsar's maritime aspirations would

---

* Disclosure: Azimut was a sponsor of The Spine of Russia.

have been better (and more swiftly) served by an expansion and development of Riga, Tallinn or Narva.

While we are on the subject of alternate histories, we can also posit that Russia might have been better served had Novgorod and not Moscow become the nation's capital half a millennium before, but the Mongols and their local tax collectors shifted history's course away from that more democratically-inclined trading center, toward a more compliant bearer of tribute.

Yet Petersburg is far from unreal. In fact, in comparison to Moscow, 650 kilometers southeast of here, Piter is a charming city graced by romantic, narrow riverside streets, impressive martial squares, and inviting parks and monuments. It also has, as we discovered during our long walk back to the hotel along the embankment, a lively neighborhood nightlife, even on a Monday night. With little effort, we discovered all sorts of pleasant bars (British and Mexican, to name just the two I remember) where one could pop in and warm up with a stiff drink against the gathering October cold.

Perhaps the city was just being kind to us. Which was rather unusual, because on most every other visit I have made to Piter, the city had been cold and bleak, not unlike a certain evening in Dostoyevsky's *The Double*:

> It was an awful November night – wet, foggy, snowy, teeming with colds in the head, fevers, swollen faces, quinseys, inflammations of all kinds and descriptions – teeming, in fact, with all the gifts of a Petersburg November. The wind howled in the deserted streets, lifting up the black water of the canal above the rinds on the bank, and irritably brushing against the lean lamp-posts which chimed in with its howling in a thin, shrill

creak, keeping up the endless squeaky, jangling concert with which every inhabitant of Petersburg is so familiar. Snow and rain were falling both at once.*

But, of course, that was fiction. And we would be leaving in three days in any case, well before November sunk its teeth into things.

The Writer

I decided we needed to include Eugene Vodolazkin, 51, in our St. Petersburg itinerary after reading his recent novel *Lavr*. It has been published in 20 languages and was released in English soon after our trip concluded. A meetup was arranged through the generous assistance of Vodolazkin's agent and translator – remarkable if only because it was set about a week in advance.

But before we can sit down and chat, Vodolazkin insists on giving us a quick tour of Pushkin House,† which contains St. Petersburg's finest museum that few know about, where he is a senior researcher. That it is inexplicably off the main foreign tourist itinerary is witnessed by the fact that exhibit notes are only in Russian.

A repository of jaw-dropping displays sure to astound any Russophile, Pushkin House is small and beautifully kept. In the Tolstoy Room there is the great writer's death mask and an amazing collection of photographs. In the Lermontov Hall there are some of the writer's personal effects, including the pencil that was in his pocket when he was killed in a duel. In the Gogol Hall there is the chair in which it is believed Gogol sat as he incinerated the second volume of *Dead Souls*.

---

* Translation by Constance Garnett.
† *Pushkinsky Dom*, not to be confused with Pushkin's House Museum.

Elsewhere there is the table where Mandelstam wrote, as well as Gumilyov's briefcase. As if all that (and much more I cannot list) were not enough, the museum is home to all of Pushkin's handwritten manuscripts, several of which are on display.

We set up a few chairs for our interview in the Tolstoy Room, and over the course of the next hour are only interrupted once, by a Russian school group scurrying through. Our discussion is wide ranging, from history and politics, to literature and international relations. Vodolazkin is erudite and articulate, the very embodiment of the Russian *intelligent*.

Born in Kiev (where his great grandfather fled after fighting in the White Army), Vodolazkin is nattily dressed and bears the slight paunch of a middle-aged college don. He speaks slowly and thoughtfully, carrying each train of thought to its full conclusion.

"Countries exist only on the basis of ideas," he notes, after recounting the sudden collapse of the Soviet Union that followed the lethargic "vegetarian communism" of the late Brezhnev era. "Fear lies at the base of every dictatorship…," he adds, and by the end of the Soviet era, the fear was gone and a huge gap had opened up between the state and its people. "By the 1970s, it was clear that the USSR would not live forever… there was a vacuum between the people and power." It is of course a view informed by hindsight, for certainly few but the most avowed anti-Soviets predicted the imminent demise of the USSR back in the 1970s or even early 1980s.

This vacuum is in contrast, he says, with today, when "power is a continuation of the will of the people… as Tolstoy said, 'a leader is merely the expression of the people.'"

In this and many of his subsequent observations, Vodolazkin is careful to underline that he is not offering his own opinions of events, but those of an outside observer. "I am a philologist," he explains, "but that also requires me to be a historian."

Yet one place where his opinion is clear is on the nature of Russia. "Russia is not some mystical, Eurasian country," he says. "It is a purely European country… It is Byzantine Europe, not Roman Europe, and it is very important that the West understand that Russia is a European culture."

The current troubles between Russia and the US, Vodolazkin asserts, "have their roots in the fact that we are so similar. The most horrific struggles are those that are between those who are similar. We are very similar, we are both messianic powers, we teach everyone how to live," he says. But there is more. In the 1990s, he continues, many in Russia felt that the country was on the brink of a new world, that Russia "would be allowed to join the world order as 'one of' the others. But understand what it means to speak in these terms to a population raised on the imperial idea. For Russia is was not about reaching for power or expansion, but simply a desire to be treated as an equal. The US and Russia are two great empires, or two large state formations, and now the idea was we don't need someone to be in charge, no one needs to be running things, we can be brothers, we can be friends; we don't need to decide who is in charge. Russia very clearly expressed its desire for equality, but the West set very strong conditions in which there could be no talk of such equality.

"Russia is a huge country, a country with huge resources. Big ships require a certain size berth in port. And Russia cannot sit in that port as if it were a little boat, because it is simply too large."

Then NATO began moving toward the East, Vodolazkin says, citing the infamous promises made to Gorbachev in 1989 that, if Eastern Europe were freed from the Soviet Empire, NATO would not move eastward. This, he says upset the international balance of power.

In fact, history shows that there were no such promises to Gorbachev. On the contrary, notes show that Gorbachev was very sanguine about NATO expansion and even saw Soviet ascension as a possibility (something even Putin posited, early in his reign), if it were turned from a military into a political alliance.[20]

"The US cannot be a single, unipolar power," he says. "There must be two poles for there to be stability." And the West itself created the second pole, he says "by pushing Russia away."

So what is it that distinguishes this new, Russian pole?

"The essence of Russia," Vodolazkin says, "is that it is a conservative nation. We are tolerant to the point where toleration turns to something else. Russia represents a return to the European idea, the Christian idea... family values." And for many Russians (here Vodolazkin reiterates that he is summarizing what he sees as an observer, a witness, that he is not summarizing his own opinions), the idea of gay marriage, he says, is a "red line."

Indeed, recent Gallup and Pew Center polls showed that 72 percent of Russians feel that homosexuality is immoral, versus 37 percent in the US.

Russians see themselves as "correcting Western humanism a bit," Vodolazkin says. "The rights of a person cannot be the ultimate end unto itself... if you think about things like euthanasia and same sex marriage, they could ultimately lead to the end of our species."

In Vodolazkin's view, Russia is still in the process of forming its much touted "national idea," and its likely endpoint will be what he calls "liberal conservatism." Meaning there should be tolerance for different ideas and opinions (the liberalism bit), but that these should not be institutionalized, that a generally conservative notion of social relations and issues should hold sway.

Finally, we turn to Ukraine, the country where Vodolazkin was born. "What the West should understand," he stresses, "is that Ukraine is not a neighboring country for Russians. For most Russians, we are all one country… No one side can win in this battle."

In this context, he summarizes, "there is no serious anti-Western opinion in Russia. We really need each other, and so it is time to return to that infamous Russian question, 'What is to be done?'… We can do much together. To quote Leopold the Cat (a popular Russian cartoon), 'C'mon guys, let's live together as friends!'"*

For my part, after our long discussion I was reminded of a quote from a scene at the end of Vodolazkin's beautifully-written *Lavr*. The novel follows the life of an itinerant healer who travels throughout Europe, across space and time, trying to redeem his fate. Near the end of the story, a Russian blacksmith is talking with a German merchant: "Oh, you will not understand anything in our Russian lands," the Russian says. "We ourselves don't understand anything here."†

The Cossack

It would be impossible to recount the history of Russia without discussing the Cossacks.

Born in the vacuum that appeared in the empire's southern and eastern borderlands when the Mongol Horde retreated, the Cossacks began their rise to significance in the fifteenth and sixteenth centuries. Originally comprised of "free adventurers" (from which the name derives) – Slavic peasants and misfits that fled to the borderlands to escape central power (or tax collectors and serf-owners), they began to coalesce into tribes or hosts. As they gained in strength, those in

---

* Ребята, давайте жить дружно.
† "Что, мол, ничего вы в нашей русской земле не понимаете, да и сами мы в ней ничего не понимаем." (Translation by Lisa Hayden, published by Oneworld.)

the West (Zaporozhian Cossacks) asserted their independence from Lithuania and Poland, and those in the East (Don Cossacks) mainly aligned with Russia.

They became vanguard mercenaries and explorers in Russia's expansion, securing the borders with the Caucasus and Central Asia and "discovering" and settling vast Siberia. Yet by the seventeenth century the power and hubris that arose from occupying and defending the empire's buffer zones combined with their traditional sense of independence, freedom, and democratic self-rule to create an incendiary mixture. Repeated revolts against the center by the likes of Stepan Razin and Yemelyan Pugachev were all either widely supported or instigated by once loyal Cossacks.

But by the end of the eighteenth century, the concerted efforts of Peter the Great and his granddaughter-in-law, Catherine the Great, at once vanquished and co-opted the Cossacks into the Russian military as a special class of fighter. They went on to play leading roles in the country's imperial wars with Turkey, Sweden, Britain, France and Persia.

Alongside this there bloomed in the nineteenth century a romanticizing of the Cossack "ethnicity" that to some extent continues to the present day. It was fanned by works such as Nikolai Gogol's brutally graphic and misogynistic *Taras Bulba* (1835):

> Bulba was fearfully stubborn. He was one of those characters which first emerged in the grim fifteenth century, in a half-nomadic corner of Europe, when the whole of primitive Southern Russia, deserted by its princes, was laid waste and burned to the ground by the irresistible incursions of Mongolian spoilers; when, robbed of house and home, men grew daring; when they settled on the ashes of their homes, amidst formidable foes and perpetual perils, and grew used to looking them straight in the face and

forgot there was such a thing as fear in the world; when a warlike flame fired the Slavonic spirit, which had remained peaceable for centuries, and begot Cossackdom a free, riotous outgrowth of the Russian character and when all the riverbanks, fords and ferries, and every suitable spot in the river country, were sown with Cossacks, whose number no man knew; and rightly did their bold comrades answer the Sultan, who inquired their numbers, "Who knoweth! We are spread over all the steppe: on every hillock will ye find a Cossack." This indeed was a remarkable manifestation of Russian strength, struck out of the people's bosom, as out of flint, by the steel of dire misfortune....

There was no craft the Cossack did not know: he could make wine, build a cart, grind powder, do a blacksmith's and a locksmith's work, and besides all this he could revel in the most riotous manner, could drink and feast as only a Russian can – all this he could do and more. Besides the registered Cossacks, whose duty it was to join the army in case of war, troops of mounted volunteers could always be mustered in time of urgent need. The esauls had but to make a round of the market-places and squares of all the villages and towns, and there, standing up in a cart, to shout at the top of their voices:

"Ho, you beer-brewers and wine-makers! Have done with your beer-brewing, your dawdling on stove-ledges, feeding the flies with your fat carcasses! Come and win knightly fame and honor! And you ploughmen, you sowers of buckwheat, you tenders of sheep, you lovers of women! Have done with following the plough and mucking up your yellow boots with mud; have done with running after women and wasting your knightly strength! The hour is come to win Cossack glory!"

And these words were as sparks falling on dry wood… In short, the Russian character displayed itself at its greatest and mightiest here.*

Come the revolution, most Cossacks lined up against the godless, heathen communists, comprising the core of the doomed White Army. Tens of thousands emigrated at the end of the Civil War; those that remained on Soviet soil were subjected to brutal Decossackization. Thousands were executed and as many as half a million (out of an estimated population of about three million) were deported. A decade later in Ukraine, the punitive Soviet famine of 1932-33 (Holodomor) killed millions in the country's agricultural regions, many of them populated largely by Cossacks.

By the time of the Nazi invasion, those Cossacks who had survived were again allowed to serve in the military, and many did to great distinction. But others also defected to the enemy, particularly those who had suffered under Stalin.

After the War, the Cossacks were disbanded from the military yet not accepted in the melting pot of Soviet society as a separate ethnicity, perhaps feared for their independent streak and complex history. But with the arrival of perestroika, for some the Cossack romanticism was again bestirred. For others, there was too much history – of pogroms, of those who fought against the Soviet Union during the Great Patriotic War. Over five hundred years, the word "Cossack" has become heavily freighted with meaning, and far from all of it good.

Nonetheless, by the time of the 2010 Russian Census, some 67,573 people in Russia identified themselves as ethnic Cossacks. We therefore knew we needed to seek out and interview a Cossack. And we found

---

* Translation: O.A. Gorchakov.

a rather interesting one far from their traditional southern homeland – outside St. Petersburg.

"RUSSIA," NIKOLAI GOGOL wrote in *Dead Souls,* "has two misfortunes: roads and fools."*

I consider this trenchant, frequently-cited quote as we bounce and weave over a back road outside St. Petersburg that is more pothole than road.

Actually, we drove over very fine roads for the first 45 kilometers out of the northern capital, including a gleaming toll road with futuristic light poles, followed by nice two-laners past dacha complexes that could double for Spielbergian American suburbia. But the last few kilometers of dirt roads are Dramamine worthy.

If that is not enough, we are on our way to see a person some have called far worse than a fool – Andrei Polyakov, 53, the ataman (head) of the St. Petersburg City Cossack Society Irbis, who is seeking to create a *khutor* – a Cossack village – in the frigid nether reaches of St. Petersburg.

A year before, in October 2014, Polyakov was censured by a council of more than 50 Cossack elders and atamans for "conduct unbecoming a Cossack." In their statement, delivered to the governor's council for relations with Cossacks, the elders promised a "detailed audit of the activity of 'the odious imposter ataman,' who in his striving for power, money and honors, has undertaken cheap public relations stunts that smack of obscurantism and that discredit the Cossack movement as a whole." Polyakov, the council said, claimed to have undertaken a range of activities that do not in fact exist, from an Orthodox Cossack Taxi Service, to a College for Cossack Cadets, a rehabilitation center

---

* The thought turns out to be rather appropriate for today's meeting, because, as will be elaborated below (page 211), Gogol never wrote it, no matter how much it sounds like he did.

for persons suffering from drug and alcohol addiction, a settlement in Leningrad Oblast's Kingisepp District, and a fishing enterprise. Irbis also falsely claimed to have sent fighters to eastern Ukraine as well as 18 relief convoys.

But the last straw was when Polyakov began calling himself "Supreme Ataman of the Northwestern Troops and All-Russian Ataman of the Union of Independent Cossacks," thereby presuming to speak to mass media on behalf of all Cossacks in Russia's Northwest. (Ataman is the highest rank in Cossackdom, roughly equivalent to Commander.)

That Polyakov has a flair for public relations is unquestionable. In May 2015, he erected a monument to Vladimir Putin in which the Russian leader is stylized to look like a Roman emperor. The unveiling evoked an inpouring of foreign media, all bouncing over the same punishing roads we have just traveled.

And this past summer, in August, Polyakov announced that Irbis would take the lead in looking for banned foreign goods in local stores. One of their members, Stas Baretsky – the super-sized destroyer whose videos of himself biting through cans of foreign beer went viral on the internet – was a bit too successful in this pursuit, and was reputedly expelled from Irbis for his antics.

Also in August, Irbis created their own money ("just a *wechsel*," Polyakov demurred, using the German word for a promissory note) to help their members buy services from one another during the economic crisis. The alternative currency was decorated with, among other things, symbols of Crimea and the faces of President Putin, Tsar Nicholas II, and Polyakov himself. The Prosecutor General was said to be looking into the matter.

POLYAKOV MAY OR may not be a fool, but he certainly has his screws tuned to a slightly different frequency, leading to a pointed exchange when he suggested there is no documentary evidence that Russia ever actually sold Alaska to America or that America paid the bill. "I only know what I read on the internet," he finally says after I bluntly report that I have seen a copy of the actual cancelled check congress issued for the Alaska payment.*

By the end of our time together, Polyakov even seems to have warmed up a bit to the American interloper and purveyor of uncomfortable truths, offering us tea and some delicious, raw, home-grown honey.

"I just want to live like my ancestors," Polyakov says, explaining why he has decided to establish a *khutor*. "To get back to the land, to farm, raise geese and goats… Soon we will have some horses here," he says, pointing to a fine lea with a small river flowing through it.

Several dogs roam the property, but it is owned by an insatiably energetic and gregarious German Longhair Pointer who goes by Alpha. There are also four types of geese, as well as goats and ducks. "I sold 500 birds this summer," Polyakov proudly reports. "Raised them all myself from chicks." A gaggle of them raise a loud ruckus during our long chat that bitterly cold morning.

Born in Eysk, Kuban, Polyakov is a bear of a man. Six foot three and barrel chested in his well-pressed blue Cossack uniform, he has a smooth, shaven head and hands like catcher's mitts. He is a doer. Although he only broke ground this spring, the *khutor* is very far along, yet there are no signs of any inhabitants other than Polyakov, and he is cagey when pressed about how many people live or work here. The property has two main buildings (one will be either a museum or mini-

---

* Treasury Warrant 9759, to be exact, with a PAID stamp dated August 1, 1868. Polyakov is merely voicing a common conspiracy theory from the Russian internet, which strangely happens to perfectly mirror the plot of Jeffrey Archer's 1986 novel, *A Matter of Honor*. In the book, the sale of Alaska was secretly a lease with a possibility for Russia to buy Alaska back in 99 years, but it had to do so before a deadline soon to arrive, and produce a copy of the secret codicil in time to prove its case.

hotel, it is not clear) and a nicely designed apiary. Alpha races around it all, desperately looking for sticks we can toss.

So why the Caesarian monument to Putin? "Because I understand him to be a true leader, a world leader of historical significance," Polyakov says. "The sort of leader who goes down in history, like Churchill, Roosevelt, Washington... There are few people like that. He returned our lands bloodlessly, without war... I can compare that to the collapse of the Berlin Wall..."

This is when Alaska comes up, Polyakov asserting that yet another wall could fall when Alaska reunites with Russia...

Statues make for good PR, but Polyakov claims that what he is most keen on is the reinvigoration of Cossack culture. "Cossacks are a distinct ethnos," he says. "We have a distinct language and a historical homeland – between the Caspian and Black Seas... Unlike many peoples in the Caucasus who were largely moved out by the Soviets, the Cossacks were simply annihilated." Polyakov says he wants to reinvigorate Cossack culture, language and traditions, having grown up at a time when Cossacks were considered "second class citizens, illiterate peasants, drunkards, even though the opposite was true." Thus his *khutor*, or farm village, located just down the miserable road from elite dacha settlements and a dilapidated *sovkhoz*.

"St. Petersburg has always had Cossacks," Polyakov explains, when I suggest that he is rather far from the historical homeland. "We protected the tsar, and all city and state buildings; the security forces and border guards were Cossacks... Petersburg is where the Cossacks first took their oath to defend Russia... The Manezh was a Cossack stable... There were four regiments... Karavanaya ulitsa 1 was the Cossack General Staff headquarters... These are things government officials don't know... By some accounts, Staraya Ladoga was founded by Cossacks. There is a memoir in a monastery that Cossacks pushed the Swedes out of there even before Peter I arrived… America was also discovered for Europe by the Cossacks, before Columbus…* India would have been part of Russia thanks to Cossacks, had there not been a palace coup dethroning Paul I…† The Cossacks conquered too much territory; the state could not digest it all. Alaska, California… there were just not enough resources to rule over all this."

To hear him tell it, "Russia only exists because of the Cossacks… we put the first Romanov on the throne… and ousted the Poles [during the Time of Troubles]." What is more, he claims, it was the Cossacks who gave the world oyster farms, olives and herbal tea. And, despite their annihilation under Stalin ("the only ones who survived were those who hid the fact that they were Cossacks"), Polyakov says their numbers are strong and they are a force to be reckoned with. Any government is going to fear 20-30,000 Cossacks and need to control them, he says. It is like a gigantic political party. "If suddenly a national leader of Cossacks arose, it would be like a Masonic lodge… If all the Cossacks united behind a single leader, it would be a fearsome force. Imagine, a organization in every city… it is a force, the only force in Russia, as Hitler said, that is capable of organizing itself."

239

There are rather few grand social achievements that the Soviet Union bequeathed Russia that do not carry the taint of Communism's suppression of individual liberties, labor camps, mass murder, or blatant

---

* More internet myths.

† Here he is at least basing his assertion on some measure of history. He is referring to a secret plot Tsar Paul I hatched in 1801 to invade India as a way to counter British interests in the region. Cossack commander Matvei Platov led some 20,000 Cossacks on a march east that got bogged down in spring flooding and mud after the plan was set in motion. They only got as far as Saratov Province, before they were called back when word arrived of Paul's assassination.

disregard for the environment. Some successes in the arts, space and sports may be mostly odor free. But education may be one of the least tarnished triumphs.

Yes, education was often used to odious ends in the Soviet era, washing innocent minds, instilling propaganda, and imposing collectivism over individual identity. But it brought near total literacy to the Soviet population, educating a vast trove of engineers, scientists, artists and thinkers who made countless contributions to Soviet and world culture. It was central to turning a backward, conservative, rural society into a modern, industrialized one that valued learning and culture.

On the flip side, of course, education, because it had so much significance in shaping the minds of the future, was unquestionably "dictated from the center," and all things were oriented toward harmonizing "the character of school-teaching at the microscopic level."[21] Yet, given the realities of geography and Russian culture, where the all-encompassing nature of laws is only matched by the will to fulfill them capriciously, there was plenty of room for localization and adapting to the needs of students. Still, famously, the primary and secondary curricula across the Soviet Union were unitary and identical. It was said that one could go into any class in any town across the entirety of the USSR and see the same lessons being taught everywhere on the same day.

In any event, the upshot is that Russia today has one of the world's finest, most universal educational systems. In 2014, the Economist Intelligence Unit ranked it 13th best in the world. And, while it may not yet have an institution with the international reputation of Harvard, MIT or Stanford,* it does have hundreds of excellent public universities, despite spending far less on education (3.7 percent of GDP) than

---

* Strangely, Moscow State University does not even make it into the top 100 of international rankings, largely because such rankings are heavily weighted by citations in professional journals, which Russian academics get little of, because so few specialists the world over know Russian.

European (5.4 percent) countries.[22] This of course means that Russian professors and teachers are vastly underpaid compared to their foreign colleagues, which only primes the pump for bribery (estimated to amount to $1 billion in 2009[23]) and corruption.

Educational reform has been on the national political agenda for the past few years, indeed since 2003, when a new, unified national entrance exam was introduced for college admissions. The stated goal was to make the road to post-secondary education more meritocratic, to create more opportunities for students educated at the periphery, and to eradicate the potential for bribery. By 2009 the new exam was mandatory nationwide, but it is too early to assess results. In 2012, additional reforms were enacted to reduce the number of university-level institutions, in order to better focus resources.

At the same time, in 2007 eleven years of education (normally starting at age 6 or 7) was made mandatory nationwide (versus 9 years previously), though students can drop out with parental approval and upon reaching majority. Few apparently do, and Russia has an admirable high school completion rate of 87 percent and some of the best student-to-teacher ratios in Europe.[24] That said, given the ongoing demographic crisis, there has been a sharp decline in students entering the educational system over the past 20 years, which will surely put excess-capacity stresses on the system down the road.

In sum, notwithstanding ill-conceived attempts to jump-start entrepreneurship through things like nano-centers, and ongoing attempts to politicize the teaching of history, Russia has a solid, tested system in place to educate and train its future workforce. Its proven strength in training fine engineers and scientists would seem to augur well in the context of a global economy with an insatiable appetite for programmers and computer scientists.

So perhaps it was not surprising that our inquiries about people doing interesting things in education led us to the doors of St. Petersburg's Lyceum 239 – a place so famous that many know it simply as 239, and to Yakov Somov.

SOMOV, 31, IS a dynamo of energy and enthusiasm. Sporting blonde, shoulder length hair, a mustache, goatee, and t-shirt declaring "Live Long and Prosper," he has found his place in life and is thriving.

St. Petersburg's Lyceum 239 has produced a mind-boggling list of famous mathematicians, scientists and humanists (from mathematician Grigory Perelman, to dissident Elena Bonner and musician Boris Grebenshchikov). Any student lingering in its halls could not help but be intimidated by the long lists of Olympiad winners in mathematics and other disciplines that are affixed to the foyer and stairway walls. (Olympiads are city, regional, national and international academic competitions that recognize superior ability in the chosen field).

Not surprisingly, the Lyceum is rather difficult to gain admission to. "There are twelve applicants for each open slot," Somov says. That's Harvard level exclusiveness. "It is a Cathedral of Knowledge," he adds proudly. Entrance is based on achievement, not economic or social status. No matter one's economic background, if you meet the school's challenging standards, you can get in. "Our motto is to evoke children's maximum potential," Somov says.

And even if a student does not gain access to its formal course of study (800 students aged 12-18), she can still gain access to the school's superior teachers, students and traditions by taking part in informal educational programs – the after school "circles," subject-specific study groups comprised of students from around the city that are free and open to all comers. Some 1,500 students presently participate in the circles.

But we are not here to sit in on lectures or talk to school administrators about the successes of Russian secondary education. We are here to see what Somov is up to.

His studio is just off the school's main stairwell. Here, under the umbrella of Lyceum 239, he and his wife Alexandra Skorodumova have, over the past seven years, created Russia's largest MOOC (Massive Online Open Classroom), Lektorium.

What is a MOOC, you ask? It is the bleeding edge of higher education. It is a place for online, self-paced learning, where a single teacher can have 35,000 students in a single class, where students study at their own speed, exploring their interests and testing their talents. To date, Lektorium (lektorium.ru) has created 40 courses in everything from biodynamics to art history, from math to engineering. They also have recorded and archived over 3,200 classroom lectures in math and engineering, now available online.

Forever.

For free.

Lektorium is also a place where teachers come to improve their skills (continuing education online, at a time that works for the teacher's busy schedule) and the classes they teach. "Studies have shown," Somov says, "that 39 percent of those studying in MOOCs are people employed in education. They are using the courses to either improve their own teaching, or to use the online materials in classes."

As a result, Lektorium has begun to focus its attention on teaching teachers how to teach their subjects better and has developed courses in 21 subject areas. It is also seeking to use its well-developed platform to offer Russia's universities a way to present their courses to the world. "We cannot create all the content that needs to be created," Somov says. "So we decided to be a platform for classes created by others."

The quality of Lektorium's video production is superb, which has led to contracts with American and other Western universities to create their own MOOC courses. Even at $25,000 or so to create a single course of 30-100 lectures (depending on the content area), the 30 plus production staffers and three studios that Lektorium can put at a contractor's disposal gives them a strong competitive advantage.*

But Lektorium and MOOC, Somov says, is also a very useful tool for students who must cope with the *proforientatsia* system, where they must decide at a relatively young age how they want to proceed in life, what education and profession they wish to pursue. By taking and testing courses via a MOOC program, they can try on various professions or areas of learning without actually making the commitment.

What is more, MOOC "preserves our teachers," Somov explains. "Due to historical circumstances, all our teachers are either over 60 or under 40. This helps us preserve the work and lectures of our older teachers for the next generation."

Somov is enthused, excited, and empowered by his work. Himself a graduate of Lyceum 239 ("we do have a record of family dynasties here," he admits with a smile), he is technically speaking an "educational methodologist," but in reality he is a cheerleader for learning, a technocrat who has dedicated his professional life to creating newer, better, more innovative educational systems, and to ensuring that Russia is at the forefront of coming changes.

And he is something of a live wire. It took every ounce of willpower in his arsenal to stand still for five minutes to have his portrait taken. Thankfully, Mikhail worked quickly.

---

* Postscript: One month after our visit, in November 2015, Lektorium was awarded the title "Startup of the Year" by the Russia business media outlet RBK St. Petersburg.

Tea Time & The Russian Soul

While our Azimut Hotel was located a bit outside the heart of the city, its position was optimal for drop-dead gorgeous panoramas of the city at sunup or sundown. It's pretty hard to compete with starting your day with a view of the sun glinting off St. Isaac's and the Admiralty.

At the end of our long, second day in St. Petersburg, we enjoyed that very view over a glass of tea in the hotel's 18th-floor Sky Bar, served by Valeria Miloslavskaya, a 20-year-old Tea Sommelier.

Yes, that is a thing.

The company Miloslavskaya works for, Chai-i-ne-Chai ("Tea and Not Tea") purveys everything from reds, blacks, greens and whites to herbals and alcohol infused brews, all prepared in the arduous yet relaxing Chinese tea serving style.

"I never dreamt this is something I would do," Miloslavskaya says, "but it turns out it is really enjoyable; it's a great way to talk and socialize with people, to learn about them while you are preparing their tea."

A third-year student in business management, Miloslavskaya says she took a year-long course to become a tea sommelier. Tea and Not Tea, she says, has 70 sommeliers who ply their trade at different St. Petersburg and Moscow establishments, all of whom are able to explain the subtle differences between different tea colors, sorts and harvest years.

SO WHAT IS it about Russians and tea?

For over four hundred years, since its introduction during the reign of the first Romanov tsar (Mikhail, 1613-1645), tea has slowly grafted itself onto the Russian soul. It is equally important on hot summer days at the dacha or after taking refuge from a horizontal blizzard, equally at home in the bathhouse and the parlor.

Yet the funny thing is that it is an "invented tradition." Neither tea nor the vessel commonly associated with it, the samovar, are Russian creations. Like the matryoshka and the potato, other staples of Russian-ness, both are imports.

Tea did not really become popular as a beverage until a century after its first appearance in Russia (making an awkward debut, when the tsar mistakenly tried to sample it as if it were chewing tobacco), during the reign of Catherine the Great (1762-1796). By the end of the eighteenth century, Russia was importing nearly three million pounds of "the Chinese herb" each year. Still, over the course of the next hundred years or so, "tea drinking as an everyday social ritual, if it existed at all, was confined to the highest echelons of Russian society."[25] Not until the 1880s or so did the drink dribble down to the commoners.

The world famous samovar ("self-boiler") also appeared in the 1770s, adapted from Mongol kettle designs by metalworkers in Tula. So, since the beginning of tea's appearance in Russia, the distinctly Russian style of tea making has revolved around this important appliance, which was typically brought out to the table after a meal was completed. A concentrated tea (*zavarka*) is brewed in a teapot, and a measure of this poured into one's cup, then diluted with hot water from the samovar, according to individual taste. Different locales developed different traditions for drinking the tea, whether sipping it through a hard sugar lump stuck between the teeth (*vprikusku*), washing it over a tongue laden with sweet preserves (as we did in Petrozavodsk), or pouring a steaming brew from one's cup into a saucer, allowing for faster cooling.

By the nineteenth century, tea drinking in Russia had become widely equated with hospitality and national identity. All the great Russian writers invoked the traditions and rituals of tea drinking, weaving them into their works. Gogol makes repeated references to tea drinking in

Dead Souls, including this wonderful passage describing the chief of police and his place in a local community:

> Generally, he was, as they say, suited to his post, and understood his job to perfection. It was even hard to decide whether he had been created for the post or the post for him… The merchants were the first to love him, precisely because he was not haughty; in fact he stood godfather to their children, was chummy with them, and though he occasionally fleeced them badly, he did it somehow extremely deftly: he would pat the man on the shoulder, and laugh, and stand him to tea, and promise to come for a game of checkers, asking about everything: how's he doing, this and that. If he learned that a young one was a bit sick, he would suggest some medicine – in short, a fine fellow!*

Chekhov, as one would expect, had a few humorous quotes about the beverage, quipping at one point, "What fine weather today! Can't choose whether to drink tea or to hang myself." And one of the characters in his classic play *Three Sisters* has the line, "Fine. Since the tea is not forthcoming, let's have a philosophical conversation."

But Alexander Pushkin, the Russian national poet, ought to have the last line. "Ecstasy," he wrote, "is a glassful of tea and a piece of sugar in the mouth."

MILOSLAVSKAYA PREPARES A fine jasmine tea for us, showing how one must first warm up the glassware, so as not to shock the tea, then does repeated "pour-overs" (in Russian the term is проливом) where she pours a bit of hot water over the tea that rests in a glass, uses

---

* Translation: Pevear and Volokhonsky..

the lid to swish it back and forth, then pours the brew into a teapot. She does this six or seven times. The first pour-over is dumped out – that is to prepare and cleanse the tea. The second pour-over is to decant the smell, the third to capture its flavor, the fourth to extract its healthful qualities. And so on.

The cynical devil on my shoulder wants to ask if she makes tea like this at home or just uses a tea bag, but the tea ceremony is a very relaxing way to end our stay in the northern capital. In addition to meeting several interesting Russians and having engaging interviews about history, politics, education, Cossacks, Tolstoy and more, we spent many hours walking the streets of this beautiful city, enjoying the cool, crisp, yet sunny weather, capturing some great images, and savoring excellent, reasonably priced local cuisine. One of the best things about St. Petersburg is how walkable it is – the historic center is both compact and flat. While we were a bit late in the year to enjoy a White Nights stroll along the Neva or the Griboyedov Canal, we did savor a fine sunset over the Admiralty, and an enchanting twilight walking along Nevsky.

The Valley of Death

Grey, cold, wet weather chased us from St. Petersburg to Novgorod. It set a properly somber tone for our brief stop at the Valley of Death (*Dolina Smerty*) World War II memorial site just north of the village of Myasnoy Bor, which is itself just north of Veliky Novgorod.

Thousands died during months of battle here (December 1941-June 1942), after an unsuccessful attempt by the Soviet Red Army to pierce the German lines and end the blockade of Leningrad. The 2nd Army was almost completely surrounded by German forces, with Soviet losses mounting as the noose was drawn tighter (the gap decreasing from four kilometers down to 300 meters).

On June 25, 1942, German and Spanish forces succeeded in closing the circle. The 2nd Army's attempts to break the encirclement failed, and it was all but annihilated. Its commanding officer, Lieutenant General Andrei Vlasov, was taken prisoner, and later became infamous as the traitorous head of the Nazi's Committee for the Liberation of Russian People.

Every year they bury new remains found near here. Rumor has it that, under the right conditions, moaning can be heard in the forests.

Interestingly, the name of the nearby village, Myasnoy Bor, which literally translates as "Meat Forest," has nothing to do with this recent bloody history. Instead, it seems to come from the time when Peter the Great was building St. Petersburg. That effort required the provision of large quantities of meat to the nascent capital, and much of it was loaded onto barges here, along the Volkhov River.

The monument is a solemn collection of mass graves with headstones, and a large central statue, just meters off the E105. We pull into a narrow turnout alongside a locked, horizontal barrier pole and step out into the freezing morning. With the traffic rushing by, it is not a peaceful place, but the memorial is respectful and moving nonetheless. Still, standing on this narrow expanse with a rushing highway to our back and swaying birch groves a hundred yards in the distance, it is difficult to grasp the scope of the murder and carnage that took place here, what it must have been like to be trapped in this open land, surrounded by enemy invaders.

Indeed, it is immensely difficult for any Westerner to grasp the enormity of the Great Patriotic War in the Russian consciousness. The scale of the war's destruction and its imprint on lives and geography here is incalculable. It did not merely destroy a generation, but forged what was left, creating a thick scab that is half pride at having won the war, half resentment for having had to do most of it alone.

The numbers are staggering. Over 10 million Soviet soldiers died on the Eastern Front, and over 11 million civilians were killed in the territory overrun by the Germans. The prewar population of the USSR was just under 200 million, which means more than one in ten Soviets perished as a result of this war, and that does not even account for postwar illnesses, early deaths due to battle injuries, shortened life expectancy due to trauma or malnutrition, etc.

By way of comparison – to grasp the scale of things, but by no means diminish the value of any life lost in any part of this horrific war – all of the battle deaths of all the Western allies on the Western front (US, UK, Canada, France, Italy, Belgium) totaled less than one million.

While the war that ended 70 years ago is passing from living memory, it yet looms large in the collective Russian consciousness as *a priori* proof that Russia always has been and always will be surrounded by antagonistic, if not openly hostile, neighbors, to whom Russia has repeatedly shown that it will not be cowed or turned from the historical path it has chosen. This powerful vein of pride and honor undergirded the legitimacy of Soviet power even during its steady four-decade post-war decline. Of late, the vein has been increasingly tapped to assert and justify the Russian state's new assertiveness in its post-Soviet sphere of influence, from Crimea to the Arctic, and to draw a starker line between East and West.

And of course, just as under the Soviet regime, the history being retold is neither complete nor subtle. Yes, there is appropriate homage paid to the millions who died, to those whose individual acts of heroism in battle or on the home front were astonishing. But there is little discussion of the decisions taken by top leadership; of the SMERSH forces that stood behind regular forces, ready to shoot them in the back should they fail to press forward; of the retributive crimes on civilians committed by advancing Soviet troops in Germany; of how the purges of the 1930s decimated the officer corps, or how Stalin ignored obvious prewar intelligence; of how those unwittingly captured as prisoners of war were transmogrified into traitors. Perhaps even 70 years on, the gaping wounds are still too raw. Or perhaps, as with the modern Russian disinclination to fully come to terms with its Gulag past, it is that negative facts from the past somehow besmirch the memories of those who died. In fact, the opposite is true. It throws into sharper relief just how extraordinary were their acts of selflessness, because the state did not deserve them, but the people, Russian society, did.

Unfortunately, it may also have something to do with a law passed in May 2014, which mandates up to five years in jail and heavy fines for anyone who tries to rehabilitate Nazism or denigrate or distort Russia's World War II record. It criminalizes things like "the desecration of symbols of Russia's military glory," but it does not define any terms, in particular what constitutes a "distortion" of the historical record.

In the Beginning

Every nation has a foundation myth. Russia's starts in 860-862 AD, with four tribes that had been forced to pay tribute to the Varangians (aka Vikings or Scandinavians): the Chuds, Slavs, Merians, and Krivichians. They apparently

> drove the Varangians back beyond the sea, refused to pay them further tribute, and set out to govern themselves. But there was no law among them, and tribe rose against tribe. Discord thus ensued among them, and they began to war one against the other. They

said to themselves, "Let us seek a prince who may rule over us, and judge us according to custom." Thus they went overseas to the Varangians, to the Rus. These particular Varangians were known as Rus, just as some are called Swedes, and others Normans and Angles, and still others Gotlanders, for they were thus named. The Chuds, the Slavs, the Krivichians and the Ves then said to the Rus, "Our land is great and rich, but there is no order in it. Come reign as princes, rule over us." Three brothers, with their kinfolk, were selected. They brought with them all the Rus and migrated. The oldest, Rurik, located himself in Novgorod; the second, Sineus, in Beloozero; and the third, Truvor, in Izborsk. From these Varangians, the Russian land received its name. Thus those who live in Novgorod are descended from the Varangian tribe, but earlier they were Slavs. Within two years, Sineus and his brother Truvor died. Rurik gathered sole authority into his own hands, parceling out cities to his own men, Polotsk to one, Rostov to another, and to another Beloozero. The Varangians in these cities are colonists, but the first settlers in Novgorod were Slavs; in Polotsk, Krivichians; in Beloozero, Ves; in Rostov, Merians; and in Murom, Muromians. Rurik had dominion over all these folk.[*]

Like any founding myth, this tale is long on legend and short on truth.

Begin with the fact that the Laurentian codex of the Primary Chronicle (also known as the *Tale of Bygone Years*), from which this famous excerpt is taken, was compiled in 1377, over 400 years after the events in question. Four centuries of oral tradition between the event and its record-keeping is bound to play loose with the facts.

---

[*] Samuel Cross translation of the Russan Primary Chronicle, Medieval Academy of America, 1953.

Second, Rurik arrived first not in Novgorod, but in Staraya Ladoga, where he ruled for a few years, then moved down the Volkhov River to Holmgard, along Lake Ilmen. Novgorod ("new city"), another 15 kilometers or so down river, is not believed to have been founded until some time later. And he arrived on the shores of Lake Ladoga not in 862 as tradition has it, but more likely 856.

Third, there is the question of the Rus. While the Chronicle alleges that they were a Varangian tribe, in fact the origins and nature of the Rus has provoked a long and unsettled debate.

Interestingly, the historian George Vernadsky places the origins of Rus in the South, not Scandinavia, and rather far back in history:

> In fact, however, political life in the territories occupied by the Eastern Slavs had originated much earlier in Southern Russia, in the social and political forms centering around the trade between the wooded regions and the pasture lands of Western Eurasia, the Black Sea, and the East.[26]

It all began with the Scythians, a nomadic, war-loving, horse-straddling tribe of Turkic-Iranian origin that roamed the southern steppes beginning in the seventh century B.C., whose dominion stretched even into the forested realms north and east of the Black Sea.

These were later joined by the Sarmatians and the Alans, also from Iran. One of the leading Alanic clans, Vernadsky asserts, "was called Rukhs, 'the radiant,' and it is from this name that Ros or Rus (hence Russia, Russians) presumably derives."[27] By the third and fourth century A.D., the Slavic Rus and Antes tribes had settled and created hierarchical agricultural societies in what is now southern Russia. At about this time, however, a century-long battle was fought in the southern steppes between the Goths, from the west, and the Huns, from the east. In the end, the Huns won out, bringing most of what is now Eastern Europe under their control.

Meanwhile, in the northern forests, the territory we now know as northern Russia was being settled by Finno-Ugric tribes from the east, and Baltic and Lithuanian tribes from the west. Both would eventually come under pressure from expanding Slavic colonization from the south, and from the Varangians, or Scandinavians, in the north.

By the middle of the eighth century, the Scandinavians had penetrated into much of northern Russia, chiefly via its rivers, and were ruling over local populations in Yaroslavl, Rostov and Suzdal. They began moving south, where, Vernadsky says, "they mixed with the Rus and even assumed their name." Yet here he notes that other historians argue that the name Rus derives from the Finnish word for the Swedes, Ruotsi, giving it a northern, not a southern origin.

In any event, it is now believed that sometime in the early ninth century an independent, self-governing Russian *kaganate* (a word taken from the Khazars, a Turkic Jewish tribe which had been powerful in the middle Volga region for some centuries, but was now on the decline) coalesced, and that it began to exert its influence, mainly through trade, but also through brutal raids, throughout the region. Indeed, archaeological evidence supports the hypothesis that Staraya Ladoga and Holmgard, along with a few other settlements, had by this time developed into active trading centers (furs for silver, largely) between the Baltics and the Caspian, and that Russian traders were notoriously crafty, suspicious and successful.

There is in fact a record in the Frankish Annals of St. Bertin (written reasonably contemporaneously to events, not 400 years after the fact), suggesting that in or around 838 a group of Norsemen calling themselves Rhos visited Constantinople, as emissaries of the Russian *kagan*. Emperor Theophilus declined the Rhos' proposal for a treaty and hindered their early return. Then, either because the emissaries feared returning home via the steppes (rampant Magyars), or because Theophilus wanted to slow their return, it was proposed that the Rhos travel through the Frankish Empire, accompanied by Greek ambassadors from Theophilus. Upon meeting the Rhos, however, the Frankish Emperor Louis the Pious quickly sussed out that they were Swedes by birth and had them detained as potential spies, this period in history being one particularly rife with Viking (i.e. Swedish) raids into the European continent.

From all this, it is clear that the Rhos/Rus/Ruotsi were but one of many intermingling tribes in the region in and around Lake Ilmen, and that their existence here pre-dated the purported arrival of Rurik. Further, it seems more likely that the purpose of calling in Varangian reinforcements was not to unite bickering tribes into a state, but to coalesce a sufficient force to secure trading routes and create a fighting force. Two decades after the events described by St. Bertin, in 860, a rather massive force of Rus assaulted Constantinople "like a bolt of lightning," disappearing almost as strangely as they had appeared.

In any event, by the end of the ninth century, the beginnings of what would become the Russian state were taking root in and around Lake Ilmen, and chiefly in a settlement then known as Holmgard, but today known as Rurikovo Gorodishche (Rurik's Settlement). It sat on a high promontory along the Volkhov River, just below where the river exits Lake Ilmen.

The Historian

Sergei Troyanovsky is late. A half hour late. We can't find out why, because his phone has been turned off. Miffed, we shuffle our day's appointments around and hope we can meet with him later.

We reconnect at lunch and cut short our enjoyable feasting on a thin crust pizza (multiple interesting topping combinations, the most surprisingly delectable of which is paper-thin slices of lemon) in a cafe near the center of Novgorod. We rush off into the rainy afternoon to meet him in front of a seedy hotel on the opposite side of town.

It is cold and wet, and there is no sign of Troyanovsky. We wait a bit, wondering what could have happened, why one of the city's most respected historians, who insisted he is very interested in meeting with us, is a no show.

Finally, Mikhail makes one last foray through the rain and into the hotel lobby, returning with Troyanovsky in tow. The historian is apologetic yet also somehow distracted. He climbs into the car and starts muttering something about how the newspaper where his wife works celebrated its 25th anniversary last night.

Troyanovsky is dressed for dryer weather, wearing a lightweight, orange down jacket and a Baltic-style cap with brim. He is slightly overweight, about 6' 2", and sports a carefully trimmed goatee.

The plan agreed to beforehand was that Troyanovsky would take us out to Rurik's Settlement, where, according to legend, Rurik came to rule over Rus.

On the way over bumpy back roads, I try to engage Troyanovsky in a discussion of Novgorod's history, of how, when it was absorbed into Muscovy by Ivan III and then destroyed by Ivan IV, Russia's last best hope for going down the democratic path – the path of Baltic mercantilism represented by the Hanseatic League, in which Novgorod was a thriving trading hub – vanished.

But Troyanovsky will not go there. He insists on speaking English, even though it is completely unnecessary. "I love Anglo-Saxon culture," he says. "Do you know where Watford is?"

I don't.

This leads to a long digression on his last trip to this suburb of London, of his time at Cambridge, of sherry and British dons.

And then our road ends.

There is a clear line of hazard tape stretched across the road, and to the right is a wide swath of red earth that looks very soft and quicksand-like. Dump trucks and graders with monstrous wheels are moving about, and a few workers are off to one side, seemingly discussing where the edge of the road needs to be.

"Just drive ahead, to the right," Troyanovsky urges.

Mikhail and I are mystified. "What do you mean to the right?" Mikhail asks. "There is no road."

"Drive on," Troyanovsky says. "Don't worry. The name Troyanovsky has pull here. I have papers that say we can be here."

Neither of us are worried about papers. We're worried about Kukisvumchorr getting mired in eight inches of rain-soaked mud. I have visions of red goop flying off spinning wheels as we try to push him out of some awful rut. I place a placating hand on Kukisvumchorr's dashboard and mutter some a quiet assurances, then Mikhail drives off the road.

THE RED DIRT proves more solid than we imagined. Yet in several places we have to navigate ruts that seem as deep as our wheel wells. How Kukisvumchorr gets us through this muck, I don't know. But after about five minutes of this (the workers don't even pay attention as we pass by; the wheels on their gigantic trucks are twice the height of Kukisvumchorr) we are on the banks of the Volkhov River, looking back towards Novgorod, barely visible through the mist and driving rain.

Nonplussed, Troyanovsky exits the car and begins explaining how this road to nowhere, which they are finally finishing at massive expense, is an unfinished construction project dating from the late Soviet era. Several massive stone pylons rise out of the river, atop which the planned road (a bypass road) was to rest. This explains the roadwork and the red dirt, which is being graded up to meet an eventual bridge across the river here.

But what we have come to see – Rurik's Settlement – is off to our left. We look downriver and just can make out the point where the Volkhov flows out of Lake Ilmen. The twelfth-century Yuriev Monastery peeks out behind trees on the river's opposite bank.

We then set off along a flagstone path for a several-hundred-meter walk in the driving rain. With each step it is getting colder and wetter. Occasionally, Troyanovsky stops to tell a story, to explain the history of the bombed out Annunciation Church we are passing (it dates to 1103 and was heavily damaged by German fire from across the river; Novgorod was occupied by the Nazis from 1941-44). He repeatedly tries to make his presentation in English, but when he can't find the words, he slips back into Russian and we move faster. Faster is what we want. We are freezing out here.

We come to the end of the path and stop before a massive, 40-ton boulder. It is a beautiful, reddish stone, granite perhaps, and measures about eight feet on each side. It was set here in 2012, on the occasion of the 1150th anniversary of the founding of the Russian state. Troyanovsky expresses his disgust that no one from the highest echelons came to the celebration of the stone's unveiling. The only major politician was the political clown Vladimir Zhirinovsky, who Troyanovsky says embraced the stone and kissed it, expressing his eternal love for Russia. Local, regional, and church officials were also present, along with representatives of the city's many foreign sister cities. They arrived at the site by boat and were entertained by performers in period costumes.

I ask what is special about the stone, which has been dubbed the "Prince's Stone" (Княжий камень). Troyanovsky looks at me as if I am slightly daft. "Because it is a beautiful stone," he says. Indeed it is, but I find out later it was hauled in from Novgorod's Batetsky region, and, since it is certainly over 1,000 years old, it was "around to witness the events of that time." But I like Troyanovsky's answer better.

Engraved on the side of the stone that faces toward Novgorod, which sits two kilometers upriver, is a quote from the Radziwiłł Chronicle, declaiming how Rurik came to found his town on the edge of Lake Ilmen:

> И прия Рюрикъ власть всю одинъ, и пришед къ Ильмерю, и сруби городок надъ Волховом, и прозваша и Новъгород, и сѣдѣ ту, княжа, и раздая мужемъ своимъ волости и городы рубити.

Troyanovsky, who seems oblivious to the cold, his down jacket now soaked through, slowly reads the old Russian script, translating it into new Russian (something to the effect of: Rurik had all power, came to Ilmer, built his city on the Volkhov and called it Novgorod; he ruled there and distributed other regions and towns to his relatives), underscoring that "this is where Russia began."

The wind picks up as we finally move away from the stone toward the overlook. Troyanovsky notices my discomfort. "You're completely frozen through, eh? Did you serve in the army?"

"What does the army have to do with anything?" I shout into the howling wind. "It's just damn cold out here!"

"The army has everything to do with it. I served in the army…" He mentions his unit and where he served, but the names are lost to the wind. "It toughened me up."

"I think I'm plenty tough," I shoot back. "It is, pardon me for saying, just a bitterly cold day and we are getting soaked through."

Troyanovsky chuckles and proceeds to point out the reputed site of a pagan memorial to the god Perun (near where the river meets the lake), and the Siversov Canal, a nine-kilometer commercial waterway built in 1804 to connect the Volkhov and Msta Rivers. It is named for the then governor of Novgorod, Yakov Sivers.

The area, Troyanovsky takes pains to explain, was settled first by Finno-Ugric tribes. The name of the lake, Ilmen, was originally Ilmer, as written on the stone. And the name Volkhov comes from Volga, which means "water that flows down," because the Volkhov, scraped out by a retreating glacier, flows from Lake Ilmen north to Lake Ladoga. He notes all this to underscore that Novgorod was always Russia's most European and Western of cities.

I recall something Aleksandr Solzhenitsyn wrote, in his controversial essay, published in book form as *The Russian Question*, on the myth that Novgorod was a bastion of democracy and that, had it not been decimated by Ivan III and IV, the future course of Russian history might have been very different (indeed, it is the point I began trying to raise in the car).

The existing myth of a flourishing Novgorod democracy in the fifteenth and sixteenth centuries is refuted by Sergei F. Platonov (*Smutnoye Vremya*, Prague, 1924). He portrays an oligarchy comprised of a small circle of the richest families, and argues that the predominance of the Novgorod elite had reached a level of political dictatorship. Mechanisms of compromise had not been honed and quarrels between feuding factions were played out, often bordering on anarchy, by throngs on the street. Platonov maintains that, in its rapid development, the social and political order in Novgorod had decayed significantly in its own right, even before it was broken by Moscow.[28]

It is a fascinating point, because I have heard Troyanovsky speak about Novgorod and its democratic history previously, but I decide it is too cold to open a new discussion that would only prolong our time in the open air, so instead I use all the body language at my disposal to get us moving in the direction of Kukisvumchorr.

Finally, as we are making headway toward the warm, waiting car, Mikhail announces that he must shoot Troyanovsky's portrait. Of course it must be in the rain, overlooking the grey river and lake.

Mikhail, who in fact did a full term of service in the Russian military, is also frozen through to the bone. How he will summon the fine motor skills to operate his camera and keep from dropping it onto the unforgiving flagstones, I have no idea. He sets up his tripod with shivering fingers and then breaks into about 30 seconds of vigorous jumping jacks that get his blood pumping enough so that he can pull off the portrait shoot. It is, nonetheless, one of the shortest sessions he has done the entire trip.

When the shoot is completed, Troyanovsky walks back toward the path, where I am hunched with my back to the wind, and asks in a provocatively rhetorical tone, "So are we to sell this all to the Asians?"

I am at a loss for his meaning, and look to Mikhail for help, but he is packing up his tripod with frostbitten fingers and in any case didn't hear what was said over the roar of the wind. Troyanovsky repeats himself twice before I comprehend his words and the meaning starts to sink in.

"What do you mean the Asians?"

Thousands of Asian tourists have come to visit Novgorod in recent years, he says. First they are here just to look around. But, Troyanovsky implies (more than implies, actually, saying he is "accustomed to his relatives and the people around him… having blue and brown eyes, like you"), it surely will not end there. "Foreign expansion… immigration by Eastern peoples is dangerous," he says.

"Why dangerous?" I ask, surprised by this turn in the conversation, not really sure where he is going.

"Because they are not interested in our history, what I have been sharing with you today… we have been chatting today as representatives of peoples who are Indo-Europeans… We are Indo-European peoples on this territory, we are the people who settled on this land, mastered it… but immigrants are arriving who are complete outsiders for us. It is a Hunnic attack on Europe… it's not the first time. How much has been endured, especially by Russia?"

He then relates a recent visit to a dig in Yaroslavl, where they uncovered three wells dated to the time of the Mongol invasion. One contained men whose heads had been chopped off, a second women who were beaten and probably raped, the third children. "There you have an example of Eastern Asian expansion into Rus, which took place 800 years ago. We are living with this. We are excavating it. It is the work of archaeologists. We should show that, look guys, what is happening in the modern world, it has precedents. There are certain things that happened well before we came along, 800 years ago, perhaps 1,000 years. We don't know much about it, but we do have some facts."

FINALLY, WE GET Troyanovsky back to the car and begin steeling ourselves for the treacherous return drive through the soft red dirt. Before we can get in the car or start the engine, Troyanovsky asks who is driving.

"I am," Mikhail says, his teeth chattering.

"Perhaps a bit of whiskey?" At this, Troyanovsky pulls from his bag a bottle of Dewar's scotch that is already one-third empty.

"Maybe later, when we get back to town?" I reply.

"Maybe right now, so as not to get sick."

I wouldn't think of insulting our guest by refusing his offer of hospitality. Plus, the weather is clearly Hebridean and a bolt of scotch is exactly what my doctor friend Dale would order in these circumstances.

I pull out our two collapsible rubber cups, which I picked up at an L.L. Bean outlet in Vermont, because I thought it would be a convenient way to have tea by the side of a road (which we have done just once so far, by the side of a Super Deep Borehole). The cups handle the transition to scotch just fine and Troyanovsky and I immediately feel much warmer. I feel bad for Mikhail, but he seems not the least bit bothered by being left out. He is itching to take on the red dirt.

As we drive back into Novgorod proper, Troyanovsky again returns to the subject of his wife's newspaper party the night before, how he refused to go because it is not a real newspaper, which leads into a rather doleful accounting of the state of affairs in Russia.

In addition to being convinced that it is inevitable that Russia will be overrun by its neighbors from the East, Troyanovsky is worried about the general lack of democratic values in Russia. Unlike in the more meritocratic West, he says, "in our country, someone can pop up at the top of the heap, without having previously proven oneself, or showing that one is a person of worth. I worked in the Academy of Sciences… all the titles mean nothing, they are all for sale. You can purchase a doctorate and zip to the heights of power with a scientific degree."

WE ARRIVE BACK at our meeting point and say our goodbyes. Troyanovsky insists on a second round of Dewars (again, "in order not to get sick"), and then asks about our larger project, and where we see Novgorod sitting along Russia's spine.

"There are three sections of the spine," he says (actually four: the cervical, thoracic, lumbar and sacral), "and I would not want for Novgorod to be associated with the lower, pelvic regions," he jokes. "At the least it should be somewhere in the middle, or in the neck portion."

"We've only completed a third of our journey," Mikhail replies, "so geographically it must be somewhere near the top."

"Well, just please remember my request," Troyanovsky says.

Then Mikhail gets out and Troyanovsky gives him a hug, saying "I hope you won't smear me."

"What do you mean?" Mikhail says, but gets no reply.

When Mikhail gets back in the car he turns to me and says, "I have no idea what that was."

Later, I notice that one of the collapsible rubber cups is missing. Perhaps it fell out and even now is lying in that sleazy hotel parking lot, its green, rubbery ridges glistening in the rain, a few missed drops of scotch caught in its half-collapsed ridges.

Three Visits

Over the next two days in Novgorod we met with three people who work in very different spheres, yet who share a commonality of action and purpose. All are seeking in some concrete way to improve the lives of Novgorodians against very difficult odds. Whether it is enhancing culture, building awareness of the city's infrastructure shortcomings, or supplementing the education of the city's youngest students, all are passionately committed to making a difference in their patch.

Back when it was at its peak, in the 1500s, Novgorod was the third largest city in Rus, with some 25,000 inhabitants. It never grew too fast, and today it is only about ten times that size, and, outpaced by the country's megacities, it ranks 85th in Russia by population. Like Petrozavodsk (260,000; in 71st place), it is big enough to be doing interesting, innovative things on the metropolitan level, but small enough to be left alone.

And yet, both cities are not being left alone. As it turns out, both have reformist mayors who are under siege from their city councils. In both instances, the council deputies (seemingly acting from the same playbook), rather than waiting for the next round of elections, are seeking to oust their mayors based on vague accusations of non-fulfillment of their duties, for not completing projects started well before their tenure, or for not adequately maintaining the city's infrastructure (mainly because city and regional tax funds are not provided in sufficient measure).

In Veliky Novgorod, in May 2015, Mayor Yuri Bobryshev (a member of the United Russia party, a master of sport in tennis, and a successful businessman) was fired by his city council. The decision was overturned by the Novgorod Regional Court in June, but in December the council was back at it, subjecting Bobryshev to another impeachment vote, which this time he survived, at least in part because the Liberal Democratic Party refused to "take part in the circus." In Petrozavodsk, as noted above, Mayor Galina Shirshina was not so lucky. She was voted out by the local council in a lopsided vote; she vowed to take her case to the courts.

Meanwhile, seemingly oblivious to the political hubbub "in the skies above," our three cutizens were going about their work.

The Activist

Novgorod is a demonstrably flat city. Reasonably compact, with wide, soviet-era streets and large municipal parks, it is well suited to be a bike-friendly city.

That is the hope, at least, of Kirill Kuzmichyov, 29, a local civil engineer who volunteers his time to Novy Gorod ("New City"), a local organization focused on making Novgorod more comfortable, environmentally conscious and handicapped accessible.

Tall, slim, with long dark hair and sharp, avian features, Kuzmichyov says his group is inspired by urbanism efforts and, in particular, by Moscow's Municipal Projects (*Gorodskie Proyekty*). Novy Gorod, according to Kuzmichyov, seeks to encourage use of public transport, bike-if-ication, accessibility for the handicapped and recycling.

Yet it is the group's handicapped accessibility activities over the past three years that have garnered it local and national attention. By encouraging journalists and citizens to sit in a wheelchair and attempt to navigate the city streets, the group has illuminated the inadequate (or nonexistent) sidewalk ramps and pedestrian transitions.

The efforts have led to official letters, and some 90 access problems across the city have been reduced to 75. While those that have been fixed "are not ideal everywhere," Kuzmichyov says, "I feel it is beneficial, it is a step forward."

Kuzmichyov is nothing if not an optimist, and it helps that Novy Gorod has a city council deputy, Konstantin Khivrich, a member of the Yabloko party, on its board. Khivrich is an active advocate for the group's causes.

But if they are going to make long term change, Kuzmichyov recognizes, they need to overcome the most difficult thing of all: "focus the society's attention on the question [of what kind of city Novgorod should be] and create a public expectation for a comfortable city...

"We want to tell people what this city can be, how comfortable it can be, how suitable... so that people will want this and will begin to demand improvements from the administration," he says. And such lobbying can be difficult when the main beneficiaries (the elderly, handicapped and underprivileged) are not those with whom Novy Gorod's message best resonates (the young, well-educated middle class).

What is more, when it comes to bikes, "people don't see bicycles as an alternative form of transportation," Kuzmichyov says. "They are seen as a form of recreation... but we are trying to overturn that stereotype..."

How have the powers that be reacted to the group's activism?

"I can't summarize that in one word," Kuzmichyov says. "But this year, for the first time at our annual Urbanfest, the mayor came and opened the ceremonies with a speech."

It is a sign of acceptance and legitimacy for the causes they are trying hard to promote. The annual Urbanfest event brings in speakers for roundtables and lectures to fill the public space with relevant ideas. Like this year, when the group brought in a leading Russian expert from Perm to talk about public transport planning.

"Public transportation is in a degraded state here," Kuzmichyov says. "For economic reasons, people are being disincentivized to use public transport, and prices are rising out of proportion for a city of this size. This leads to more use of private transport, which we don't approve of. We prefer an optimal balance of private and public transport," he says.

The driving force behind Novy Gorod's activity is the recognition that, if a city is not comfortable and suitable for its residents, people will not be engaged in the city. They will pull back or, worse, move away. Handicapped people will stay home; those who cannot afford public transport will not go out and engage with the economy; young people will move to bigger cities.

What gives Kuzmichyov hope is an exchange that the group carried out with Novgorod's sister city of Bielefeld, in Germany. Visiting that city, which is similar to Novgorod in industry and size, helped Kuzmichyov and the other members of Novy Gorod to understand their goal, to see what it would take to get from A to B. What was encouraging, Kuzmichyov says, is that "the people we met with, the specialists, say that they had the same exact problems 20 years ago."

The Director

"We are building an island, an island where culture is possible," Nadezhda Alexeyeva, 48, says, sitting in her pleasant office at the back of Novgorod's Maly Theater – home to an independent drama company that is known for its often edgy, thought-provoking productions.

The island metaphor is apt. Alexeyeva and her Maly are surrounded by rough seas: youth who don't know how to appreciate the theater or are fleeing to big cities, meager city and regional budgets for the arts, and a dire economic situation that makes finding sponsors nearly impossible.

Yet they press on. The Maly is a beautifully kept small theater. Great attention has been paid to decor and presentation, from the neat, brightly lit staff offices, to the foyer's Da Vinci wall drawings and slick parquet floors, from the elegantly simple refreshment stand to the efficiently organized stage lighting racks.

Even more importantly, the passion and loyalty of the Maly's actors and production staff is palpable. They are doing a final dress rehearsal for their new production of H.P. Lovecraft's *The Outsider*, to debut the following night. It is a story of loneliness and imprisonment, of self-awareness and social norms. A creature escapes from a castle prison, only to discover it has been kept there to hide its hideousness.

But Alexeyeva is not staging this in a standard way. "Theater," she says, "is not only what happens on stage, but in the audience." The performances are limited to 50 audience members who, when they arrive, are greeted and offered refreshments by strange, Gothic creatures ripped from the pages of *Frankenstein*. A pianist and cellist torture music at the back of the foyer, and a tall character removes his head and hands it to a hobbling midget. Finally, when the mood is set, a vampiric narrator enters the foyer and delivers a long monologue by way of introduction. Then the creatures begin rounding up the audience and herding them toward the theater, tying black blindfolds around their eyes and leading them to two long benches facing one another in a blackened chamber.

The blindfolds will not be removed. For the next 20 minutes, the audience is in utter darkness while actors deliver the text of Lovecraft's story, with copious moaning and gnashing of teeth. At the end (when the creature goes running back to his prison, horrified to discover his own ugliness), the theater doors are opened and the audience is allowed to remove their blindfolds and move out into the light.

It is a powerful experience, and typical of Alexeyeva's Maly. "Even when we present the classics," Alexeyeva says, "we try to do it in a way that raises contemporary issues." Indeed, last year they happened to unveil a staging of *The Trojan War* just as the war in Ukraine was getting started. And another production they have on is a staging of Mark Haddon's powerful novel *The Curious Incident of the Dog in the Night-Time*, which, among other things, is about difference, about how society deals with autism. "It is very easy to love someone who loves you back," Alexeyeva says. "Autism shows how hard it is to love people who don't express it back to you. This reflects back on society."

Five foot two or three, and as energetically expressive as you would expect a 25-year theater veteran to be, Alexeyeva is a force of nature. A single question releases a torrent, as if she has been keeping words bottled up for two decades, waiting for an attentive listener. But then Alexeyeva is not the sort of person one suspects bottles anything up. She bemoans how not just Novgorod, but all small cities are dying when it comes to the arts, how the youth of today don't know how to relate to plays, because they do not get the sort of cultural training that used to be common. Globalization, she says, is pulling young people to the cities, ripping them from their roots. Even young actors see their time in provincial theater, she says, as a stepping-stone, a way to get to Moscow or St. Petersburg. And it's not like she can use pay as an incentive to keep them in Novgorod.

The financial side of things is endlessly challenging. About 50 percent of the Maly's budget comes from government sources, 40 percent from sponsors, and just 10 percent from audiences. Even with tickets priced at just R250-300 ($5 or less), Alexeyeva says, "people these days just are not willing to pay to be spiritually uplifted."

"It was so different in the 1990s," Alexeyeva says, speaking of when communism ended and everything was simultaneously falling apart and opening up. "People had the feeling that we were all changing the world together… there was at least a sense of unity. The system had collapsed and we needed to build something together."

Today, she says, things are entirely different. Everyone is focused on consumption, and the government "is creating a new mythology. But we are a huge country and don't need a mythology. We need actions…"

A few minutes earlier, in a related train of thought, she had commented, "Nothing good comes from uniting around something against something else." It is an eerie echo of a famous quote by Anton Chekhov, one of Russia's finest playwrights: "Love, friendship, respect, do not unite people as much as a common hatred for something."

So what is her vector going forward? "To protect the people around me," she says. "In both the human sense and economically... so that the people on our island not just continue to exist, but continue to develop.... You just have to keep moving, because even in the darkness there are stars."

The Entrepreneur

Andrei Morozov, 35, had a bit of an epiphany soon after he and his wife had children.

He had begun to worry about the education and upbringing of said children, and so, being a trained journalist, he began to do research. What he quickly latched on to was the maxim pronounced by the Japanese education theorist Masara Ibuku, that "after three, it's too late."

By the time kids get into kindergarten, Morozov says, they are put into regimented programs and classes where teachers don't have enough time for quality one-on-one instruction, where kids therefore cannot learn the essential skills they need to think independently. "It's lost time," he says, time when kids could be developing.

Morozov's research led him to Yevgeny Belonoshchenko, who has started eight schools in Yekaterinburg and 20 across Russia as a whole, integrating the work of Igor Matyugin on early childhood learning and memory. The idea is to teach children critical problem solving skills through fun, interactive, intense one-on-one sessions over a period of eight months. The focus is on building reading, memory, and knowledge retention skills. The result, Morozov says, is a "super-*chuvak*"* – a child well prepared to take on the learning and educational system that he or she is about to enter.

The proof of course will be in the doing, and Morozov's storefront learning center, located on the ground floor of a new residential area in Novgorod, had only been open a few weeks when we stopped by. Morozov is slim and fair-haired, with a neatly trimmed beard. He dresses simply, in dark slacks and a blue, crewneck sweater.

"Children won't see the effect of this work for about a month," Morozov says. "And parents won't see it for about two months."

Yet such schools, which Belonoshchenko is franchising, while Morozov prefers to chart an independent course, are profitable. "There are 3,000 students and 20 successful, profitable schools already in operation," he says. In just 3 weeks of operation, he has recruited 25 young students and expects to have 50 by next month this time, and as many as 125 per month when he is running at full steam.

During our visit, seven-year-old Danill Tsvetkov is being taught in a classroom next door by a teacher Morozov hired after extensive vetting and interviews. She is a very cheery, amiable type, and at one point during our interview comes out with a workbook to show Morozov. There is a rebus puzzle that she and Danill just can't work out. She and Morozov struggle over it for about five minutes until Morozov finally solves it and there is laughing all around.

Born in Siberia, Morozov moved to Ukraine when he was very young and grew up there. On a lark, because his hometown had a sister city relationship with Novgorod that allowed for easier college entry options, he applied to a journalism school here. He got in and has lived in Novgorod ever since.

---

* A slang word perhaps best translated as "bloke" or "fellow."

A successful mass media online portal followed, but Morozov soon saw the writing on the wall. "Journalism is a different breed here," he says, "and investigative journalism can lead to a head thumping." It was not a difficult decision to leave that line of work and move into something that truly interested him: helping children.

"I believe in the philosophy of small things, of doing a single, focused thing well," Morozov says when asked why he has stayed in Novgorod, rather than take his business to Moscow. "I can do things here easier and better… I am trusted here." Eventually, he could see himself moving to the capital if the venture works out and he can build it to the sort of scale he is interested in. He is particularly interested in building on the current program to develop ways to teach children 5-7 years old basic financial skills.

"But I am comfortable wherever I am," he says. "I like this city, but it is not important *per se*. It is not a question of geography." For him it is something else entirely. "The main thing is to be fully realizing my potential, to work in a way and in a place where I am comfortable, doing excellent work that is effective."

The Feldsher

When President Vladimir Putin returned to the Kremlin in 2012 for his third term, one of the things he pledged to tackle was health care reform. An admirable and daunting undertaking, to be sure, and so the past three years have seen huge changes in this, one of Russia's largest entitlement programs, a tattered link in the fraying social safety net.

In the Soviet era, health care was technically free to all, but getting decent care required *blat* (influence and connections) and bribes. Since the end of the Soviet era, health care has been comprised of a complex mix of private and public health care facilities. While free health care (on which the state has increased spending per patient ten-fold over the past decade) continues to be a right enshrined in Russian law, in reality the system is overstressed; getting top quality care means paying for private doctors and hospitals. And paying more – at least twenty five percent more over the last few years, to the tune of $8.7 billion (or over twice the country's annual budget for health care), says Russia's Audit Chamber.[29]

The general principles behind the recent reform of the state health care sector were logical: optimize delivery systems, bring smaller facilities in under the umbrella of larger ones, eliminate redundancies, staff and equip fewer hospitals, but do it better. By reducing the number of facilities (and, thus, doctors and nurses), it was argued, health care salaries could be increased. The goal, according to the Health Ministry, was not to reduce the overall level of medical care, but increase it "by a more effective distribution of resources."

Unfortunately, the results have so far been far from optimal. There have been massive doctor and health care worker layoffs, shuttering of rural primary care offices without putting in place the promised general practitioner replacements, and the wholesale closure of thousands of hospitals and clinics. Patients are waiting longer for routine procedures and now must pay for tests that were free just a year ago (or pay bribes to get to the front of the line for "free" tests).

The reality is stark. According to the government's own statistics, from 2005 to 2013 the number of health facilities in rural areas fell by 75 percent, the number of district hospitals fell 95 percent, and the number of local health clinics dropped by 65 percent. Over 17,500 towns and villages now have no medical infrastructure, and residents of 11,000 settlements must travel more than 20 kilometers to reach a doctor (and likely much farther to reach a hospital), yet over a third of such settlements have no public transport.[30] In Moscow, 10,000 medical workers lost their jobs in 2014. Not surprisingly, just 19 percent of Russians in a 2014 poll said they were satisfied with the current medical system. [31]

Further, under the guise of "optimization," the reforms seek to commercialize hospitals and health care and to shift the financial burdens of health care from the federal budget onto regional budgets, and onto individuals. But, as three well-informed observers wrote in 2015, "With all attention focused on the bottom line, nobody worries about the increased mortality, longer periods of illness, shorter healthy life spans and rise in disabilities that have resulted."[32] Indeed, according to the state's Audit Chamber, in the first year after the reforms began, there was "a 3.7 percent increase in in-hospital deaths... or almost 18,000 additional deaths."[33]

IF YOU LOOK in a dictionary under "salt of the earth," you might just find Vladimir Nikolayevich Simonov listed there.

For 39 years he has worked as the feldsher in the village of Krasniye Stanki, the last village on the E105 out of Novgorod, before it joins with the M10 for the frenzied, three- or four-lane blitz into Moscow.

Slim and fit, Simonov has a bright light in his blue eyes, and an easygoing, quiet manner. It is easy to imagine confiding all of one's uncomfortable medical issues in him, and getting sound, straightforward advice in return. He is quick with a smile and seems mystified that anyone would be interested enough in what he is doing to want to write about him or take his picture.

A feldsher is a primary care medical professional in rural Russia. It is someone just shy of a fully trained medical doctor, yet able to prescribe drugs, provide obstetrical care, diagnose and treat basic health issues, and refer patients for care at nearby hospitals or clinics.

"When I started, we had about 800 residents [in Krasniye Stanki]," the 61-year-old Simonov says. "Today there are about 500. It's less, yes. It's a village. Most of the population is elderly…"

Most of the care Simonov provides is prophylactic, and the most common ailments he treats are heart related, given the age of his patients. Simonov does most everything himself – "five minutes seeing a patient, three days doing paperwork," he jokes when we first enter the creaky old wooden home that contains the medical clinic (though it turns out the extent of his paperwork is mainly writing up visit notes in patients' files). He has a medical assistant to do simple things like take temperatures, draw blood and keep the *pech* (old Russian stove) stoked, with the latter perhaps his "most important job" in these cold climes, Simonov laughs. If patients need any acute medical care, or any tests, like x-rays or blood work, then they are sent to specialists or to the hospital in Proletarsky, eight kilometers away. One assumes, given the new health care realities, that some or all of those services are paid.

Simonov is responsible for providing primary care – including in-home visits where necessary – not just for residents of this village, but for anyone within a 25-mile drive. "We all know each other here. I know all my patients by their name and *otchestvo* (patronymic), the year they were born, what they suffer from" he says. "I see someone approaching and immediately can tell if they need an ambulance or not." He was born and raised in the village (his family worked on the *kolkhoz*, the communal farm, which has since evaporated), went to medical college, served in the army, and then came back here to work. He has never doctored anywhere else and rarely gets away for vacations, because there is no one to step in when he is gone.

We talk about the differences between doctoring in the US and here, and he is fascinated to learn about how much paperwork must be done, about the insurance system. While there is private insurance in Russia, basic medical coverage is still free, as are many medicines to many groups of people, and the extent of his insurance paperwork is filling out visit information on a 3x5 inch slip of paper that gets sent on to the companies. Most significantly, unlike in the US, he does not have insurance companies breathing down his neck, telling him to minimize his interaction-time with patients. "If it takes five minutes, it takes five minutes," he says. "If it takes an hour, it takes an hour." (This is in contrast to doctors in Russia's big cities who report that the new reforms advise that they spend no more than 12-14 minutes with patients, even though the reality is never that simple.)

As it turns out, Simonov is technically retired, but he continues to work because he loves the practice and the people. "If I left tomorrow, I don't know who they would get to replace me. It's not likely they would." He feels he has developed a trust and relationship with his patients, "something that only comes with years of work," and does not want to let them down. Even if he stopped working, he says, people in the village would keep coming to him for medical help.

When asked what he would like to change, Simonov thinks for a moment. "As you see," he says, "we are located in a private house, one that is not really suitable for this [work]..." Indeed. There is no computerization of records (though that is becoming widespread in cities), and patient records are kept in simple paper folders that lie stacked about neatly in his office, which is adjoined by an examination room in one direction, and the waiting room (seven uncomfortable chairs and the *pech*) in the other. There is no technology, and just one visible medical reference book. The aging linoleum floors whimper and crack underfoot, and the waiting room is lined with yellowing, Soviet era health care posters.

Yet Simonov does feel his work has done good, that after the difficult period of the 1990s, people are taking better care of themselves in the village. Of the 500 or so residents, he says, maybe only ten have a serious drinking problem, and critical medical emergencies are rarities (over his 39 years he has only had to handle two sudden births with women who could not get to the hospital in Proletarsky).

Doctors are well respected in Russia, but notoriously underpaid. I put that fact to Simonov to probe if that is something he would like to see changed. "A person does not go into medicine for the money," he says with a smile. "I enjoy helping people."

Pie Town

Our driving objective for the day was Valdai, a lake resort town about one-quarter the distance between Novgorod and Moscow.

About mid-afternoon we came upon Krestsy, a village founded in the fourteenth century that historically was a place where travelers changed horses or carriages when on the road between the capitals. When the train line was installed between Moscow and St. Petersburg, it bypassed the town, turning it into a backwater. Today it has just over 8,000 residents.

Over the past two decades, however, Krestsy has transformed itself into a modern pit stop for drivers along the E105 (called the M10 here).

As you approach the southern end of town, you start to see smoke billowing from little wooden huts, pop up tents, and fold up card tables. The smoke is coming from wood-burning samovars, and their emissions are like a billowing shingle, signaling to passing cars that "we're open for business."

Despite the town's long, historical role as an important way station, it seems to make no appearance in Russian literature, except perhaps in the Symbolist novel of Fyodor Sologub, *The Petty Demon*, which takes

place in an anonymous provincial town like Krestsy and was surely informed by the ten years the author spent teaching in the provinces,
including his first three in Krestsy.

The novel is not for the faint of heart, telling the story of a sadis-
tic teacher going slowly mad and tormenting all those with whom he
comes into contact. The main character, Peredonov, has no redeeming
qualities whatsoever – indeed, his last name has since become synony-
mous with the horrible character traits he expressed:

> His feelings were dull, and his consciousness was a corrupting and
> deadening apparatus. All that reached his consciousness became
> transformed into abomination and filth. All objects revealed their
> imperfections to him and their imperfections gave him pleasure.
> When he walked past an erect and clean column, he had a desire
> to make it crooked and to bespatter it with filth. He laughed with
> joy when something was being besmirched in his presence.[34]

A psychological study of evil, *The Petty Demon* is also an indictment
of provincial life: "It appeared as if the inhabitants of this town lived
peacefully and amicably – even happily. But it was only in appearance."
It shines a light on that concept so vital for any Russophile to understand: *poshlost* – an almost untranslatable word that, in its vilest sense,
connotes a scabrous, obscene, and immoral crudity; in milder usage it
is simply a shallow sleaziness. Vladimir Nabokov perhaps captured the
meaning of the word best when he transcribed it as *poshlust*:

> Russians have, or had, a special name for smug philistinism –
> POSHLUST. Poshlism is not only the obviously trashy but
> mainly the falsely important, the falsely beautiful, the falsely clev-
> er, the falsely attractive. To apply the deadly label of POSHLISM

to something is not only an aesthetic judgment but also a moral indictment. The genuine, the guileless, the good is never POSHLOST.

Poshlost could well be used to describe the 50 or so ramshackle, tacky huts and vendor tables that line each side of the road at what is called the Yamskaya Sloboda ("Coach Settlement") outside Krestsy, all offering pretty much the same thing: tea, coffee and pies. For incredibly low prices. We stop for a cherry and *tvorog* pie and Mikhail chats with the young girl, Alyona, who sells them to us. Her mother has been selling pies here, eking out a living, for 16 years, she says. She helps out on the weekends by filling in and giving her mom a rest.

As we sit in the car (out of the rain), enjoying our warm pies and tea, Alyona huddles with a girlfriend, who is monitoring a spot two tables down. When a car pulls up in front of the girlfriend's table, she darts off to snag the client before he can move on to another seller, who is offering exactly the same thing for exactly the same price.

Valdai

If you Google Valdai, the first thing that will come up is the Valdai Discussion Club, an annual conclave of talking heads who gather to discuss the world's problems:

> The club's goal is to promote dialogue between Russian and international intellectual elites, and to make an independent, unbiased scientific analysis of political, economic and social events in Russia and the rest of the world.

Founded in 2004 and named for the lake because this is where the first event took place, the Valdai Discussion Club in recent years has met in Sochi. It is largely an opportunity for academics, policy makers, and representatives of the Russian state to wrestle with the notion of "wither Russia," and to make foreign policy statements within the guise of a quasi-academic forum.

Aside from that, Valdai's claim to fame is as the location of (a) posh lakeside dachas, including an uber-posh retreat oft-visited by the current occupant of the Kremlin, and (b) Iversky Monastery, founded by Nikon (the Patriarch whose tenure in the 1600s set in motion the Russian Orthodox Church's "Raskol," or Schism). All of this is set inside a national park, declared across 1,500 square kilometers here in 1990, encompassing the town, lake, presidential dacha and monastery.

"There is paradise in heaven and Valdai on earth," Nikon supposedly said.

How can we *not* stop here? All the more so when our searches turn up an "Eco Hotel" just inside Valdai National Park. Done.

The hotel turns out to be a large log building similar in style to our residence in Medvezhegorsk, or what might be found in the Ozarks. We reach it over a bumpy, loosely-packed sand trail that winds through a forest. It is a family friendly establishment, staffed by helpful young locals, some of whom I would inadvertently roust from their crash pads on the couch of the 24/7 bar when I came downstairs for an early morning cappuccino.

The setting was pleasant and very safe, and at first I thought the Eco in the name might refer to how they cut corners and economized on some of the construction and interior design (they definitely tapped the low bid decorator). It turns out the Eco is in fact because they grow and/or make many of their own food items, from cabbage and moonshine, to preserves, *tvorog*, cheese and more. The staff were very pleasant and helpful, but there was the feeling that we had arrived in the shoulder season, after all the hard work of the summer had passed, and everyone was a bit exhausted, but also a bit exhilarated.

After a nice, quiet dinner, Mikhail announced that he had discovered in the bowels of the Eco Hotel a billiards table (on which, I later discover, the pockets were only 1/16 inch wider than the balls). He insisted that it was essential that we have a game. I unwittingly gave in, and must admit to the fact that, in this titanic battle of Good vs. Evil, Black vs. White, Russia vs. America, America was defeated by Russia. More exactly, America went down in flames without any help from Russia, when America's low-skilled representative accidentally plonked the red ball (which stood in for the 8 ball) into a corner pocket. Sorry America.

Disgusted, I retired to the cozy couches in the 24/7 lobby bar and nursed a scotch while catching up on some writing. As I did, a young girl brought in a tiny kitten (it could not have been more than a few days old, its eyes barely opened) from some unclear situation and showed it around, asking anyone if they wanted to adopt it. Of course no one did or could, and soon the kitten ended up wandering around on its own around the lobby, letting out mews the pitch of a sparrow's chirp. I was dumbfounded that no one else was worried about this tiny creature's welfare or that someone might trip on it in the dimly lit lobby. But no one did.

Finally, I went back up to my room to continue writing, where a tiny thrush landed on my balcony and repeatedly threatened to stroll in the open window.

THE NEXT MORNING, after a nice breakfast of kasha and sausages, we walked along the foggy lake for about an hour, taking pictures of the oddly carved animals and the waterfront, before packing up and heading into the town proper.

By the time we drove into downtown Valdai, our trip odometer read just over 2720 kilometers. Not once in our entire journey south from Kirkenes had we yet been stopped or in any way hindered by a Russian police officer.

This seemed rather unexpected. So, if Muhammad would not come to the mountain, the mountain known as Kukisvumchorr would have to, well, you know…

We had an 11:30 AM meeting arranged and approved to meet with Ivan N—, an *uchastkovy* (kind of like a beat cop) in Valdai, to whom we had been introduced through a friend. We arrived in town an hour early, so decided to walk around separately and do some photography, never mind the overcast, gloomy weather.

I set off to the east side of the main square and walked up a few streets before heading down to the waterfront. On the way, after passing a small street market, I happened upon a rather interesting burned-out building that had shredded green construction material hanging from its façade. It was rather compelling, artistically – the texture and color of the fabric and the scorched wood carvings.

After I took a few shots, I crossed the street to head down to the lake. An elderly babushka yelled out to me.

"You, in black, stop for a minute!"

Oh boy, I thought, here we go. I readied myself to answer questions about why I was trying to blacken Russia's image by shooting only its bad side.

The woman, who introduced herself as Nina Nikolayevna, wanted to know what I was up to. "Why is everyone always photographing this building?" she cried. "Why can't they tear it down already? In Belarus, everything is very well kept and painted. If something like this happens, they raze the building and clean up after it. Here, no. Just dirt everywhere and disorder."

"I was just photographing it because it was interesting, artistically speaking…" I replied, searching fruitlessly in my memory for the Russian word for texture.*

She seemed uninterested. What she wanted to do was unleash a litany of complaints about the state of her town's disorder and dirt. Nina Nikolayevna volunteers a few hours each week at the local evangelical prayer house near the town center that I had noticed when I walked up the street, and she wanted to know why someone let people put up ugly little tents nearby, selling baked goods and knitwear (I didn't mention that I nearly bought a pair of gloves).

Nina also wanted to tell me, unsolicited, a bit about her life. How she had lived in Murmansk Oblast for 40 years, then moved to Belarus with her husband, and now for the last dozen years or so has lived here. She likes the climate better than in Murmansk, and especially likes that it does not stay dark here for six months in winter, but she is not fond of how dirty things are.

Later, Mikhail and I, comparing notes, felt that Valdai was actually a pretty clean little town, as Russian provincial towns go. No trash wafting about, and not much dirt collecting in the gutters. Most of the wooden houses, however, even along the lakefront, were rather run-down and sad looking. But the newer areas of town were decently maintained, and there were a few stores and some nicer cafes. (One even sold Ritter Sport Mint, our official trip mascot, if that is a mantle chocolate can assume.) It was hardly as nice as I expected the town to look, given that it is a dacha town and tourist center (Iversky Monastery is directly across the lake and there are several museums, including one for bells).

As Nina Nikolayevna and I parted ways, I crossed the street. I had not gotten five feet before a man called out to me. "Stop," he said.

---

* That would be текстура (textura), although the Russian and English cognates do differ slightly in meaning.

He didn't look like an official of any sort. Rather the opposite, actually, and overweight and unkempt to boot.

As he approached me, Nina Nikolayevna returned back across the road and cut him off with a torrent of invective, accusing him of some past misdeeds to do with her pastor, and generally read him the riot act before moving on.

He, for his part, asked her to please stop lecturing him.

I just stood watching their social interaction, because, well, that's what I am here to do.

After they finished, the man came over to me and apologized. He said that none of what she said was true, that he was just a guy trying to make it through life the best he could. "And I noticed that you are not from here," he says, working his way to his close. "I don't suppose you could spare fifty rubles, eh?"

AFTER CIRCUMNAVIGATING THE small town separately, Mikhail and I enjoyed some tea and a Ritter Sport off Kukisvumchorr's backside, then walked ten minutes up Gagarin Street to our meeting with the local *uchastkovy*, exchanging dark banter about going in to the police station but not coming back out.

Ivan – six foot tall, well fed, with a buzz cut and nicely pressed uniform – met us outside the building, which was surrounded by a high, iron fence. He looked like the sort of fellow who used to be rather muscular, but had over the last ten years let himself go. Or perhaps he had never had the muscles and just let himself go anyway.

"You are, I believe, here to see me," he says as we approached the building.

A statement, not a question.

We exchanged handshakes and followed Ivan inside to his office, where we began to set up for the interview.

As Mikhail began to explain what our project was about in more detail, we were joined by Maxim, who did not give a last name nor a patronymic, but who introduced himself as *dezhurny otdela*, or the senior officer on shift, saying that he had a few questions.

Maxim had the same build as Ivan, only he was a bit shorter and wore not a uniform, but jeans and a grey turtleneck. I knew the minute he sat down that the planned interview was either off the schedule or would now be closely monitored. In any case, our social interaction lasted just 11 minutes 57 seconds. Which I know, of course, because we taped it.

Maxim stated that, since we had called to set up the interview, he had been in touch with the police press bureau in Novgorod, and he wanted to know what sort of publishing house we represented and if we were a mass media outlet.

Mikhail rolled back his introduction and explained our project again, how it was crowdfunded, that we did not "represent any publishing house," *per se*, that we were talking to people all across Russia, to create a book, etc.

"So, this book of yours, what genre will it be? Documentary?"

"Yes," Mikhail says. "Documentarian, it is sort of a view of modern Russia."

"And it will consist purely of interviews of people?"

"No, not only. There will be descriptions, photos… It will be about 200 pages, and probably about 60-70 will be text, the rest photos."*

"You understand, we have been informed that the interview format presumes journalistic activity. You chat with a person, do an interview, and for journalistic activity, if you are not a freelancer and don't represent some kind of organization… you must nevertheless have accredita-

---

* We had not, incidentally, agreed on any such text to photo ratio. In fact, the coffee table book is to be about 80 percent imagery, 20 percent text.

tion. Do you have accreditation, in particular as members of the mass media?"

"I do, only it is in the car." (Which was about a half mile away.)

"And your colleague?"

"He is the editor of the magazine *Russian Life*," Mikhail replied. "We are simply working together on this book."

"But does your colleague have accreditation?"

"He is an editor, so he is also a journalist—"

"You understand," Maxim says, "if you want to do an interview, then you need to have accreditation."

(At this point Mikhail started to get exasperated, because he felt they were asking for something that really did not apply in this case – an accreditation, the sort of thing one gets for a conference or event. In fact, what Maxim had likely been told is that a foreign journalist needs to be accredited. Basically, they were talking past one another.)

"To get an accreditation, basically you write a letter," Mikhail continued, "then maybe after a week, get an answer, maybe yes, maybe no…"

"Let us agree then, since you do not have an accreditation… well, you do, yet your colleague from the United States does not, as I understand, if you desire to undertake some sort of interview here, which is journalistic activity in Russia, then you must receive accreditation. If it takes place without accreditation, then accordingly, you are breaking the law. The rules for a foreigner being in the country say that, if he is going to undertake journalistic activity, then he must have accreditation. Otherwise, he may be turned over to the Federal Migration Service… because he has been traveling the country on, say, some kind of guest visa, and has been undertaking journalistic activity… That's the essence of what we are talking about. And we, as representatives of law enforcement bodies, we cannot violate that law, and give an interview to a person who does not have accreditation."

"Then maybe I can do the interview?"

"Well, let's proceed like this. If you have an accreditation, let us take a look at it…"

"What I have is not accreditation," Mikhail finally says. "Perhaps you don't understand. Accreditation is a kind of formal procedure… For the mass media, you write a letter saying you want to be present at some event. For an interview, you don't need any type of accreditation. There is just no general concept of accreditation for an interview."

"But accreditation for journalistic activity—"

"No, no no… there is no such concept of accreditation for journalistic activity… There is a press card, and that's it. Accreditation for members of the press to work as journalists, to do journalistic activity, this concept does not exist. "

"Nonetheless, it is specifically presumed that this material that is being gathered, meaning doing an interview, it will be used in the West, yes? In the mass media?"

"No, it will be a book."

"Well the mass media can cite the book… and we will not be able to protest in any way, because you did not have accreditation… and so the objections will be directed at us."

"Let's try this. I have a proposal."

"Okay, fine."

"Perhaps you can be present, take part in the interview, and if you are not happy with something, say you don't like some question—"

"No. We are just small fry here… and we have been strictly… this is a government organization… Our department for working with mass media has strictly instructed us that, if there is no accreditation, do not give the interview. Ask to receive an accreditation, and if you receive it, 'you are welcome'."

"Well, we are traveling on down the road today."

"Well, yes, unfortunately… And they asked that we warn you that, if this sort of journalistic activity is done without accreditation, it is grounds for the application of administrative measures."

"Why did you not just immediately say by phone that you would not give the interview?"

"We did not know that you did not have accreditation."

"Oh, hm," Mikhail vigorously wipes his face in frustration, "it's just that I am a journalist and you are speaking about an accreditation for an interview. But there just is no such thing…"

"I am not going to argue about a concept. It's possible you know more about it."

Totally frustrated, Mikhail is now about ready to blow his normally cool stack. But he also seems to have realized this is a non-starter, so he decides to flip things back on them. "How do you see it? What is an accreditation? What should we give to you, in order to conduct an interview?"

"Prior to my departure," I interject, "I specifically put this question to the Russian Consulate in America, 'Here is what we are doing. We will be collecting information and talking with people… and will be creating a book. Do I need some kind of journalistic visa? Do I need some kind of letter?' The consulate said no, you don't need anything like that. If they had said, 'Yes, you need this, this and this,' then I would have gotten it…"

In fact, the consulate was very supportive of our project all along, even stepping in and waiving the normal $160 fee for my visa.

"Clearly there are different opinions…" Maxim replied. "Nevertheless, get an accreditation, and you are welcome."

"Okay," Mikhail says, undeterred, "what is an accreditation? How should we receive it?"

"I would suggest you do a search on Google, as to what a press accreditation is… I can answer questions about the Criminal Code, as an officer of the law…"

"Well, you see, you say we need to obtain accreditation, but we don't know what that is. I know what it is. You don't know what it is!"

"You don't have an accreditation, do you?"

"You can't request an accreditation from us because it is not required. We simply don't need it to do an interview."

"Accreditation is not necessary?"

"No."

"Of a foreign citizen?"

"No."

"Okay, fine, we have different views," Maxim finally says, proving himself the coolest head in the room.

"Accreditation… listen, again…" Now Mikhail lapses into instruction mode. "I understand that the interview will not take place, but for your understanding. A journalist needs accreditation only in order to attend some sort of official event… How does one get it? Some official event is going to take place. The journalist finds that next week there will be this special event. As a journalist, I write a letter: 'I would like to attend this event.' That's it. That's accreditation…"

"That is your opinion as a Russian journalist. But as relates to someone who is a foreign citizen?"

"Exactly the same."

"I don't know. Ilf and Petrov, when they wrote *One Storied America*, did they have accreditation?"

"No," I interject. "They simply traveled."*

"They did not write about receiving permission, accreditation, even though at that time relations between our countries were not very good?"

Here there is a lot of back and forth and it is difficult to make out any specific conversation on the tape. Things have deteriorated. Finally Maxim breaks through.

"Request from the consulate permission to conduct journalistic activity, if it is an interview format. Understand, you will travel, or you have been traveling, through many cities, and you may be asked why you are conducting an interview without permission as a journalist... I think it should be easy for you to get. I have no doubt... and then we would gladly chat with you."

"Well that would clearly not be you, then," Mikhail says.

"Well, unfortunately, but that's how it is."

WE NOW KNOW that both sides were right. Mikhail was right that accreditation is generally event related. But Maxim was right that the Ministry of Foreign Affairs does accredit foreign journalists – but that is for foreign media outlets. Which is not something we were representing. We were working for no one but ourselves (and our supporters) on this project, and it would certainly be a stretch to call a coffee table book mass media.

We are a writer and a photographer creating a book. We are not reporting on events (except those which happen to us in the course of our travels) and we are not seeking access to government facilities or events.

---

* Later, after I returned, I checked with Anne O. Fisher, an expert on said trip who translated the authors' work into English. She said she was not certain, but felt that most likely they likely had some sort of special accreditation or dispensation.

The US, for its part, does require visiting journalists (who are employed by foreign media outlets) to get a Media Visa, but does not, like Russia's Foreign Ministry, require accreditation upon entry. The US law seems chiefly to be targeted at keeping foreign individuals from coming to America and stealing US jobs. It does not seem to have any special provision for private individuals who are traveling to the country to write a book.

Tver or Bust

The impending rain, combined with the unwelcome reception at the police station, led us to flee the lake area sooner than planned. We had thought about visiting Iversky Monastery, but the rain portended a lack of photographic opportunity and so we decided to press on to Tver, with a brief touristy look-see at Torzhok.

Only the Torzhok stopover also did not go as planned. Distracted by our discussion of the accreditation spat, we missed the town's first exit off the E105/M10, and the second one, even though it clearly indicated that it too led to Torzhok, did not offer a route back across the river. We only succeeded in making a lot of train commuters angry at us for plugging up their street with our little German vehicle. So, rather than beat an ignominious retreat back up the E105, toward the storm that was shadowing us, we continued south to Tver, arguing over what really happened in Valdai, and what it meant for the rest of the trip.

FOR THE FIRST time we had no appointments in our destination city. At Tver, we were at nearly the expedition's halfway point, so we decided we needed a short pause, a chance to catch our breath and reassemble our forces for the forthcoming assault on Moscow. (Translation: we need to spend several hours on wifi, tying up loose ends, answering emails, editing posts and photos.)

En route, we made reservations at a hotel that had decent ratings, was close to the center and that was, well, cheap.

What we should have paid more attention to was its address: 38 Sovietskaya Street.

We arrived just before dusk and decided that, from the outside, the establishment looked more or less fine (although the two leather-clad fellows loitering out front were questionable). As we entered the front doors, we saw only a sketchy blue cafe to the right and stairs straight ahead. So naturally we climbed the two flights of steep stairs, thinking, "Hm, this is an odd sort of hotel lobby."

When we reached the top floor we were informed by a very nice hall monitor slash key lady (Clue #2) that we had walked right past reception – it had been on our left as we came in the front door and were distracted by the neon blue cafe.

So we tromped back downstairs and entered the nondescript door we had passed by so cluelessly. A middle-aged, unsmiling attendant awaited us behind a chest-high desk.

Now, throughout this trip we have taken all officious, Soviet-style demeanor as a personal challenge: it is our thankless obligation to get these souls to lighten up a little, to crack a smile. Usually all it takes is a bit of back and forth banter (jokes at the expense of the clueless American are particularly effective).

This one was a tough cookie, however, probably because all the check-in procedures needed to be done old school: with handwritten forms, multiple stamps and signatures, and overly-complex instructions. The breakfast *talony* (vouchers) each needed to be stamped and signed by her four times, with four different, forged signatures.

But crack her we did. We not only got a smile, but also some reasonably sincere directions of where to stroll that evening before dinner: "Just go to the statue of Lenin and follow in the direction he is pointing, down Tryokhsvyatskaya Street, the pedestrian zone."

Our precious breakfast *talony* in hand, we trudged back up the stairs and showed our passes to the hall lady, who gave us each one of those iconic, numbered fobs that look like a cross between a sink stopper and a blackjack, with a room key attached as an afterthought.

We entered our rooms and stepped back in time to the 1990s, when stodgy Soviet hotels were being upgraded with cheap East European linoleum, compressed Yugoslavian wood furniture, and Bulgarian wallpaper – it is definitely a "distinctive look." There was very little room to move around between all the furniture and fixtures, and the finish carpentry was bizarre: wide crown molding sealed the bathroom sink to the wall, staples held down the floor trim.

But, on the flip side, the hotel was clean and safe, and the staff were friendly and helpful, and very gifted in the art of forgery, should that skill be required.

On the other flip side, the wifi was horrendous.

Still, we were sure to give the Hotel Seliger high ratings so that others could enjoy this blast from the past as much as we did.

TVER IS A fairly typical provincial post-Soviet city. The center is in need of a bit of maintenance and is comprised of mostly two- and three- story buildings, many built in the St. Petersburg manner with an inner courtyard. The pedestrian zone was well-kept, however, and mildly busy for a cold weekday evening, with people out strolling past the Baskin Robbins, coffee shops and a few elite clothing shops and/or their knockoffs.

We circled around to the embankment, where nothing was going on (strange, why wouldn't you go out for a stroll along the water when it is dark and 30 degrees?), and on the way back toward our hotel stumbled upon a truly fantastic place for dinner, Manilov, named for the character in Gogol's *Dead Souls*:

> God alone could say what Manilov's character was. A class of men exists whom the proverb has described as "men unto themselves, neither this nor that – neither Bogdan of the city nor Selifan of the village." And to that class we had better assign also Manilov.

Manilov the restaurant was anything but characterless. Decorated in light, understated colors, its walls were hung with nineteenth-century photos and lithographs. The waitresses were uncommonly patient and deeply knowledgeable about the 12-page menu full of interesting dishes like Potatoes with a Surprise, Dvoryansky Salad, Borshch with Garlic Donuts and Sour Cream, and all sorts of *vareniki, pelmeni* and *golubtsy*. Mikhail who, shall we say, can eat like a *bogatyr* if the need arises, was flummoxed, unable to choose between the many mouth-watering options.

We supped like a couple of Chichikovs, and, thanks to the strong dollar (or is it the weak ruble?), the whole thing rang in at just $25 (German beer included).

The next morning, our *talony* entitled us to a very hearty breakfast (*syrniki* anyone?) at the basement cafe next door. The pleasant young waitress needed none of our anti-Soviet agitation, though it would have been nice if she had not made me suffer through a cup of instant coffee and told me straight off that espresso was available, provided one wanted to part with an astronomical R70 ($1.15).

Maybe I just looked like a guy who didn't have R70 to spare.

THE 175-KILOMETER DRIVE between Tver and Moscow has an interstate feel to it – two lanes in either direction, separated by a median. Yet we still must slow down to 60 kph through each village that lines the thoroughfare. The condition of the village homes and roads improved markedly as we transited from Tver to Moscow Oblast, and the landscape began to change from the swampier flatlands more typical of Novgorod (which legendarily saved it from the Mongol hordes) to one with more hills, fewer trees and more farmland.

About 100 kilometers from Moscow we stopped at a roadside fast food joint that advertises its *ponchiki* (donuts) with gaudy overstatement on brain-numbing red and gold billboards. Sadly, the *ponchiki* were limp and lukewarm and did not live up to the hype.

In a few places (Emmaus, Mokshino), the landscape suddenly opened wide, with sweeping views of the Volga and/or appended reservoirs. But the sky was not amenable to photography, so we pressed on.

For some of the final stretch, we diverted to a gleaming new toll road (road open, tolls not) that ran between Solnechnogorsk and the outer ring road.

Meanwhile, Ira – our artificial intelligence navigation device – was stymied by local developments. She led us down a dead end road manned by a surly parking lot attendant who said the road in front of us, the one we could clearly see, was not in fact a road, or at least not one we were allowed to traverse. We backtracked and ended up having to drive halfway to Petushki to travel the needed final block west.

But it was worth it. We were staying in another Azimut Hotel, conveniently located just a cobblestone's throw from Moscow's Tulskaya metro station. The contrast with last night's soviet-luxe hotel was profound. We were warmly greeted at reception, efficiently checked in without any stamps or signatures, and sent up to our rooms where a nourishing plate of fruit awaited. Best of all, the electrical outlets were where we needed them (instead of, Soviet-style, hidden behind the headboard), and the coffee was not instant.

The Center

Moscow is a barrel chested, steroidal river city where *naglost** digs its heels into the cracked pavement and where everything is done on a scale that seems designed to fulfill someone's dreamscape expectations. The architectural, metropolitan backdrop is monumental, ever-changing, almost cinematic, but the foreground is a village tableau. Lines of kismet tangle with neighborhood identity and coincidence to build bonds of family and relationships that are the city's lifeblood.

It is not quite a melting pot, more of a samovar, where, unlike lots of big cities, many people you meet actually *do* seem to come from here. They are the warm, steady waters that hold the city together. But there are also millions of immigrants from Russia and beyond. Central Asians, Caucasians, Europeans and Asians, with their own tight, insular communities in distant boroughs and gated communities, provide a heady mix. And then there are the selfie-stick toting, matryoshka-seeking tourists.

BY NO MEANS did we have the thinnest shred of an illusion that two days spent in the capital during our trans-Russia expedition would leave us with any sort of complete portrait. That is not our intent. Instead, as with all the other places we are visiting, we hoped to pluck a few inter-

---

* A virtually untranslatable word that enfolds the ideas of pushiness, cheeky impertinence, nerve and an almost crude insolence. Sort of a chutzpah born not of charisma but self-righteousness.

esting stories out of the millions humming about us to supplement our gathering portrait of modern Russian life.

The Singer

We stop outside the front gates of the Gnesin Russian Academy of Music on Moscow's Povarskaya Street.* The address sign reads 30/36, but we have been told 38. Something doesn't add up.

A trio of friendly young students immediately asks us what we are looking for.

"A girl," Mikhail answers with a wry grin.

"There are plenty of those here, take your pick!" a young female student jokes.

Before we can ratchet the repartee up a notch, Mikhail connects by phone with our subject, Alexandra Turchenkova, who is waiting just inside the Academy's front door, apologetic for having misstated the address.

The foyer hums with an invigorating mix of hormones, music, chatter and hard-heels. We pass through security, climb a few flights of stairs, then zip down a series of long hallways lined with practice rooms. As we pass each one, classical music seeps out through the doors – violin, tenor, piano, soprano, cello. In the hallway itself, a balalaika student is tuning up for a lesson and a violinist is running through some scales.

Contra to our usual interview procedure, in this instance we are doing the photography first and the interview second, because this was the only time we could get a room. Space is at a premium here at Gnesin.

---

* Gnesin was founded in 1895 by the three Jewish sisters Gnesina, all of whom graduated from the Moscow Conservatory with distinction. It is located in the heart of Moscow and considered Russia's second best elite music school, after the Moscow Conservatory.

And, as we shall find, so is a place of quietude for taping an interview; it is as if we have found ourselves inside an intense musical hive; during our interview, an officious queen bee will quiz us about what we are doing just sitting around – idleness is not prized here.

We go down a final hallway and enter a small recital room Turchenkova has reserved for 15 minutes, close the doors, and Mikhail digs into his portrait work.

To say that Alexandra Turchenkova has charisma would be like saying Mozart knew something about music. The camera loves her and she oozes a charm, intelligence and presence you usually only see in seasoned actors or stage performers. After the portrait, she sings *O del mio dolce ardor* for us so that we can have some "action" shots. Yes, the room fills with her crystal-clear mezzo-soprano voice, as one would expect with any talented vocal performer. But there is more: she is uncommonly expressive, dramatic and enthralling as she sings Gluck's tender and soulful declaration of love.

Charisma is not something that can be taught, even in a place of Gnesin's calibre. Either you have it or you don't.

Turchenkova has it.

"You cannot just stand there with your hands at your sides and sing," Turchenkova replies when we comment on her performance. "The composer is trying to express emotions and ideas, so you need to understand them and transmit them to the audience."

Odd as it may seem, this is not where Turchenkova expected to end up. She was actually trained as a linguist and a French translator. But she has sung all her life and loved it. A few years ago she suddenly decided to follow her passion, to make music her life. She was living in the United States at the time and working with some vocal teachers there. When she started thinking about where to study, she realized that most of the good teachers she had in the US had studied in Russia, at Gnesin or the Moscow Conservatory. So she decided to return home to Moscow.

But getting into Gnesin is not easy. Unlike many institutions in the US that require merely an application and an audition tape, Gnesin requires five exams, including in Russian literature, music theory, solfeggio, and vocal skills, as well as an interview. If you fail to accumulate the required points for any of the five exams, you are out. No appeals. Do not pass Go. Done and gone.

Turchenkova not only had this set of challenges before her, but, at 27, she was also several years older than the average applicant, who typically applies right out of high school or a music school at the age of 19 or 20.

"I arrived for my interview," she recalled with a smile. "The security guard asked what I was here for, and I handed him my documents, saying I was here to see the entrance interview committee. He looked at the dates in my passport and said 'Whatever would you need to see the interview committee for?'"

Now in her first year (of four) at the academy, Turchenkova says she fits right in. "I cannot live without this. When I entered here, I understood that this was my home," she says. "It's always interesting for me to be with musicians, to make music..."

A typical week includes about three hours of one-on-one vocal training. "All practicing must be done in the presence of a teacher," she says. Technically one is not even allowed to warm up without a teacher present. Which means our photo shoot slash impromptu performance was actually a figment of our very colorful imaginations.

"The first job of a musician is to be a professional," she says. "And the second is to take our music to the public, if one has the chance… I of course would like to develop classical music in Russia, which has a huge tradition, huge potential… I want to show young people that this thing called classical music is very interesting, especially opera… the main thing is to have patience, to listen, to want to understand…”

As to her future goals, “I am Russian,” Turchenkova says. “I want to live in Russia. But if I can perform outside Russia too, that would be wonderful. Either way, I can’t not sing.”

Which is a fine thing for those who will get to hear her perform.

The Single Mother

We start our second day in the capital with a late morning meeting near Novoslobodskaya metro. Diving into the bowels of the Moscow Metro after more than a year’s absence is like meeting an old friend for a drink in an old haunt that has been recently renovated – familiar and yet not. It is as clean and efficient as ever and continues to modernize, adding stations, opening its 200th at the time of this writing. There is now wifi on most trains, which means that today more riders are reading from tablets or phones than from paperbacks or newspapers.

The rainstorm that dogged us north of here has passed over the city, leaving behind cool, dampened streets. Finding the appointed apartment takes some searching (there is no earthly logic to the numbering of Russian apartment blocks), and we wander through a curiously chic neighborhood that seems almost Parisian, with narrow streets and six-story Stalinist high rises, peppered with tasteful yards and playgrounds.

We have come here to meet Marina Kozlova, a 31-year-old single mother of two. Trained as a lawyer, Kozlova practiced for several years, but now does the work only as much as she needs to in order to pay the bills. Otherwise, she has chosen to chart her own path. She spends a greater part of her life taking care of her two young children (each with a different father) and photographing them and the world around her in an engaging, high-contrast, black and white style that edgily celebrates life, love and friendship. It has earned her wide accolades and over 12,000 followers on Instagram (@solaristika).

Kozlova is the polar opposite of a helicopter parent, not attempting to contain or over-direct the energies of her two young children so much as parry their actions and interact with them in a style far from the Russian norm. "My main task," she reveals, "is to keep them from killing themselves or each other. Most important is that things are calm, pleasant and happy, for me and everyone around me. If things are good for me, it will be good for them." She speaks frankly and openly with her children, she says, answering all their questions. "I try not to limit their desires," she says. "They should choose themselves what they want to wear, whom they want to play with, with whom they want to live (I asked [my six-year-old daughter] Marta if she wants to live with her father, and she says 'No!')..."

This is in contrast with the more authoritarian, directive parenting style that prevails in Russia, and was particularly prevalent in past generations. And certainly for Kozlova herself. "My mother was wonderful," she says. "She decided everything for me, including what I would grow up to become, and I thought that was just the way it was supposed to be. But when I turned 30, I suddenly realized that my entire life had been constructed not by me, but by someone else. This is of course a huge tragedy... everything I had been doing up to that point is not what I wanted to be doing. I don't want that [for my children]... but I also don't believe that a mother should put her life on hold just because she has children and subordinate everything to that..."

Does her un-Russian parenting style ever get her any reprimands from the courtyard babushkas or other people in her building?

"We have strange people living here," Kozlova laughs. "There's a babushka living upstairs. She thinks there is a hole in our ceiling through which evil seeps into her apartment… She constantly knocks on the floor and complains that we are too loud."

"Am I a good mother?" Marina asks. "Yes," Marta answers, flitting about the kitchen in a pink princess dress. "You would be even better if you photographed me less."

Marta is clearly happy to have been able to skip kindergarten today, so as to be part of the photo shoot, and hams it up in front of Mikhail's camera – she is a natural in front of the lens, and thus the subject of many of her mother's best images.

Meanwhile Lev, 18 months, is upset that we are not going out to play on the new playground. It was erected almost overnight in the neighboring courtyard and has numerous towers and bastions meant to mimic a kremlin.

We attempt to distract the children with some interesting cookies we picked up near the metro station – some sort of individually-wrapped waffle and chocolate treats – but that only works as long as the cookies last; Lev is actually more interested in unwrapping all of the cookies than eating them.

Slim with striking, angular features and large, aquamarine eyes, Kozlova has numerous flamboyant tattoos (including one in Hebrew she declines to translate or explain). "Once I started, I couldn't stop," she says as she prepares coffee for us in her tasteful two room, Ikea-decorated apartment. She has been surprised, she says, that so far no employer or client has had any trouble with her body art.

"Somehow, I never saw myself in the role of a mother with several children," Kozlova says. "But that's how life worked out."

She says she is "happily divorced" for over a year from her second husband (and just recently kicked out the "next" man). "It was not my first divorce," she says, "and so I feel really good about things… I divorced Marta's father when I was pregnant with her; I decided I just could not live with him any longer. Then I got remarried for some reason, got pregnant with Lev, and again divorced… You know, it's just difficult for me to live with someone… I start to feel uncomfortable, constrained… I meet someone, spend time with them and hook up… that just seems to me to be a more acceptable form of interaction. Our [Russia's] social and moral norms seem a bit strange to people from more progressive European countries. My mother has more or less made peace with this, realizing her daughter is not like everyone else."

"What do you mean by making peace?"

"People say, 'Oh, Lord, how can it be that a woman lives alone with two children, each from different fathers? How has she made such bad choices? They do not have a complete family…' But I think that the main thing is that both mama and papa are happy. And if they are somehow not happy together, then they should not try to keep it going 'for the children's sake.' On the other hand, one should probably be more careful about choosing one's partner, so as to not divorce them after a few months. But, it is what it is…

"I think that the only reason two people should live together is because of Great Love," she continues. "Other things, like for the children, for convenience, etc., those are not enough."

The hardest thing about being a single mother, Kozlova says, is having to do everything yourself after having gotten used to having someone else to turn to. Moscow, she says, is not the easiest city in which to bring up children. It is not built for children or mothers with carriages, and so every errand becomes an expedition. "But every grown person is an independent adult and can cope with just about anything," she says.

What would she like to see change to make her life easier?

"Change the country," she jokes. "I think we are talking about huge, systemic changes that we will never live to see. Change the people… change the infrastructure… the main thing is that in Russia the indi-

vidual is not valued at all as a person. Ideas are valued, but not people…
it is such an elementary thing, but it is also so global."

So, why not leave?

While Kozlova says she "has the documentary prerequisites" for
emigrating to Israel, she is, for now, not interested in that. "My family
is here, my language, my history… There, I don't know the language,
I don't have a job, I am alone with two children who also don't know
the language, and I am insufficiently brave to just pick up and go off
somewhere without any form of support…"

As to the future, Kozlova is disillusioned about what is going on in
Russia. "It's difficult to guess what will be even a year into the future,"
she says. "Two years ago I would never have expected things could have
turned out how they are now. I had illusions that there would be some
sort of changes. But all the changes have gone in the other direction. I
don't know… I am not so strongly tied to any country or place, should
things get really bad. If things are calm, we will be calm."

Interestingly, when she talks about things getting bad, she is not primarily talking about economic realities. Yes, she says, it has an effect
on your life when prices for basic goods go up threefold. "But I am not
talking about economic changes, but social ones," she says. "This is no
longer a comfortable place to live, socially; it has become difficult to
look at people, to talk with them. Of course I have my circle of friends,
people who think like I do, but the rest of the country, it's a nightmare
what is going on in their heads – they are embittered, aggressive, unhappy, and this is what oppresses me."

To some extent, she says, for the past several years she has sought
solace through personal fulfillment, through meditation, yoga, searching through new experiences, and of course through her photography.
She will continue to seek and look for a better situation, she says, and

the ultimate determinant of what the future holds for her children is her own happiness. "If things are good for me," she says, repeating a sentiment she has expressed more than once, "it will be good for them."

The Chefs

In a quiet Moscow neighborhood about a five-minute walk from Russia's busiest (and first ever) McDonald's is the popular restaurant TWIN2 (with the 2 reversed). It is the brainchild of Sergei and Ivan Berezutsky, 29-year-old brothers and twins born in Armavir, Krasnodar Krai.

As the father of twins, I naturally start by mentioning this fact and say I am curious how twins handle working together.

"Of course it is not easy," says Ivan, smirking, "we finally decided to divide the kitchen in half and we each have our own areas. That seems to work."

The twins are utterly different, in both appearance and demeanor. Ivan has a slightly rounder face and features, and is the talkative one, perhaps more comfortable and used to dealing with inquisitive journalists. Sergei has narrower features and his mind is clearly in the kitchen. Frankly, I found it odd they would suggest a six PM meeting, with the dinner rush lurking just over the time horizon. But then things happen according to a different schedule in Moscow. The dining room, they tell us, won't fill up until nine, so they have time to spend with us.

The decor is light and modern, but also cozy and warm, with rust-colored walls. A huge chandelier made out of wooden tennis racquets hangs in the center of the main dining room. And the bar is backlit and colorfully tiled. Quiet music – hardly the norm in Russian restaurants – purrs in the background.

TWIN2 specializes in "new Russian cuisine," Ivan explains. To them, this is not about creating new takes on old dishes, like Beef Stroganoff or borshch, but sourcing food products from across Russia's many agricultural and climatic zones and then turning them into unusual, healthy meals, often in surprising presentations.

"Take our tasting menu," Ivan says. "We pair foods that look a lot alike, but which taste completely different, and present them in a surprising way. It is just like with us. We look a bit alike but are completely different people."

Every other month, the brothers travel to some distant corner of Russia in search of new items for their menu. "We want to prepare things no one else can," Ivan says.

Some time ago, they traveled to Altai (a remote, mountainous region in Siberia, near the border with Kazakhstan) in search of cheese. Their Toyota Outlander died, Ivan says, so they took horses further into the mountains, where they found a cheese making factory built in the 1930s that was making really fine cheese, while a newer site closer to civilization was "using the same raw materials, and making completely inedible stuff."

The main obstacle to their goal of harvesting all that Russian cuisine has to offer is logistical, it can be difficult just convincing local providers to even sell to them.

"Take the Far East," Ivan says. "They have a great assortment of fish products, but only a certain selection of them get shipped anywhere. Why? Because there is demand for them, there is no problem selling them, and that's all there is to it. The other fish don't get shipped. Why? Because in principle no one needs them."

"And they don't ship in kilograms, but in tons," Sergei inserts.

"Exactly, no one is interested in your 10 kilograms and won't ship it for you," Ivan continues. "So we have to turn down certain things because there is no way, physically, to get them to us. Or take herring for example. It is always salted (preserved), because it is very oily and spoils rapidly. Yet it is very tasty when fresh and has long been popular grilled. But we can't get it delivered fast enough to do that. We went to Solovki… and there they grill it because they catch it and grill it right away – it is twenty times better than salted or marinated herring… but we don't get it shipped because it spoils too quickly and it also can't be frozen, as that also spoils it."

Russia is a big country, and when it comes to food, logistics rule.

"When we worked in St. Petersburg, we got our mussels from the White Sea. Here in Moscow, the mussels come from the South, from the Black Sea," Ivan says. "They are much better from the Black Sea, but Petersburg gets them from the White simply because it is closer… both the strength and weakness of our country when it comes to food is its size and its many climatic zones. We are doing our best to overcome this, to serve unique foods from all over Russia, but it is difficult, very difficult."

Despite their young age, the twins have a wide breadth of experience and enviable accolades. Initially, they gained their cooking experience separately – Ivan in St. Petersburg, Sergei in Moscow – and both have worked at restaurants abroad – Ivan in Spain, Sergei in the US. Both are "world champions" in cooking, by their reckoning the only Russian cooks in their age group to receive this honor.

The brothers decided to unite their passion and talents in December 2014, and brought in a third partner to handle the business side of things. They have garnered good reviews and are cooking to packed houses – as one would have to in order to survive in Moscow's competitive market.

And one of the hottest objects of competition is personnel. The Moscow restaurant market is so saturated that the industry is plagued by massive turnover of staffers chasing the quickly depreciating ruble. The brothers say they have countered with the only move that makes sense: creating a work environment that is interesting and challenging for those who work there, something they can take pride in. And they are very proud of their nouveau Russian cuisine.

"There are classic dishes like Beef Stroganoff, cutlets, puree, borshch..." Ivan says. "For us, the main thing is the produce, the items without which Russian cuisine cannot exist... Real Russian produce, this is what we use to make our dishes. Yet we don't do classic dishes, but new ones... Tastes change and diets change. Previously, everyone ate fatty, heavy foods, but now everyone is watching their figure and wants less fatty food... So we don't prepare 'old Russian cuisine,' because it is heavy... but we do get all of our produce from within Russia."

This has been their guiding principle since even before the imposition of Western sanctions and Russian counter-sanctions severely constrained the quantity and quality of foreign foodstuffs imported into Russia. The approach is based on principles and philosophy, not the tactics of necessity.

"We have lived and worked in different countries," Ivan continues. "There, they use their own meat, their own fish, to make their dishes. But we [in Russia] always used others' meat and fish and produce to make our food!... Every Russian cook knew French or Italian ingredients better than our own. What kind of nonsense is that? We have excellent produce with which to make our food."

"Here is one very specific example," Ivan says. "Yesterday this farmer, a farmer from Moscow Oblast, came into our restaurant with truffles, white truffles. And the strangest thing – these were from just outside Moscow, from Sergiev Posad. White truffles! The aroma and taste of the white truffles, of course, were not the same as white truffles from

France, they are weaker. But they are *ours*! And he dug them up with a shovel and half destroyed them. With a shovel! It's just crazy."

Sergei interrupts: "Truffles, *white* truffles, from *Moscow Oblast*. And he just came to us by chance, can you imagine? And he was just mashing it back and forth in his hands like…" and Sergei mimes someone making a big snowball out of a precious white truffle, cringing at the thought.

"It used to be," Ivan says, "that everything abroad was good and everything made in Russia was no good, to put it lightly. Even if the food was lesser quality, because it came from abroad it was better… But now people have traveled back and forth to Europe, tried all the cuisines and they have eaten their fill. They want something of their own… After the sanctions and counter sanctions, basically all Russian restaurants are using only Russian produce. And the main thing is that people like Russian produce, Russian cuisine."

Take cheese. Even before the sanctions, the brothers say, several companies went abroad, studied cheese-making techniques, acquired equipment, and are now making it in Russia. There is good cheese, they say, to be had from St. Petersburg, on a par with what can be had in Europe.

Then the brothers compete with each other to expand on a list of companies and products, of rare fish and unusual local dishes that can only be found in Russia, that have yet to be truly discovered, truly enjoyed. But of course that is not the main thing…

"The main thing," Sergei says, "is that people's mentality is changing, that they are willing to eat Steak Tartare or carpaccio made from Russian meat, instead of frozen and shipped from abroad."

Roads and Fools

God of snowstorms, god of potholes,

every wretched road you've trod,

coach-inns, cockroach haunts and rat holes,

that's him, that's your Russian god.

Бог метелей, бог ухабов,

Бог мучительных дорог,

Станций — тараканьих штабов,

Вот он, вот он русский бог

Pyotr Vyazemsky, "The Russian God" (1828)*

As mentioned above, when speaking of Russian roads, it is common to quote Nikolai Gogol: "Russia has two misfortunes: roads and fools." The only problem is, he never wrote it, as far as anyone can tell. The phrase has also been alternately attributed to Nikolai Karamzin and Mikhail Saltykov-Shchedrin, also likely erroneously. Nonetheless, the aphorism continues to be widely cited, even if its provenance is uncertain.

We have traveled nearly 3,500 kilometers on Russian roads so far this trip, and I can honestly say that the overwhelming majority of main

---

* Excerpted from *The Penguin Book of Russian Poetry*, edited by Robert Chandler and Boris Dralyuk.

roads have been very well maintained, and many seem to be recently paved. Admittedly, we have been traveling on the main *trassa* from north to south, and once you leave that in the cities and in between places, the pavement does get spottier and bumpier. But no worse than New Jersey, which is hardly something we expected.

Huge investments have been made to make the main north-south artery better, wider, safer, and smoother. And there has been great progress.

The problem, of course, is that the fools remain.

I have driven around much of Europe, Canada and the United States, and I can honestly say that nowhere have I met a higher percentage of more impatient, pushy and foolish drivers than in Russia. The fast drivers drive faster, the bad drivers drive worse, and the rude drivers are unspeakably so. They don't tailgate so much as climb into your backseat. And if you are driving a bit slow – as in just 10 kph over the speed limit on an open road – some take it as sport to pass you with only the slimmest of distance between vehicles.

That said, fools exist everywhere, and even here they are well within the minority.

As a counterbalance, the courteous people can be amazing, offering copious directions to the wayward, or a gas siphon for an Abkhazian who comes up short between stations. One of the finest road customs among Russians has to do with passing on long, two-lane roads. When you are trying to get around a big semi and can't see around it, the semi will sometimes do the looking up the road for you, and will blink his right blinker when it is safe for you to pass, or his left if it is not. After you pass, you blink your safeties for a few seconds, to transmit a "thank you" back to the driver. I asked Mikhail how this came to be an embedded custom and he had no idea, but it must have started somehow, organized or not. This needs to come to America, stat.

And then there are the service stations. Clean, usually with plenty of food items and often cafes, they offer roadside conveniences that were simply lacking 20 or even 10 years ago. Not all stations are created equal, of course, and we limited our stops to "good" stations, which means state-owned brands like Lukoil, Gazprom, Rosneft or BP, which are plentiful. Private stations were not on our preferred list for buying gas, but we did stop at several for refreshments, ever on the hunt for good chocolate (Ritter Sport Mint) and coffee (passable in many locations thanks to the ubiquitous pod-based, automated cappuccino makers). I have yet to see a standard drip brew type coffee pot you see in every coffee shop and diner in America. For better or worse, Russia seems to have leap-frogged that stage of development.

Where Eagles Soar

The road from Moscow to Oryol is mostly a wide, four-lane affair with a center divider, and the sort of smooth, clean surface we have been spoiled by over the last several hundred kilometers.

By the time we hit Serpukhov, the traffic has lessened, and by Tula the landscape starts to change. It seems to have been hit with a vicious infection of birch trees: suddenly, over a distance of a dozen or so miles, we start to see birch copses and forests everywhere. Yes, there are still a few pine trees here and there, but the deciduous trees seem to dominate the rolling hills south of the capital.

The Sushka River near Pushchino marks another change. The land opens up into broad farmland reminiscent of Western Pennsylvania, Iowa or Ohio. Clearly, we are now in the transition zone between taiga and steppe.

RATHER THAN STOP at a cafe for lunch, we opt for fast food at a gas station. Mikhail decides to be brave and order up a sausage on a bun.

Behind the counter, dressed in Rosneft canary yellow from head to toe, is a surly, impatient rhino of a cashier of the type we have been fortunate to meet only at Rosneft stations.

"What kind of sausage do you have?" Mikhail asks.

"We have Danish, Bavarian, smoked." (У нас датская, баварская, копченая.)

"Give me a tasty one," (Дайте мне вкусную.) he says, trying to be clever, riffing on the rhino-cashier's adjectival descriptions, as if Tasty were a brand option.

There is a long, uncomfortable pause in which he stares down the Rosneft rhino-cashier, determined not to blink, hoping to break through her Soviet facade.

"We don't have any Tasty ones," (У нас вкусной нет.) she finally says. "Danish, Bavarian, smoked…"

"Okay, give me smoked," Mikhail says, defeated, blinking.

Being rather more conflict averse, I opt for a bag of nuts, some chips and a coke.

Every road trip should have a lunch like this. Just one.

WE ARRIVE IN Oryol at dusk. The trip odometer reads 3522 km.

We check into the Hotel Oryol, located on Sovietskaya Street (have we learned nothing?), right near a central square. It is actually a rather impressive, municipally owned hotel that was built by German prisoners of war after World War II (very little of the city was left standing, and much of the center, as well as the railway station, was rebuilt with war prisoner labor) in the Stalinist imperial style.

It is here for the first time (Day 17 of the trip) that a hotel requests my Statement of Arrival of a Foreign Citizen at the Place of Residence

(Бланк уведомление о прибытий иностранного гражданина в место пребывания), supposedly to be issued by our previous hotel. Apparently this is something I should have received upon checkout in Moscow, which of course is news to me. I gather it is one way that certain "polite people" can economize on their effort in tracking my whereabouts (and that of any other foreigner). I am always happy to make other people's job easier, but I must reveal the uncomfortable fact that such a statement was not issued to me.

"Without this, we cannot check you in," says the pretty yet officious young night manager at the Hotel Oryol on Sovietskaya Street.

My red-tape-averse travel partner starts to get his hackles up and begins expressing his undiluted opinions about this "soviet establishment" almost loudly enough to be heard by the overfed security guard wedged behind a desk in a distant alcove. I am uncomfortable with this and sense a confrontation coming. Thankfully, the manager herself offers a way out of the corner she has painted us into. She asks for the contact information of our last hotel and says she will get in touch with them herself, to have them email over an electronic copy of our Statement of Arrival.

Thanks, internet.

IF YOU ASK a Russian what Oryol is known for, they will probably first mention the Oryol-Kursk Salient (Орловско-Курская Дуга), the infamous southern front in World War II where the world's largest and most destructive tank battles took place. It was decisive in turning the tide of the war.

Some might also know that Gennady Zyuganov, head of the Communist Party of Russia, was born here, as was Pyotr Stolypin, the pre-revolutionary prime minister whose reforms fell far short of the mark. More literary types might know it instead as the hometown of Ivan

Turgenev, Nikolai Leskov, Afanasy Fet and Leonid Andreyev, or the site of Turgenev's famous "Literary Nest."

But Oryol meant none of these things to us as far as trip experiences went. For us, Oryol will forever be associated with dance.

We had decided we wanted to seek out a ballet school somewhere in the provinces, and so we thought we would try Oryol. Little did we know that the city is home to the impressive Oryol Choreographic School (OCS).

In 2014 OCS was ranked as one of the best dance schools in all Russia, and in the recent Third All-Russian Competition among extracurricular educational institutions, OCS took second place in the Central Region (a wide region of Russia comprising much of the agricultural belt). Some of its alumni have even made it to the pinnacle of ballet: the Bolshoi or the Mariinsky.

Raisa Rychkova, OCS's 61-year-old straight-talking director, says her school is "Not just about dance. We are educating the children to be so much more. It's not about being in this or that company, but about preparing them to be able to discuss the arts, to be well-rounded, upstanding adults..."

Some 600 students aged 4-18 come here three times a week for two- or four-hour classes in all aspects of classical dance (modern dance "is not our style," Rychkova says). The school moved into its gleaming new 5,000 m^2 facility just over a year ago, after spending its first 33 years in a dingy, unsuitable 650 m^2 building closer to the town center.

The new building (which sports a tiara over its entrance) is due in large part to the school's success preparing students for some of the country's top ballet academies and companies. Eight students last year went on to such institutions.

The school is supported by municipal funds for overhead, by municipal scholarships (about half of each incoming class's students have their tuition paid by the city) and by fee-paying parents. Students must of course pass rigorous testing to assess if they are ballet material.

It is Wednesday, which means it is on-stage rehearsal night for the 80 top students in the school's ensemble. They are preparing for the school's upcoming 35th anniversary performance, but Rychkova also has them do a few assorted numbers for the visitors' benefit, including one they performed for the 70th anniversary of Victory in the Great Patriotic War.

There is something powerful and inspiring about watching young people dance, free of inhibition and yet not fully polished in their technique. It is a raw, engaging beauty. The hour and a half rehearsal zips by.

Just before the end, Rychkova calls over young Irochka, an 11-year-old pixie of a girl, to sort out some details of her schedule. After she leaves, Rychkova tells me that Irochka will be going on to an academy some five or six years from now. Even in someone that young, Rychkova says, it is "already apparent" that she has a future in ballet.

THE NEXT NIGHT we walk three kilometers in bracing 30-degree weather to the Railway Workers Cultural Hall. The grand, colonnaded building (also built by German war prisoners) stands directly opposite the railway station. In the square between them is a massive, striking sculpture of an eagle made from branches and twigs (*oryol* is the Russian word for "eagle").

Inside, a popup flea market selling coats and hats occupies the grand spaces of the Stalinesque lobby. We climb a side stairwell that empties into a warren of offices and ballrooms. This is the nightly home of the Oryol Dancing Sport Club, presided over by Marina Gorbacheva, 49, a slim, poised redhead with stylish glasses and colorful, knitted, opera-length gloves that leave her fingers exposed.

Gorbacheva is leading what may well be the cutest dance class in the known world. You have not experienced true joy until you have watched poised seven-year-old boys and girls whirl about the dance floor in well-rehearsed waltzes and mazurkas.

The main hall has a wainscoating of patterned blue carpeting, with sky blue walls and colorful crepe paper decorations, perhaps to distract from the wide plaster molding at the crown of the walls that features dust-caked, embossed hammers and sickles.

As soon as we enter the room, I am approached by Tonia and Matvei, who have been dancing for 4 and 7 years, respectively, and who want to tell me in their very fractured English how they like dancing because it makes them happy. Matvei is something of a Slavic Billy Elliot, whirling and dancing about the room with ramrod perfect posture. It is clear he loves this activity with every fiber of his being.

Gorbacheva has the dozen kids stand straight-backed for a long time in four neat rows with arms up in the shape of a U, their heads flat and straight, then walks around placing *talony* (coupons or tickets) on the heads of each child who is standing with good posture. (*Talony* will be handed out throughout the class for performance or for winning games. At one point I am asked to judge which of four rows did the best in one competition; I pick the one with the kids who seem to be getting the least *talony*.)

In the next exercise, the kids cut perfect squares on the dance floor. They move together as smoothly as silk. It is amazing to see how comfortable the boys and girls aged 7-11 are with each other. There seem to be no worries about cooties, no angst about holding hands with the opposite sex. It takes me back to fifth grade, when I played the scarecrow in our school's production of *The Wizard of Oz*. So awkward was it, at that age, to be required to skip around the stage hand-in-hand with "Dorothy," that even today my aging scarecrow brain retains vivid memories of those sweaty-palmed rehearsals.

Exercises to learn the more difficult moves are interspersed with free-wheeling activities, where the boys and girls race around the room or spin about like breakdancers. It lets the kids blow off a bit of steam and act goofy, helping them keep their attention better focused during the learning exercises. The kids truly seem to enjoy every aspect of what they are doing and there is no sign they are even the slightest bit jaded, even the older ones.

The exercise ends and Gorbacheva calls the students over, saying, "What do I have here?" She is holding up a limp rubber chicken and gets giggles and obvious sorts of replies from the kids. "Okay let's go back out there and then we'll decide who is like this little guy," she says.

The scarecrow exercise resumes; more *talony* are distributed.

At the end of class, the kids total up their *talony* to find out who the "best" student is today. Seven-year-old Gleb comes out on top – he was an amazing spinner.

BALLROOM DANCE WAS a popular sport in Russia decades before *Dancing with the Stars* became a thing in the West. Russia has city, regional and national competitions, and three national dance federations ("because everyone wants to be in charge," someone jokes, explaining intricacies that are impossible to grasp).

The adult class begins around seven PM Before it can start, Margarita approaches and starts quizzing me in English about where I am from and what I am doing here, but in a friendly way. Then, from across the room, Nick, a former ship's mate, starts rattling on in an English that Margarita did not know he had, about how the two of them are dance partners and are known as "The Master and Margarita."

The Master, Margarita, and four other pairs of men and women, most of whom seem to be in their forties, start their warm-ups, walking around the room mimicking graceful birds to 1980s dance music. It is interesting to see normally staid, reserved Russians engaged in this passionate, fluid sport. The New Englander I have become thanks my lucky stars that I am not a Plimptonian journalist, and that I am not in Kansas with Dorothy.

The class breaks in two, with the more advanced pairs going into the adjoining dance room with Sofie Perelygina, 25, the attractive, poised lawyer who has brought us to this class. One of the pairs, Larisa Ilynikh, 52, and Valery Nikolayev, 58, is uncannily loose and fluid as they move about the floor, with an agility that belies their ages. They are both married, but not to each other, and have been dancing together for three years. They come to classes twice per week, or every day in the lead-up to a competition, where they "basically always win," the intense Nikolayev says, smiling.

Ilynikh, who has been dancing for nine years, says it has made her more sure of herself, she now has a better sense of self-worth. Nikolayev, a college professor and psychologist who has been dancing all his life (and doing karate for 30 years), says he has written over 50 books, but gets far more satisfaction from the month-long process of mastering a new dance.

The Priest

History cannot often be painted in black and white. And the pages of Russian history have interminable shades of grey. Consider one of the most revered local sons of Oryol, General Alexei Yermolov. Few generals in Russian history have been as decorated and celebrated, yet he was twice bounced out of the army by suspicious tsars, and to this day some feel he is the most odious symbol of Russian imperialism.

Alexei Petrovich Yermolov was born in 1777 to a wealthy noble family that had its roots in Oryol *guberniya* yet lived in Moscow. A military career was chosen for him early. By the age of ten he was enrolled in the elite Preobrazhensky Guards, and before his twentieth birthday he had distinguished himself in battle against the Poles.

Yermolov was a tough, charismatic character who, as we say these days, had issues with authority. In 1798 he was arrested on suspicion of taking part in a Smolensk-based officers' political discussion circle that exchanged ideas in writing that were at best insulting to and at worst part of a conspiracy against Tsar Paul. Yermolov spent a month in Petropavlovsk Fortress Prison and was exiled to Kostroma along with the Cossack Matvey Platov (the two became fast friends), where he used his "down time" to study Latin under a local priest.

In 1801, after Alexander I took the throne and assented to the assassination of his father, Paul I, Yermolov was pardoned and returned to favor. Over the next decade he experienced a meteoric rise through the ranks. By the time of Napoleon's 1812 invasion, Yermolov was Chief of Staff of the 1st Western Army and an aide to General Barclay de Tolly. True to form, he actively argued against Barclay's (and Alexander's) strategy of defensive retreat (not to be contrary, he asserted, but because he thought it endangered the homeland; he turned out to be wrong), yet he also fought heroically at Smolensk, at the all-important Battle of Borodino, and through the rest of the war.

Yermolov had little but scorn for Petersburg court life, for the "Germans" who populated the officer corps, and for non-noble commanders. All of this continually got him in trouble and led his superior officers to little trust him. Yet he was beloved by his troops for his friendly and informal way of dealing with subordinates, his larger-than-life personality, his Herculean physical stature, and the countless anecdotes of his outrageous behavior. Indeed, many of the younger officers saw Yermolov as an inspiration for the Decembrist Revolt (and he is said to have warned the gifted writer Alexander Griboyedov of an impending raid, allowing him to destroy his papers).[35]

In any event, after his heroic exploits in the defeat of Napoleon, Yermolov was appointed Commander of the Caucasus, where he served for a decade, simultaneously holding the position of ambassador to Persia, where he negotiated a peace treaty and was elevated to the rank of General of the Infantry. It was during this assignment, however, that Yermolov (whom Tsar Alexander I once said was "black as the devil but armed with as many skills") acquired and cultivated a reputation for unbridled brutality toward local tribes, while at the same time establishing fortresses, towns and roads in the name of the empire. As a result, Russians tend to see in Yermolov a symbol of heroism and "great exploits" (romanticized by Pushkin and others), while native peoples of the Caucasus almost universally revile him as an imperial oppressor. As one historian wrote, "he was responsible for implementing a series of policies that were at the time hailed as vehicles for civilizing the benighted Caucasus frontier, but today might very well be called state-sponsored terrorism."[36]

Finally, in 1827, Yermolov's star fell. He had been viewed with suspicion by the newly crowned Tsar Nicholas I for his supposed involvement in (or at least inspiration of) the Decembrist Revolt. Reports back to St. Petersburg that he had invited exiled Decembrists to dine at his officers' table certainly did not help. He was discharged and lived out the rest of his days (30 years, it turned out) on the family estate near Oryol. When he died, he was buried at Holy Trinity Church in Oryol, according to his wishes, so that he might lie beside his father. Yet Yermolov is not buried in the huge graveyard that adjoins the church, and that is filled with heroes from many wars, but just inside the church's eastern wall.

FATHER DIONISIUS, 26, leads me into an apse off the church's main sanctuary – a cozy, inviting space topped with a soaring dome. He moves aside some chairs and a screen and I see the simple white stone plaque on the wall: "Hero of the Patriotic War of 1812, Artillery General Alexei Petrovich Yermolov, 1777-1861."

Father Dionisius notes that the church takes great pride in its role as Yermolov's final resting place, yet he recognizes the difficult truths of Yermolov's later years. History can be hard to reconcile, a fact certainly not lost on a priest of the Russian Orthodox Church – an institution that for most of the past century has been repressed, abused, coopted and infiltrated, all the while fiercely clinging to its claim as the spiritual bedrock of Russian society.

In fact, the role and influence of the church in everyday life has been declining in Russia since the early eighteenth century. Petrine reforms, modernization, and the church's own effort to impose a "vertical" of power, led to a decline in the influence and significance of the parish church, and the parish priest, in Russia's social, economic and, eventually, spiritual life.[37] By the time the Russian Revolution came, Russian society was becoming increasingly urbanized, industrialized, and secularized – while at the same time fascinated by sideshow spiritualists.

That, of course, is not to say that the church lacked influence or significance. By no means. Before the outbreak of the First World War, in 1914, there were over 55,000 churches and over 500 monasteries in Russia. Over the next two decades, however, most of these would be shuttered or demolished, thousands of their priests imprisoned and/or murdered, and hundreds of thousands of believers sent to camps or simply shot.

Officially, the Soviet state declared itself tolerant of all faiths, but in reality atheism was integral to communism, and no competition for Russian hearts or minds was to be tolerated. An underground Church, loyal to the last non-Soviet Patriarch, Nikon (who died in 1925), lived on in the shadows for several decades.

A modest reprieve was given to the Orthodox Church in 1941, when Stalin decided that rapprochement served the state's interest in uniting against foreign aggression. But the cooptation of the institution and its showpiece churches, with their state-approved clergy, carried the taint of collusion. It also deepened the split with the Russian Orthodox Church in emigration.

Cycles of repression and relaxation continued through the post-Stalin era, and it was not until glasnost in the mid-1980s and the 1,000-year anniversary of the "baptism of Rus" in 1988, that a true loosening began. Over the past 25 years, the Orthodox Church has steadily returned to favor, gradually regaining the trust of Russian society, without dwelling on the difficult seven decades of history that followed 1917, though there were some notable hiccups in the 1990s, when the Church was caught taking advantage of its non-taxable status to profit from the import of high margin goods like cigarettes and alcohol.

Today, various polls of Russians paint a picture of a population that considers itself overwhelmingly Russian Orthodox (somewhere between 45 and 75 percent). Yet this speaks more to national identity than religious belief or practice. Few Russians actually go to mass (15-20 percent attending once or twice per year) or adhere to Orthodox religious practices like fasting or prayer. And only 40 percent of Russians who call themselves Orthodox say they are certain God exists; another 30 percent say they are fairly certain there is no God.[38]

FATHER DIONISIUS IS a gentle, easy-going soul who is well-spoken and carries himself with the air of the provincial intellectual that he is. Beardless, with auto-tinting eyeglasses and an early-onset, middle-age paunch, he was educated in St. Petersburg as a historian and well on his way to obtaining a Ph.D. At about the point he realized that taking the next step to becoming an academic historian would require learning ancient Arabic, he says he had a revelation that drew him into the church. He suddenly realized this was to be his life's calling, despite the fact that he had no previous ties to religion or the church.

We are talking in a bright Sunday School classroom that is jammed full of desks and houseplants. Late morning sunlight streams in through the south-facing windows, warming the thick, rose-colored walls.

Born and raised in Oryol, Father Dionisius has been in the priesthood for six years, and is married with two children (Orthodox priests can marry before being ordained, but cannot remarry if they divorce or their wife dies). He knew, upon joining the church, he says, that he would end up here, because that is how the Orthodox Church works. The vast majority of priests are sent back to serve in their home districts after being trained at the seminary.

Because he is so young, I ask how he sees the differences between young priests of his generation and the other priests who served through the Soviet era.

"The modern generation of priests can be immediately distinguished from the older generation of the spiritual body, which is now 70 or 80 years old, and which was ordained in the Soviet era," he says. "Modern clergy have no idea what it means to serve under persecution; they have no idea what it means to serve under an atheistic government… the older clergy know these things; they know what a secret baptism or marriage is… Our generation is completely different. It was raised in conditions of religious freedom, and even a certain degree of goodwill on the part of the government, which, on the one hand has its positive aspect, but on the other has a negative aspect, because it can make a person feel like he is a part of a huge corporation that will always defend him…

"However, the main thing is that many well-educated people are entering the clergy, many people who have extensive secular work experience, whereas in the Soviet era anyone with a good education would have faced heavy pressure not to enter the clergy. The KGB would do everything in their power to keep such people from entering a seminary… to keep them from being ordained."

The persecution of that era, Father Dionisius says, gave the church "massive internal experience in non-violent resistance. Yet there have been certain consequences… we have become accustomed to speaking in the way we spoke 30 years ago… But this is a rather different time, which demands a rather different type of discussions… more openness."

And Father Dionisius says he feels that his generation of clergy is generally more open to dialog with people of different opinions and ideas (believers and non-believers; those who may pose more uncomfortable questions). In the absence of government persecution, he says, "we have learned that no one can harm the church like we can. Our own personal errors will be the source of any persecution we will suffer. When there is no external pressure, any mistake will be noticed. And it will lead to a judgment of the entire body."

What about the widely perceived view that the newly revived Russian Orthodox Church is but an arm of the state (something that would seem confirmed by polls that show most Russians think of the ROC more as a political party than a spiritual beacon)?

"Christianity has 2,000 years of history dealing with the State, and the Russian Orthodox Church is no different," Father Dionisius says. "As a rule, the church must serve in the conditions that its government sets... If there is one thing the Church learned living through the Soviet era, it is that significant changes can happen in a matter of days or months. And thus the Church tries to support the government when it does things that are good, that benefit society… yet the Church excludes itself from political battles… Nowhere in the charter of the Russian Orthodox Church does it say that you must have certain political views. Religion is about one thing, politics another. There is an adage I like. Unfortunately I don't know who said it – you can Google it, but the essence is true: 'A church that enters into service of the state becomes a widow after there is a change in power.'"

THERE ARE FOUR priests serving at Holy Trinity, which has some 60,000 parishioners, broadly construed. Father Dionisius and the other priests all serve in weekly rotations. The first week he oversees daily church services; the second week he is on call for things like baptisms and burials, as well as services; in the third week, he gets five days of rest. Yet every priest must work all weekends. "That is one of the hardest things to get used to," the young priest says, "working every weekend no matter what."

And of course there is the difficulty of being a clergy member in society, coping with how people deal with your outward appearance as a priest, while inside you are just another human being. "There are many difficult things in the internal life of a priest," Father Dionisius says. "For example, the hardest thing about being a priest is burying a child, or receiving a final confession from someone dying from a painful illness. Yet these are those things that service is made of. On the one hand, these are the hardest things, on the other hand, these are the reasons you are serving, to be with people when things are bad."

But such service is made more difficult because Russians lack the language, the experience of spiritual life. "You need to understand what

Russia is," Father Dionisius says. "Russia is a country that went through seventy years of state atheism. That makes it very difficult for anyone to have any type of conversation with a priest. People have many stereotypes about the Church, and they are very unfamiliar with real Christianity. The parishioner has not read the Gospels… there is no Christian cultural layer. Or perhaps there is, but it is very thin. It is now the church's job to rebuild the lost cultural layer that was Christianity… but to do it without pressure. Not to force people to listen to you, but to speak in such a way that people want to listen."

When asked if he has any particular "trick" (*fishka*) for dealing with people, for getting them to hear his message, Father Dionisius' answer is simple: "The only *fishka* a good priest should have is to love people and be able to talk with them honestly… If you want to be a good priest, you simply need to give people your attention and show mercy…"

AS IT TURNS out, at the time of General Alexei Yermolov's death, Holy Trinity was a rather modest church, and Yermolov was initially buried in Trinity's graveyard, alongside his father. In fact, for a few years after the famous general's death, there was no grave marker, not even a wooden cross, to mark his remains.

Then, in 1864, Yermolov's son Victor approached the church's priest about erecting a monument for his father. The priest counter-proposed that work be undertaken to expand the church so that it would include and enclose in an apse the Yermolov family tomb. A new oaken floor would cover the sanctuary, and the altar would be expanded and placed on a stone foundation. The work was completed in 1867 and father and son, along with Alexei's wife, were interred beneath the eastern addition.[39]

A century and a half later, in 2012, workers were renovating the church, replacing the rotting oaken floorboards with marble, when they discovered construction waste beneath the boards. In the process of removing that waste, the workers discovered evidence of vandalism of the Yermolov family tomb. The press even reported that a general's epaulet had been sighted among the wreckage.

Experts were called in from Moscow to examine the situation and to discern when and how the vandalism had taken place. Forensic scientists and archaeologists examined the site and concluded that the vandalism likely occurred in the 1930s and 1940s, based more on logic than exacting evidence.

"If we delve into the history," said Asya Engovatova, of the Russian Academy of Sciences, at a December 2012 press conference, "it is clear that, in the nineteenth century or before the Revolution, when these graves were respected, such vandalism could not have take place inside a working church. What we know from history indicates that the church was closed in the 1930s, then it housed all sorts of economic institutions. After the war it was opened and again became active. Most likely, the period of looting coincides with the period when the church was empty and inactive."[40]

In 2014, the Yermolov family remains were re-interred in a newly restored memorial and a special service was held. But the most telling words about the incident were spoken two years earlier, by Engovatova at that 2012 press conference. "On the one hand we have before us a serious scientific task, yet on the other hand there is the great social significance of what has happened – its moral aspect. Why, at the time, did no one report this? We don't know, there are no documents to answer this question. A historical mask covers this complex period in our history; for a time, great people were not respected. This is a problem for thousands who were buried, and not just for the Yermolovs… What they [the vandals] were looking for, we can only guess."[41]

AFTER OUR MEETING with Father Dionisius, we spend much of the rest of the day wandering downtown Oryol, soaking in a sudden burst of sunshine. The city has a nice central pedestrian area, where we enjoy an excellent lunch and speedy wifi at a locavore cafe called Kitchen (not *kukhnya*, but "Kitchen" written out in Latin letters). There is also a well-kept (if deserted on a Thursday afternoon) riverside park where Mikhail gets in some interesting street photography. That evening, we end our stay in the City of Eagles at a sports bar that serves decent local beer and pumpkin-sized hamburgers.

It is late by the time we return to our elegant, Soviet hotel with its towering Ionic columns, majestic foyer, eerily quiet corridors, and bureaucratically efficient desk clerks. I nod to the thick-necked bodyguard on duty in the lobby and can't help thinking of all the regional Communist Party plenums that must have been housed in this German-built palace, of the whispered deals in the colorful hallways, bartering scarce goods for influence, or vice versa. It feels a bit as if we are ensconced in a cozy, pink and green, marble-lined time machine, enjoying the overripe fruits of Soviet excess (which for us translates to the fact that the rooms have more than one available electrical outlet, meaning we can not only charge our phones, but our computers as well).

In the morning, before we depart for points south, Mikhail and I enjoy a filling *prix-fixe* breakfast of oatmeal, cold cuts and juice. Then I throw the efficient young waiter off his game by ordering a cappuccino (of course there is a machine). It turns out this must be paid for in cash, yet no one has arrived with the change drawer yet, so the poor kid is forced to trust that a money-grubbing American will come back later to make good on his debt. He betrays his nervousness by reminding me three times of the need to return, which makes me suspect it is his pay that will get docked if I forget or neglect to show up to pay the R30 (fifty cents). Had he known I rolled into town without a Statement of

Arrival of a Foreign Citizen at the Place of Residence, he might have reminded me a few more times.

The Navigator

I knew that sooner or later Ira would come between us.

I do not trust Ira. Mikhail trusts her implicitly.

We have agreed to disagree on this point, but the problem remains. Ira has her own personality and that was bound to come into play.

Ira, you see, is the third member of our entourage. She is our navigator. More specifically, Ira is the name we have given to the app on Mikhail's phone that taps into Yandex Maps and GPS signals to tell us where and how to turn, and how to get to where we need to go.

God forbid we should use a printed map or atlas.

In most instances, Ira's influence and input is benign. Like a knowledgeable local, leading you by the hand through dark city streets back to your hotel when you don't know your way. Which she has done quite often.

But sometimes she gets things wrong and, of course, never admits to it. Other times we ask her to please do things one way, yet she insists on doing it another, even after leading us to believe that she was going to do as we asked.

Ira and I didn't hit it off because I'm a map guy. I really need to pull out an atlas or map and get the bigger picture of my location, to match up physical objects with their location and orientation on a map. It helps me get my bearings and connect with my environment.

To me, using Ira is like looking at a map through a straw. She is a need to know sort of person and only tells you when the next turn will be, and how soon – often with insufficient advance notice for getting around that big, black-smoke-belching beet truck. Mikhail seems okay with this, and loves to joke about my allegiance to cartography. "Why don't you look at your atlas," he says, when we are flailing about, lost in some provincial city. Which means, of course, that I must lose no chance to point out Ira's failures whenever she leads us astray.

This morning, on our way out of Oryol, Ira continued to insist that we head out of the city via one road, while we had asked her to chart our path via another. We assumed she was following our instructions, but then we came to an intersection with an arrow pointing left for Bryansk, yet Ira told us to go straight ahead. I insisted we should turn left (Bryansk being our destination), Mikhail said "No, Ira says go straight." So we went straight and then I pushed a bit more and Mikhail zoomed Ira out a bit (the four-straw view) and realized she had ignored our instructions.

Words were exchanged. I got upset at Mikhail for trusting Ira more than me. Mikhail got upset at Ira for not following his instructions, and at me for assuming he and Ira were colluding against me.

Ira, for her part, was silent.

Until she announced that she had recalculated our route.

ON THE WAY out of the city, we stop for gas and some road food. I buy a double espresso. The cashier yells at us for mistakes another customer has made, which are somehow compounded by my wanting to pay by credit card instead of cash. Actually, she is mostly just yelling about the general situation, but since we are the only patrons inside the station, she looks at us when she is yelling, and I take it personally.

When we finally scramble out of the store, we are loading the car up with the road food and Mikhail asks me to pull Kukisvumchorr around to the side of the building; he needs to take 20 rubles back to the attendant to finish quieting her down as part of some complex commercial exchange he cannot explain and I could never understand.

I hop in the car and zip over to the side of the station, then look out the rear view mirror and see my double espresso lying spilled on the pavement behind me. I had stupidly put it on top of the car to open the door, and now Kukisvumchorr has a long brown stain down his side.

Is there nothing this car won't suffer on our account?

And no, I do not go back into the station to replace my spilled double espresso.

Changing Course

Today we said goodbye to the E105 (which heads south to Belgorod and Ukraine).

Originally, our plan after leaving Oryol was to drive to Kursk, then blitz east to Saratov, spend a day there, zip down to Volgograd for a day, and then come back west toward the Black Sea. But distance and time are taking their toll. We want to spend less time driving and more time meeting people. So we made the difficult decision to "straighten our spine" and reduce our mileage, lopping off the Saratov-Volgograd sidetrip. Maybe, we muse, we will do a Volga River book someday…

The new plan is to head west to the village of Chukhrai, to visit Laura Williams, a long-time contributor to *Russian Life*. She has lived in that remote village, which lies about two hours south of Bryansk, for 20 years, with her husband, photographer Igor Shpilenok, and their son.

About 50 kilometers down the road, we began discussing our plans and schedule for the coming days. It turns out Mikhail made an appointment for 11 AM the following morning in Voronezh, and it cannot be changed. This means that we will have to travel 500 kilometers to get to Voronezh in time, which in turn means leaving Chukhrai at 4 or 5 in the morning. But that would be no way to spend a proper visit, especially since Chukhrai is 7 kilometers from drivable roads and, whenever we decided to leave, Laura would need to shuttle us in her ATV to where Kukisvumchorr was parked.

We pull over to the side of the road and discuss our options, in the end deciding that the only viable solution is to change course. We will drive most of the way to Voronezh, to the town of Yelets (supposedly a beautiful river town), spend the night there, and then drive just 70-80 kilometers to our meeting the following morning.

This took us east over rougher two lane roads, through rolling hills of black earth and birch trees. Fall is holding on tight here. There are long stands of birch trees beside the road with bright yellow-orange leaves still clinging to their branches. And in the fields they are harvesting the last of the corn and sugar beets, while other fields are entirely covered with a low green grass – a winter hay crop.

We see a man tending a flock of geese in a field and Kukisvumchorr is charged at by a village dog. Somewhere, miles from any village, we see a Corgi running all by its lonesome, as if it is in training for a Corgi Marathon.

There are numerous sellers of preserves (pickles, mushrooms, fruits), potatoes and apples along the road, often bunched in groups of four or six every few kilometers. We drive by one grove of sellers and Mikhail yells out, "Pears, they are selling pears! I want pears."

I have seen this before.

Mikhail will not be denied. When he decides he wants something, he will continue to insist on its absolute necessity until the desire is sated. It's actually a very useful character trait in a photographer – when he sees a shot he wants to get, nothing will stop him. Nothing.

We pull over at the next grove (no, we cannot turn around, we must continue to move forward!), yet all we see are apples… apples… and more apples… No pears.

We decide to get some apples.

Mikhail chats with the seller, but she refuses to have her picture taken. She does tell us, however, that the apple we have chosen is called "In Memory of Michurin" (Память Мичурина), which honors the great apple breeder and geneticist Ivan Michurin (1855-1935) who originally hailed from near Tambov and cross-bred and created over 300 new types of fruit. He was famous for the saying, "We cannot wait for favors from Nature. To take them from it – that is our task."

I wonder what Michurin would have made of GMOs, and consider that this is actually a rather appropriate saying, given that we have ditched all hope of any pear-shaped favors and accepted our pomaceous fate. The apples are excellent – both tart and sweet without being too much of either. Like a Gala only with a fuller, more natural flavor, and a steal at only 100 rubles a bucket (a bit over a kilo, thus 75 cents a pound).

As we descend over the next rise, we see another group of fruit and potato sellers. The second one on the left is selling, of course, pears. We do not stop.

WE ARE NOW driving through the breadbasket of Russia. In case anyone asks, yes the earth really is black in the Black Earth Zone.

I had insisted we drive east over a lesser track (single line on the atlas) to reach our main (thick yellow) *trassa* into Yelets. The cars are far fewer in number, and the class B roads are rather bumpy and sketchy in places, but still better than a spring dirt road in Vermont. I had hoped such a route would offer different, more interesting views than what we see from the larger highway, but this is not the case. The legacy of massive *sovkhozes* and *kolkhozes* (state and collective farms) means there are not many small, interesting villages here, and certainly no stand-alone homes like in American farm country. Occasionally, from just off the shoulder of the road, there rises a cinderblock bus stop painted the colors of the Russian flag. At one point for several dozen miles the road is lined by large piles of harvested sugar beets. The eight-year-old boys in us surge to the surface, and we stop to climb the irresistible piles.

УРОЧИЩЕ (*UROCHISHCHE*) IS a Russian geographical term that is rather difficult to translate simply. It is the word for a place that is different from the environment or geography that surrounds it. It is an anomaly, like a copse left to grow in the middle of a farm field, or like a swamp or some unusual geographical border between two places.

There is an *urochishche* in Oryol Oblast, near the town of Livny, that is known as Lipovchik, perhaps because it includes a copse of linden trees (*lipovoe* being the adjective for linden or lime). In the fall of 1963, a young history teacher, Oleg Yakubson, was taking his students for a hike through Lipovchik after some heavy rains when they stumbled across uncovered bones that turned out to be human remains. Investigators were brought in and concluded they were World War II remains, as fighting had been particularly fierce in this area. The bones were reinterred and the matter was not investigated further. After all, the 1960s was not a time for digging up the past; many of the past's gravediggers were still around, clinging to power.

Thirty years later, in the early 1990s, the matter was looked into again, and it was revealed that Lipovchik was actually the site of a mass grave for some 423 victims of the Stalin-era purges in 1937-38. In December 1992, a memorial was finally erected to the victims, whose names have since become known. And each year there is a procession to the site of the memorial. It takes place at noon on October 30, Russia's annual Day of Remembrance for the Victims of Political Repression.

Which also happens to be the day we are driving through Livny.

Unfortunately, I only uncovered these facts and this history after the trip was over, while investigating the history behind an entirely different sort of anomaly we encountered on the outskirts of Livny. Driving down a fast, two-lane road (the R119) we were about 15 kilometers west of the town when we spotted a massive bayonet rising out of the earth. As we drew closer, we saw that it was set atop a dome-shaped hill, emblazoned with words that spelled out in stone, "We believe in Russia. We take pride and remember."

Known as the Burial Mound of Glory (*Kurgan Slavy*), the monument was opened on the 40th anniversary of the end of the Second World War, in August 1985, and commemorates the fierce and bloody battles that took place here. It is a striking and powerful monument, rising out of the peaceful, newly harvested beet fields and cornfields that surround it.

Among amateur historians and those interested in places of cultural interest, there is a saying, "Always read the plaque." Here is what the brief plaque at the Burial Mound of Glory says:

> In the fall of 1941, the fiercest of battles with the German-Fascist invaders took place on the territory of Livny District and the approaches to the city. On November 25, the city of Livny was occupied by the Germans. With the participation of units and formations of the 13th Army, commanded by General Gorodnyansky, on December 25, 1941, the city was liberated. During the taking of the city, the 143rd and 148th rifle divisions particularly distinguished themselves, as did the 150th tank brigade. The battles in the summer of 1942 were particularly heavy around the

villages of Dubrovka and Zhernovka. On January 28, 1943, units
of the 13th Army under the command of General Pukhov fully
liberated Livny District of the German-Fascist invaders.

According to other information provided at the site, some 8,000 residents of Livny died for the freedom and independence of their homeland, and some 3,000 troops died in the 1941 retaking of the city.

Livny (current population 48,000) is just one provincial town in the
Russian heartland, and we stumbled across it quite by accident, the result of a sudden course change we made just hours before. Yet in ret-
rospect it is hard not to be affected by the difficult history of its pair of
anomalies – one we visited, and one we did not. Taken together, they
speak volumes about the horrific events that devastated Russia in the
middle of the twentieth century.

WE ARRIVE IN Yelets at dusk. After some searching, we find our hotel in a scrappy, well hidden corner of the city center. There is just one
sign for the turn-off from a one-way street into the parking lot. We miss
it once, do a long loop around several one-way blocks during rush hour,
and then almost miss it again the second time around.

The hotel had good ratings, but the digs and clientele are coarse. We
discover later it is a preferred lodging for long-haul truckers (though
there are no rigs in sight), and the decor and finish is a step below do-
it-yourself quality – notably, the "pipe" connecting the toilet drain to
the sewer looks uncomfortably similar to a flexible plastic dryer vent.

After a few minutes settling in, having no success hopping onto the
hotel's wifi, I pop out to the lobby to double-check the password. I am
surprised, but not unsettled, to see two police officers in the hallway
that passes as a lobby, chatting with the manager. For some reason, I
deduce that they are talking about me – the foreigner – because their

conversation becomes quiet and guarded as I approach. After the police leave, the night manager says there are new rules of the Federal Migration Service that require the police to stop by all hotels daily, checking on the registration of residents. It seems an implausible explanation, and the timing is more than coincidental. As later events will show, I probably should have felt unsettled.

Dinner is a light affair at a cozy cafe named "Jem," because it got better recommendations from locals than the other central cafe, "London."

In the morning, I look out my window to see that my room has a "Moscow Courtyard" view that would make Vasily Polenov weep. In the distance, a pastel blue church topped with a golden dome glimmers beneath rose colored clouds. Its neighboring bell tower is encased in scaffolding and partly occluded by a block-concrete apartment building. In the foreground, beneath the window, the courtyard is littered with tires and ramshackle storage sheds, interspersed with barren bushes and the chaotic metal rooflines of nineteenth century dwellings.

Almost lost in my Polenovian reverie, trying to capture the scene from my window, I see Mikhail slip out under cover of pre-dawn darkness to explore the city. He found the town largely empty of people, and so headed down to the river embankment.

I, meanwhile, fantasize about a dark, hot cup of coffee on this cool morning, the last in October, then remind myself of a fact I looked up last night for some masochistic reason: Yelets is officially 208 miles from the nearest Starbucks. I make do with an instant coffee from the hotel's canteen and a surprisingly decent bowl of porridge.

Yelets, Mikhail said after returning from his exploration, reminded him a bit of St. Petersburg, with its courtyards and aging façades. Yet in contrast with that vibrant northern city, most of the buildings here seemed empty or in need of repair. Many wooden houses have survived the ravages of history, unlike in cities and towns further west that were utterly decimated by the war. Yelets was fortunate in only being occupied by the Germans for four days in December 1941.

On the evening of December 2, the machine guns fell silent, the explosions faded away. Looking out the window in the twilight, we could see walking down the other side of the street a line of soldiers in green overcoats. "Germans," my mother said. My heart sank. The gate rumbled. Mama crossed herself and went to open it. Two solders with machine guns entered. One of them pointed Mama into the other room and forced her to open the wardrobe – he was looking for Russian soldiers. I stood at the door and trembled, my knees knocking together. The other soldier stood opposite me, and I got the impression that he was also trembling; he did not seem the gallant victor. The day before, early in the morning, someone had knocked on our window and then two Red Army soldiers came in, asking Mama for some civilian clothing, tossing aside their overcoats. Mama buried their overcoats beneath the snow in the garden. She didn't tell me about it until our boys returned. She held on to the overcoats for a long time, waiting, in case the soldiers suddenly returned.

The Germans were in the city just four days. They rummaged about the stores, even though there was nothing there [a few days before the Germans arrived, the city distributed all goods and produce to local residents], they broke windows and made a mess. In Vosnesensky Cathedral, which had been closed before the war, they set up a stable. Neighbors said that the Germans rode around on carts, knocking on windows, gathering up any warm clothing they could.

For three days it was quiet. On the fourth, the shooting began again. Cannons thudded and bullets flew through the city. As we only found out later, it was the Red Army's general offensive along the entire Western Front. On the morning of December 9, the sky was barely lit when the neighbor girl ran to our place, "Auntie Polly, our boys are here!"

"Are you lying, Nina?"

"It's Lenin's truth!"* – that was something we said at the time.

"Well, if you can yell 'Lenin' on the streets, that must mean it is true," Mama affirmed.

Then we saw our soldiers in their grey overcoats, their rifles at the ready. They walked down the center of the streets, looking cautiously from side to side, but the Germans had gone.

– Excerpt from a memoir
by Yelets resident Maria Sapyrkina[42]

The Meat Farmer

It takes just a few hours to make the drive south from Yelets to Ramon through rolling Black Earth farmland. We are going to meet Ilya Nitsenko, 31, Vice President of Strategic Development at Zarechnoe, a local meat company.

We arrive in Ramon a bit early and discover it is the site of Princess Oldenburg's Palace, a partially renovated neo-Gothic residence on the edge of the town, overlooking a picturesque ravine. We walk

---

* Честное ленинское.

the grounds, killing time before our meeting, but balk at paying an entrance fee to see a half-renovated palace; Mikhail watches a wedding photo shoot that is taking place in the frigid garden, and I dive back into the car to warm up, and to do a bit of digging on the history of this place.

The palace was built from 1883 to 1887, after Tsar Alexander II gave an estate in Ramon to his relative, the Duchess Yevgenia Romanovskaya, who was Princess Oldenburg by marriage. The duchess went on to do much to develop Ramon and its surrounding region, most notably building a world-class candy factory in the village.

The building's Germanic style, and its unusual history as a strange but appealing import, to say nothing of its resident's impact on the region, turns out to be an uncanny historical echo of what we will see in the next few hours.

NITSENKO IS ABOUT an hour late for our meeting, which gives us plenty of time to explore bustling Ramon, to enjoy instant, in-car cappuccinos from a Rosneft gas station on the edge of down, and to take a roadside catnap.

Finally, Nitsenko phones to say he is minutes away and we are to meet him by the side of a road that leads to his factory. He drives up in a well-equipped black Land Rover and rolls down the passenger side window to let us know to follow him. Apparently it's not an easy place to find. He is younger than either of us expected.

Kukisvumchorr has a tough time keeping up with the black SUV over the next 15 kilometers, as we wind through three or four small villages and settlements, hoping Ira will be able to pick up our breadcrumb trail and lead us safely back to the main highway.

Finally, we pull up to some sort of large agricultural facility (tarps held down by tires; feed piles; round silos; John Deere tractors; and just beyond the rise, cattle in feed lots).

It looks a lot like an American farm, except that American farms don't generally have a security perimeter. We drive through a gate and park alongside Nitsenko's SUV. He gets out to greet us and quickly shifts to fluent, colloquial English. It is a welcome change after three weeks of almost non-stop Russian.

Slim and fit, dressed in new grey tennies, black jeans and a black spring jacket, Nitsenko is about 5' 10" with short, dark-brown hair and wears sunglasses to staunch the bright mid-morning light. He is clearly relishing the chance to speak English. Or maybe it is just that he is passionate about what they are doing here, about this 12,000-hectare American-style farming operation in the middle of Russia's Black Earth zone.

"Eight years ago," Nitsenko says, "I didn't have any idea where Voronezh was. Now I am here full time, loving what I do."

Nitsenko was raised and educated in the US, graduated from Boston University, and was working in real estate in Miami when his entrepreneurial father, Sergei, called him and told him they were flying to Nebraska to learn about raising beef from the world famous Krebs Ranch.

What the Nitsenkos and Zarechnoe have done is create a Nebraska corn-fed Black Angus marbled beef operation less than an hour outside Voronezh. They have been at it since 2008, and what they have built in seven years is jaw-dropping.

It is an entirely verticalized greenfield operation, from genetics and insemination to calving, pasturing, feedlot, slaughterhouse and packaging. They grow their own corn and hay, do their own breeding, then raise the livestock all on their own land (with a long-feed,

200-day regimen that takes the animals from grass-fed to corn-fed just before slaughter). Then they slaughter and package the animals in their own facility. "It's necessary," Nitsenko says. "It's the only way… in 50 years, this might not be the most efficient way, but now it's the only way."

In 2008 they were the first company in history, Nitsenko says, to import Black Angus bulls and heifers into Russia (10 purebred bulls along with 250 red heifers) and they now have eight farms with over 60,000 head of Black Angus cattle. The feedlot alone can hold 24,000 head. "Everybody thought we were crazy," he says. "And this is all the idea of my father. He's a crazy guy." But crazy in a good way, because the operation is prospering and there are expansion plans on the books that would triple the size of the feedlot over the next few years.

Much of the machinery is also imported (including a "Haybuster" that chops up 60 tons of hay bails an hour and, Nitsenko jokes, "cost $640,000 – two Maseratis"), mostly all from America. "We are one of the biggest purchasers of John Deere [in Russia]," he adds.

But the most important thing they have imported is know-how. The entire intent of the enterprise is to take all of the best knowledge and practices from Europe and the US, and plant them firmly in Russian soil. "This is nothing amazing," he says. "This is just something we took and adapted to Russia."

THE THING IS, Zarechnoe got started eight years ago, long before there was any talk of sanctions or embargoes. Now, with the push to feed Russia without relying on imports, Zarechnoe is sitting pretty, set to benefit from the country's drive to import substitution.

"We had no idea this was coming," Nitsenko says. "No idea this situation was going to happen. Our business plan was to compete with imports…"

"But now there are no imports," I note.

"And that's a bad thing," he says, "because competition is good. Because people get used to something really good, and they have nothing to compare it to. This is why we want competition… Actually, if they opened up to American imports tomorrow, American beef would be about 30-40 percent more expensive than ours."

We stand looking out over the well-kept feed lot. A brisk wind blows clouds across a brilliant blue sky. The stock are mooing continuously, either because we are bothering them, or because it is feeding time. We stop the interview so that Mikhail can do his environmental portrait of Nitsenko. He positions him just inside a gate, where his grey designer tennis shoes are threatened by the moistened mud. A few curious steer stand behind him, peering at Mikhail's lens.

"EVERY STEAK STARTS on the farm," Nitsenko says as we gather over coffee in his conference room, "it's all about genetics and feed." And stress. Or the lack thereof. "The key to success in this business is minimizing stress," Nitsenko says. Stress leads to unhappy cattle, which leads to bad meat.

This meant moving 1.2 million cubic feet of dirt to tailor the feedlot landscape to within a precision of 5 centimeters, so that rain and snow runoff are optimally channeled, so that the animals have shelter from the wind and rain, so that they are not stressed by the grades in the land.

It also means that, throughout the facilities, and especially in the slaughterhouse, the company has, Nitsenko says, sought to meticulously implement the recommendations of noted animal rights activist Temple Grandin.

Later, we tour the slaughterhouse. We are of course expecting Upton Sinclair's *The Jungle*, but instead are met with what seems like a twenty-first century hospital. The cleanliness and organization of the facility is breathtaking. We are visiting on a Saturday, so the building – where 275 locals work, producing up to 150 tons of meat per shift – is empty and cavernous, quiet as a morgue. Yet the facility was slaughtering and packaging beef just the day before, and we don't so much as catch a faint whiff of blood or meat, so clean is the two-year-old slaughterhouse.

We note how impressed we are with the state of their facilities and Nitsenko describes the common scene at a public food market, where many Russians still buy their beef, and where the meat lies around on marble slabs in the open air, assaulted by flies. "Seriously, why would you buy your meat like this, when you can have it packaged and in a grocery store with a 40-day shelf life?"

Why indeed.

But of course the proof is in the eating, so that evening (which happens to be Halloween) we head into downtown Voronezh, to the upscale Grand Cafe Ampir restaurant, once a famous movie house. They offer Zarechnoe's Prime Beef brand steaks on their menu for about R1,500 ($25).

In the interest of proper journalistic investigation, we order up three steaks (we have invited along a local journalist who has helped us make contacts here). Neither of my two Russian table companions has ever had a Nebraska, corn-fed marbled-beef steak (most "steak" cuts in Russia are tough and leathery, overcooked and overly lean), so I advise them to order them cooked medium rare.

The verdict is unanimous. The steaks are incredible. Tender and juicy, sweet and well-marbled. Too many years ago to count, I cooked thousands of steaks in restaurants, working my way through college as a cook. And I have eaten countless rib-eyes ever since. Without reservation, it was one of the ten best steaks I have ever eaten.

There is a telling quote on the website of Krebs Ranch in Nebraska, the place that the Nitsenkos went to learn about cattle raising: "Some men make things happen, some men watch things happen, and others wonder what happened."

There's no wondering here. An enterprising Russian family decided to make something happen, to plant one of the best bits of America in the Russian heartland. Through intelligence and hard work they have created a superior enterprise, an enviable product line, and are proving that good things can come from US-Russian collaboration, that everyone involved can win.

Well, unless perhaps one is a Black Angus steer. But that is a different issue altogether.

The Sheriff

Between the feed lot and the feeding on steak we made a few stops. The first was at a very difficult to locate police station on the southeast side of Voronezh. We were determined that our nationwide "sampling" of interviewees include a policeman. But, given the reception we got at the police station in Valdai, we were a bit wary.

Those fears turned out to be unwarranted.

Alexander Cheryomukhin is soft-spoken and immediately likable. It is late afternoon and he meets us in the parking lot, where he is having a smoke, and we take his photo first, before the light fades. Then he walks us back to his office, where the nameplate on his door indicates that he is deputy director of the division – meaning second in charge of the station.

Just 28, married (his wife also works for the police), with a five-year-old daughter, Cheryomukhin is a stolid 5' 9", with rounded features, thick black eyebrows, sympathetic eyes and a ready smile. In short, rather far from the stereotypical Russian police officer one expects, particularly in the provinces.

Yet we soon learn that Cheryomukhin is far from your average cop. In fact, in a 2014 internet contest he was voted the best *uchastkovy* in Voronezh Oblast, and the fifth best in all of Russia. Yes, it was an unscientific poll, but it still is a reflection of the esteem Cheryomukhin has in his city. Locals are not going to take time to vote for a crooked cop in an anonymous poll.

And actually Cheryomukhin is not a cop but an *uchastkovy*, which requires a bit of explanation. The name derives from the Russian word *uchastok* – meaning a plot of land, a district, or a delineated region. Thus the *uchastkovy's* responsibility is to oversee and police his plot of land or, more specifically, the 3,000 or so people who live there. Probably the closest American analogy, Cheryomukhin says, is a sheriff.

In any event, Cheryomukhin says he has visited every family, and been in touch with every person under his purview. And the information he gathers (names, addresses, professions) gets compiled into a "passport" – a written survey of this *uchastok* that is subjected to quarterly review.

"The *uchastkovy* takes part in protecting social order, but the main function of a plenipotentiary *uchastkovy* is prevention," Cheryomukhin says. "Preventing crimes and law-breaking. We carry out prophylactic work with previously convicted individuals. They get out of jail, and, so that they don't repeat their crimes, we meet with them, talk with them, help them find work… if people abuse alcohol, we explain to them that this is harmful, bad, they need to stop. If necessary, we propose treatment… We also play a big roll in the investigation of serious crimes, which as we know mostly have their roots in domestic disputes. It's rarely like you see in films… If some problem arises, say a fight or dispute in a family, we can put the family on a one year prophylactic program, where there are periodic checks on them."

This has been Cheryomukhin's work for the past nine years. Originally, he thought he wanted to be a criminal investigator, "but that turned out to be basically desk work," he says, and being an *uchastkovy* is people-to-people work, to which he is better suited.

Mikhail asks him how it was he was voted the best *uchastkovy* in the city.

"I got the most votes," he says, guilelessly.

It takes a few minutes to explain that we don't mean the mechanics of how he won the contest, but why people voted for him.

"How did you become a good cop, so that they would vote for you?" Mikhail asks.

"How to become a good cop? That's not the right way to approach it," Cheryomukhin replies. "You just need to work, to fulfill your responsibilities. I helped a lot of people. People call me with any sort of question. Anything. Someone gets in a fight with her husband. Someone else is in a very difficult living situation. They just come around to talk. Babushkas, they're alone, they have no one to talk to. They come, sit, talk. And that makes it easier for them… I don't even know how to explain it. I give them time, attention… Everyone needs an *uchastkovy*…"

We then ask if he can recount an interesting case from the recent past. He tells his story in a laconic, humorous style that shows he is as good a storyteller as he is a listener.

It was May, last year. We received a call. Someone stole a babushka's goat. I show up and start questioning people, and find out the goat was stolen during the night.

"My husband died and now it's just me and the goat," the babushka says. "She's like a friend to me, we talk. Like a house pet. How am I going to live without her?"

I think, I have to find her. I start asking around, everybody. Maybe someone took her to eat her, I think. Nothing, nothing, nothing.

Then someone calls in to the station. "Someone new has moved into the area. She has a goat."

So I go out there. There's no sign of the woman, or the goat.

We have this method, "door to door rounds," when there is a crime. You go door to door looking for witnesses… talk to people. Maybe someone saw something, heard something. There is always a witness. So I start making the rounds.

"Yes, there was a goat," [someone says.] "And the woman too. But she left and the goat was left behind, roaming free. So we gave her to another babushka, who already had another goat." I know this babushka, so I go visit her.

"Valentina Filipovna, here's how it is… why didn't you call?"

"How was I to know it was a stolen goat?" she replies.

Well, then we had to get a positive identification of the goat. Yes, a positive identification. So I gather her up, go back to the station and pick up an investigator, and together we think, how are we going to do this?

We go to see the woman and gather two witnesses. And the babushka begins calling the goat by name, and she goes right to her.

Later, the investigator finds the citizen who took the goat and we bring her in. She doesn't resist. She tells us her story.

"I was walking by one night and a goat was crying out. It was hungry. I felt bad for her. I took her from the hut where she was tied up and fed her and gave her water. Then fed and watered her some more. Then I let her go."

Funny, no? In fact, she was a foreigner… from Uzbekistan.

It is a low-key story, not the stuff of television murder mysteries. But most of life is mundane, and if an *uchastkovy* is doing his job right, Cheryomukhin says, serious crimes and murder, in particular, are very rare. In his nine years of service, he says with a visible sense of pride, he has never had to use his weapon.

"The way an *uchastkovy* works," Cheryomukhin says, "this forms the public's opinion of the police as a whole. Because the *uchastkovy* is the first person people turn to…"

And what makes a good cop?

"You must be neat in your outward appearance," he replies, "because, as the saying goes, 'You meet someone based on how they are dressed, but you stick with them because of their mind…'* He should be tactful, and well educated in the law, because people rarely go to see a lawyer; mainly they seek out an *uchastkovy* for legal help. So you have to know civil law, criminal law, housing law… Thus, an *uchastkovy* should have a higher legal education… When he retires [after 20 years] an *uchastkovy* can become a judge or a lawyer."

The way in which they are in touch with the community means that the majority (two thirds by Cheryomukhin's estimate) of all crimes in Russia are solved by *uchastkovy* officers. "This is because they know everyone…" Cheryomukhin says. "For the most part, the *uchastkovy* is

---

* Встречают по одёжке, а провожают по уму.

creative work… you have to use your mind. People are different, and you have to know how to approach them in their own way…"

For all of that, Russia's front-line crime fighter and social worker brings home about R39,000 a month ($630 at the time of our interview) and works a five-day work week during normal business hours. But he can be called in at any time, especially if there is something serious. In fact, one of the main duties of an *uchastkovy* is to be called to the scene whenever there is a death outside a hospital.

The *uchastkovy* has a long tradition in Russian society. From the time of Peter the Great to March 1917, they were known as *okolotochny*, from the word *okotolok* – meaning neighborhood or ward. And, despite an often derisive attitude toward some arms of the police (road police, in particular), the *uchastkovy* seems to enjoy a rather positive public perception, underscored by films and serials from the Soviet era to the present. The most recent incarnation was a 2009 TV series called *Uchastkovaya*, featuring a woman educated as a jurist who moves to a new town and takes a job as an *uchastkovaya*, so as to have a shorter commute. She finds herself dealing with everything from difficult adolescents to alcoholics, and thieves-in-law (inveterate criminals).

The show has a generally upbeat message about the honesty and dedication of public servants, and could well be summarized by the thought Cheryomukhin expressed when we ask, in the end, if there are any difficulties in his line work he would like to see changed: "If a person is positive, there are no difficulties in the work," he says, smiling.

Kukisvumchorr's Banya

Our final stop of the day is at a Volkswagen dealership in downtown Voronezh. One of our local Voronezh contacts, Dmitry Chembartsev, a car enthusiast, has arranged for Kukisvumchorr to have a long overdue banya, while we sit in the dealership and munch cookies and tea while being interviewed by a local journalist.

Kukisvumchorr (that's his superhero name, his Clark Kent name is 2015 Volkswagen Polo) has indeed suffered much on our account. First there was the harrowing trip though the tundra to find the Kola Super Deep Borehole. I was certain we were going to leave an oil pan or axle out there among the massive boulder piles and end up having to hike back to Nikel, dragging our suitcases behind us through muck, mud and mine tailings.

Rain and dirt battered Kukisvumchorr all the way from Murmansk down to Karelia. And he was assaulted by God knows what sort of toxic fallout in Monchegorsk. We two journalists got a black banya deep cleansing in Kinerma, but Kukisvumchorr only got a dirt parking spot next to our log home.

Kukisvumchorr held up under the strain, not complaining in the least whether the dirt was Petersburgian or Muscovite. I believe it was on our way out of Moscow that one of us suggested that perhaps we ought to leave Kukisvumchorr unwashed for the entire trip, so that, upon the trip's completion, he would be able to boast the accumulated dirt from the entire 6,000-kilometer Spine of Russia.

Neither of us stopped to think that this might be a cruel fate for Kukisvumchorr. Because the thing is that getting a car washed here can be a bit of a chore. Drive-through car washes are still a novelty, as are even the multi-chambered, cinder-block, self-wash units that are littered across the US. It varies by city, but mostly people take their cars to places that do a very thorough inside and outside cleaning, which means you have to drop your car off for an hour or more, and sometimes even make an appointment. And often the wash locations are not exactly in the center of things.

So Dmitry's arranged car wash in Voronezh was a perfect solution, though the idea of washing off Murmansk dirt in Sochi still retained a certain appeal.

We left Kukisvumchorr behind in the VW cleaning chamber, feeling a bit like parents leaving their kid at kindergarten for the first time, and went in for our interview, which went well, except for the fact that, while we were waiting and being interviewed, Mikhail hit the wall. We had neglected to feed ourselves all day, and the running around and relentless producer's work finally got the better of him. He had a bit of a lie-down and some tea and cookies, and that seemed to revive him, mostly.

About an hour later, we went out to the parking lot to pick up Kukisvumchorr, but he was nowhere to be found. Well, actually, he was right in front of us, but we didn't recognize him without his layer of Barents Sea salt mixed with Black Earth dust, or his tell-tale espresso stain streaking down the driver's side of the car. And the inside was spotless, like it had never seen a Ritter Sport or a stray "In Memory of Michurin" apple core.

Refreshed and renewed, we thanked Kukisvumchorr's Voronezh allies and pressed on to our final appointment of the evening, otherwise known as dinner.

Voronezh Dreaming

After some late night Halloween shenanigans in the hopping city of Voronezh, I slept in longer than normal and descended to the hotel lobby in search of breakfast. Half of the hotel was under construction and half not, so it was not entirely clear where one was to go for breakfast. Perhaps they told us when we checked in. If so, I had forgotten…

I approached the reception desk and asked the young woman behind the counter where I needed to go. There was an inexplicable expression of discomfort on her face. "Breakfast is on the second floor," she says. As I walked away, out of the corner of my eye I saw her nod to some men sitting in the lobby's faux leather couchettes.

As I turned to head back to the elevator, they walked swiftly to intercept me. They were four plainclothes officers of the Federal Migration Service (FMS). One of them flashed an ID and asked if I would mind "having a little chat."

First of all, I am not certain this is really a question. More of a command. And second, my brain is rarely engaged before I have a first cup of coffee, and that was clearly not what they were offering.

Trust me when I say this is not a good way to start your day.

IT SEEMS THE FMS received a report from a citizen they could not name ("unless this came before a court," they say, though the logical conclusion is that it was our policeman friend Max, back in Valdai, as he had all but threatened such action) that I was engaging in journalistic activity in Russia without having Ministry of Foreign Affairs (MFA) accreditation, and thus was in violation of certain FMS rules.

I explained the nature of our project, and admitted that, yes, I was a journalist by profession, but that we were not doing what one would call straight-up journalism (reporting and investigating news for a media outlet), but something more like citizen journalism (meeting with people, getting acquainted with them and sharing the stories of their life, work, passions, etc., through a book).

It was a fine line, sure, but I drew it nonetheless.

They honed in on the fact I was "conducting interviews" and that this was what made my activity journalism, and thus a violation.

After about 30 minutes of back and forth, they essentially told me that Mikhail, as a Russian journalist (who requires no accreditation, merely the guts to assert that as his profession – no mean feat in Russia), could conduct interviews and I could sit in on them and then write about whatever I liked. In other words, I simply could not ask any questions.

I suggested that this arrangement was rather absurd (if memory serves, I also made an unsubtle reference to Kafka). By their expressions and the tone of our exchange, I could tell they agreed. They actually seemed like decent guys just doing their job; they had gotten a report and they were required to follow up. I'm not really sure why it took four of them to fulfill this function, but who am I to question Russian operational efficiencies?

It is however ironic that we set out on this project with the intent of showing the world the Russia that lives behind the headlines, behind Russian stereotypes, yet here we were getting tripped up by a stereotypically nonsensical Russian regulation.

Some might say I should have known better, that I should have gotten MFA accreditation before this trip began. Perhaps. Only here's the thing: I made very specific inquiries with the Russian consulate in New York about this, telling them exactly what we were going to get up to and where we were going to go. I was told by a knowledgeable employee of the MFA that a business visa was all I needed.

But the really important issue here is something no regulations or accreditation can address: how is journalism to be defined?

Is it journalism when a novelist travels to Russia, meets with its people in various settings, some pre-arranged, some not, and then subsequently tells true stories about those meetings in a book, magazine article or blog?

Is it journalism when someone takes photos of things she sees on Moscow streets and then shares them with her 100,000 Facebook or Instagram followers?

Is it journalism when a foreign traveler shares real-life Russia travel stories on a publicly available blog that thousands read?

Is it journalism when a journalist by profession travels to Russia as a private citizen (on vacation, say) and later shares stories in editorials and features about people he met or things he experienced?

I understand why governments feel they need to regulate the press, particularly foreign press. Usually they cite concerns like public safety, security and official secrets. But most often governments are just trying to avoid answering uncomfortable questions, like why they sent our children to die in a war no one needed, why they can't fix the roads and bridges, or why one of their number was on the take.

And this is why citizens must continually push back against any and all attempts to restrict journalistic activity, to regulate it and force its practitioners to obtain special permissions, passes and accreditations. People not only have a right to know what their governments are doing in their name, they have a right (within legal limits, of course) to speak and write freely in whatever medium they see fit.

As I write this, I have just finished reading an article about Wyoming, yes America's Wyoming, which passed a law in 2015 that makes it a crime to "collect resource data" from any "open land," meaning any land outside of a city or town, no matter if it's federal, state, or privately owned. And here's the interesting part: the statute defines "collect" as any method to "preserve information in any form," which includes taking a photograph, if the person gathers that information with the intent to submit it to a federal or state agency. So, take a picture of a polluted river and send it to the EPA to ask them to do something about it, and you could end up in jail. The statute unquestionably violates the First Amendment of the Constitution, yet it was signed into law by the state's governor.

In many cases and most countries, the press is the only institution in a position to call governments and their employees to account for their actions. Yet around the world the media gets a bad rap because of a few of its own bad apples, or because they are an easy target for xenophobic, authoritarian politicians who can lock them up with impunity, arguing that they are acting against the interests of the state (which interests get to be defined by politicians rather than journalists).

The newspaper publisher Gil Thelen once defined journalists as "committed observers" – the people embedded in a community (local, national or international) who are out there paying more attention to specific issues, so that citizens will have the information they need to make better decisions. But in another sense, and particularly in our new, hyperconnected internet age, are not all concerned and committed citizens journalists, gathering and sharing the stories of the world around us?

To quote the American Press Institute, in its definition of journalism, "History reveals that the more democratic a society, the more news and information it tends to have."

The opposite also tends to be true.

"I HOPE OUR meeting has not put a damper on your enjoyment of our city," one of the FMS officers said as they were leaving. He mentioned a few worthy tourist sites, then asked whether I had gone out celebrating last night, given that it was an American holiday (Halloween). As he left, he flashed a smile that would make an orthodontist weep.

Of course it put a damper on things (and put me off my breakfast). How could it not? What I experienced was just a homeopathic dose of what an errant Russian could be subjected to by the police, and it pales to insignificance in comparison with what went on in the Soviet era. But I did get a whiff of the reality of the individual's powerlessness before a Bureaucratic State, and the whiff made me sick. All the more so because the day before we had met what we felt was the epitome of a fine Russian police officer, only to be met 24 hours later by the system's flip side.

I did, however, take some comfort in one fact. Before we headed out for the day, I stopped by the front desk of the hotel to question the nice young woman behind the counter. She apologized profusely that my stay at the Azimut Voronezh had been disturbed by such "unpleasantries," and I assured her that it had nothing to do with them. "Yet," I asked, "can you tell me, were these four fellows waiting for me here long?"

"Since early in the morning," she said. "And they were here last night, waiting for you to get back. But they left around midnight when you had not shown up."

This was hilarious. And it explained the dentally-challenged officer's off-hand question about my night on the town. The one time on the trip I stayed out late, I unwittingly outlasted four FMS officers, forced by duty to waste their Saturday night loitering in a hotel lobby for a journalist to finish celebrating Halloween.

I'm surprised (and impressed) that they were not just a little bit peevish when we did finally meet.

Time for a Drink

When one thinks of Russians and the alcohol they imbibe, one naturally thinks vodka. Russians did, after all, invent the stuff 600 years ago (don't tell the Poles), and the country's six-century affiliation with the "little water" (the literal translation of "vodka") has been bipolar: enthusiastically satisfying growing demand and profiting wildly off its tax revenues, while repeatedly being brought low by its devastating ill effects – from alcoholism and poverty to social strife and early mortality.

For this reason, a succession of tsars and commissars alternately expanded and restrained trade in vodka, depending on whether they needed the tax revenue or worried about its societal effects (the former normally won out). But the main thing was always control: from 1895 until the break up of the Soviet Union, the production of spirits in Russia was a state business. No wonder, given that vodka taxes at times covered 30 to 40 percent of the state budget.

The effects were predictable. It was estimated that 15 percent of the Soviet population in the 1980s could be called alcoholic, with the sort of social costs one expects: alcohol abuse became the single largest cause cited for divorce; by the late 1970s, life expectancy for Russian males had dropped to just 61 years; between 1960 and 1987, there was a population loss due to alcohol abuse in Russia of some 30-35 million persons; 74 percent of all murders committed in the early 1980s were committed under the influence of alcohol, as was the same proportion of rapes; in the early 1980s, 75-90 percent of absences from work were related to alcohol; economic production was said to drop by up to 30 percent following weekends and paydays; by one estimate, the economic losses from alcohol abuse in the 1980s were three times the amount taken in through taxes on alcohol.[43]

These brutal facts lie behind Soviet President Mikhail Gorbachev's anti-alcohol campaign begun in 1985 (which is the more likely reason he is so loathed by ordinary Russians, rather than for the breakup of the USSR or the economic reforms that did not go far or fast enough). It tends to be given a bad rap, but actually the campaign succeeded in cutting public alcohol consumption by up to one fourth. Life expectancies stabilized, birth and death rates dropped, alcohol-related deaths on the job and off went down, and the birth rate went up. Divorces declined.

Yet, as admirable as these changes were, the public was gravely dissatisfied with the means to these ends; Russians resented sobriety by government decree. And the government, for its part, executed its anti-alcohol program unevenly, and on the sand castle foundation of seven decades of socialist falsehoods. So it was little surprise that, as early as 1987, the cash-strapped Soviet government began relaxing many of its restrictions on sale and distribution.

The market stepped into the breach. Less than a year after the USSR evaporated, in 1992, Russian President Boris Yeltsin signed a decree abolishing the 68-year-old state monopoly on the production, import and sale of vodka, replacing it with a system of free production and trade of hard liquor based on licensing. It was a very Russian solution to the problems of the monopoly – to completely overturn the status quo rather than tinker with it. The *Financial Times* predicted at the time that "the lifting of the state monopoly on vodka is political suicide for a country where economic and other difficulties provoke the people's desire to drown them in wine."

Russia was flooded with new brands, but also with moonshine, cheap bootleg spirits and shady foreign knockoffs. Consumption soared to around 15 liters per capita per year, but counterfeit vodka proliferated, as did cases of alcohol poisoning. The state responded with taxes and excise stamps, but the bootleggers and criminals were always a step ahead. And taxes were so unfathomably low that it was easy for legal producers to keep prices down, which has made vodka a cheap salve in difficult times, pushing Russian per capita consumption of spirits back up to some of the highest levels in the world.

Vodka, so pure and elemental, so ideal for warming the despondent soul in the long dark northern winters, is the sort of drink one would expect to arise from a northern culture with a communal peasantry, where long winters and tortuously short growing seasons meant back-breaking labor intermitted only by community-building social feasts and drinking bouts. What is more, the unique ability of vodka (unlike wine or beer or even mead) to act as an accompaniment to any manner of feast or food (whatever is on hand), plus the fact that it can be distilled from any type of grain or organic matter (again, whatever is on hand), makes it all the more popular. And, when it was discovered that the best vodka resulted from filtering with birch charcoal (not oak or pine, but birch, the tree of the Russian taiga), well, what more need be said?

Yet mead and beer also have long histories in Russia, and, two decades ago, some argued that the best way to wean Russians off vodka was with better quality beer (Russian beer always had a poor reputation). Only things didn't turn out to be quite so zero-sum.

In the 1990s, foreign companies rushed in and bought up former state breweries, soon controlling over 90 percent of the Russian market. Quality improved and consumption soared from around 15 liters per capita in the mid-1990s to over 80 liters per capita by 2007. But then the 2008 economic crisis struck, and the state pivoted away from its non-policy toward alcohol to one aimed at reducing consumption. Using taxes, advertising bans, market levers and the prohibition of sales through street kiosks, it has reduced beer consumption by around 25 percent over the past half-decade. Vodka consumption has also fallen, but only to around 12 liters per capita per year, which brings to mind the Russian joke, in which a host asks the newly arriving guest, "What'll it be, vodka... or beer?" "Beer as well," comes the reply.

Starting about ten years ago, this complex environment dominated by elephantine beer and vodka producers witnessed the arrival of a new, smaller, more exotic animal: craft brewers. It began when younger Russians brought up on decent foreign beers began looking for the next thing. First they sought out small batch brews from abroad, where the craft brewing movement had been underway for a decade or more. Then brewpubs appeared in the two capitals. Finally, the first intrepid craft brewers began setting up shop: Vasileostrovskaya in St. Petersburg, Odna Tonna in Moscow, Jaws from the Urals, and Labeerinth from Kaluga. Now, small brewers are turning up in cities across Russia, but they are not always easy to find. So you have to ask in every restaurant you visit. Sooner or later, someone in the know will point you in the right direction. We finally got the contact we were looking for in Voronezh.

AFTER MAKING OUR way to a rotten industrial backyard hidden behind a boxy furniture store on the city's outskirts, we parked Kukisvumchorr on a sidewalk and walked across the street into a cramped warehouse.

Pavel Rukavitsyn, 25, asked us to excuse the mess, saying they had sought the least expensive production space possible. Then he led us down a treacherous flight of metal stairs (pitch: 90 percent, tread width: 4 inches) into the brewery. When Mikhail and I try and fail to get their little plastic booties to cover our tanker-sized feet, Pavel says, "Oh, forget it, we'll just do a cleaning later."

Ravencraft brewery – raven because that is the English for "voron," as in Voronezh; and craft, because this is craft brewing – consists of three rooms and a narrow storage closet. Brewing vats and storage tanks are crammed into the two back rooms with nary an inch to spare; the storage closet is packed with drooping bags of malt and shelves holding spare parts; a couch, two desks and a shelving unit comprise the start-up's office; the bottling room is a side table near the vats. Nonetheless, they are producing eight tons of beer a month, or 16,000 bottles. Most of their product sells in larger markets, like Moscow and St. Petersburg, where interest has been booming of late in craft brewing.

"There were only about five craft brew pubs in Moscow a year or so ago," says Kirill Belikov (@moscowbeergeek), who is in town to collaborate on a brew and sits in on our chat. "Now they are multiplying like mushrooms and geeks like me are treating it like a game, to see how many different brews they can taste, forgetting what they have tasted even a week before."

Rukavitsyn introduces his partner, Ilya Yuritsyn, 26. While Rukavitsyn is short and stout, Yuritsyn is tall and broad shouldered, with a partially shaven head and a funky haircut. The two met somewhat by happenstance in a Voronezh technical college, where both were studying beermaking. Rukavitsyn chose the course of study because he did not know what else to do; Yuritsyn selected the institute because it was the one closest to his home. After graduation, both worked at a local brew pub, which was a good way to get some experience, but they soon discovered that the owners were not interested in trying new things, in experimenting. So they decided to strike out on their own and make "intelligent" beer.

The company, Yuritsyn explains, has four investors: "my two parents and Pavel's! At first I borrowed R200,000 from my parents and thought that would be more than plenty. It turned out we needed about R2 million [$50,000 at the time] to get up and running."

The brewery's first batch was bottled in 2013 and Yuritsyn figures they will hit break even (and be able to pay back their parents) about 18 months from now.

The duo has done plenty of experimenting, now that they are on their own, from a Jack-O-Lantern brew for Halloween to a Horseradish Lager, a Garlic Ale and IPAs. They have 10 basic brews and test a new recipe every month or so.

The toughest problems they face, Yuritsyn says, are business related. "When we went to technical school, [Pavel] thought he would be a builder and I thought I would be a mover. Turns out we were both right," he laughs, explaining that in a small business like theirs, they have to do a bit of everything. And, as one hears across Russia and around the world, their biggest challenge is finding good people. The second greatest challenge? Government red tape. "Sometimes the government makes regulations targeted at mega-breweries like Baltika," Yuritsyn says. "But they also apply to tiny crafters like us." This can be anything from accounting practices to sanitary regulations, and they can have a stultifying effect.

On the other side of the balance sheet, international sanctions and counter-sanctions have actually helped Ravencraft, the partners say, because they have raised prices on imported beers so that craft beers are now competitively priced at the upper end of the market.

Their dream? To verticalize their business in order to be able to source all their raw materials locally. Of special concern is hops, which they can now only get from abroad. During Gorbachev's alcohol crackdown in the 1980s, they say, hop production was all but halted in Russia. The country is now the world's largest importer of hops from Europe (the world's major producer). A hundred years ago, before the Bolshevik Revolution, Russia was largely self-sufficient in hops and ranked among the world's top producers of the vital beer making crop.

The partners see only upside potential in Russia's beer market, which has boomed since the 1990s, when most of the major players were bought up by large Western brewers. They estimate that craft beer represents less than one tenth of one percent of the market, whereas they figure that in the US it is 10 percent of all bottles sold and 20 percent of all dollars spent. And the Voronezh market is also taking an interest. "We have actually taken about nine calls [from local restaurants] in the past month," Rukavitsyn says.

But with that comes competition. Even from the big boys.

"We heard that some big brewers are going to start printing 'craft brew' on their labels," Rukavitsyn says, which could be problematic, because there is no accepted definition for craft brew, either by the government or among consumers.

THROUGHOUT THE ENTIRETY of our interview, I have followed the protocol agreed upon with my FMS friends several hours before: remaining silent, only noting down thoughts, facts and quotes worth remembering (and of course keeping the digital recorder running). And this is difficult, because I was the one who pushed for us to find some craft brewers, and I am the one who orders beer at dinner, while Mikhail orders fresh juice or tea.

My inability to ask questions puts a damper on things. We agree later that we are going to have to find another way to manage this.*

After the interview is over and the portrait shoot is complete, I ask where we can sample some of Ravencraft's brews in town (not an interview question, just chit-chat). They look at their watches and suggest that it is plenty late in the day to try them here, and Rukavitsyn scurries

---

* The solution, it turns out, is Russian simple. When we first meet with a contact, we make it very clear that we are not conducting an interview of any kind. We are just a couple of curious men who have stopped by for a chat, because we have heard they are doing interesting things, so we thought it would be nice to get acquainted and learn about their life and work.

off to the cold storage, returning a few moments later with armfuls of brown bottles. Happy to oblige, I sip the Jack-O-Lantern (technically called "Empty-Headed Jack") brew and the Garlic Ale. Both are nice, but a bit unusual. I typically can't handle more than a half-pint of flavored beers. I note that I prefer a hoppy IPA, and they dash off to get a bottle of their "American Style India Pale Ale."

That sample bottle turns out to have passed its expire date and has gone flat. None of us can take more than a sip.

As we ready to leave, Rukavitsyn starts assembling two bottles each of four different brews for us to take away, methodically stamp-dating and applying labels to the bottles. It is too much, I protest, but Russian hospitality is not to be tangled with lightly. In the end, we humbly accept the gift and pull ourselves up the steep metal stairs (more of a ladder, really) toting a clinking plastic bag. Later, in the interest of journalism, we sample one beer each night. The IPA is very nice, but we decide that the Horseradish Ale is far and away our favorite.

AS WE LOITER a bit outside the broken down warehouse, chatting about this and that (weather, football, our project's goals – again, definitely not journalism, just chit-chat) before we drive back into the city, Rukavitsyn points to some large humps in the ground just beyond where Kukisvumchorr is parked. They are nuclear fallout bunkers, he explains.

He does not say it like he is revealing a great secret of the Soviet era. This is something everyone here knows, apparently. This industrial area used to produce some important technical device or other for the military, Rukavitsyn says, so there are bunkers everywhere beneath our feet, in the event of a military attack. Today, the bunkers are decaying and it's all the authorities can do to keep kids from sneaking in to party there.

Ironic. The four men in leather coats were worried about me asking questions, while common citizens freely dispense 30-year-old military secrets without the slightest prompting or query.

Information just wants to be free…

PART FOUR

The South

Toward Two Seas

It was a common gesture of fraternal hospitality during the Soviet era to name hotels after cities in the Eastern Bloc. Thus Moscow had the hotels Belgrade and Budapest, and Voronezh, apparently, had the Brno, built in 1984. For its part, Brno had an exact replica of this hotel. It was called – wait for it – the Voronezh.

Our hotel formerly known as Brno is conveniently in the center of Voronezh, but it was under re-construction, so if you got off on the wrong floor you could be met not by the crisp, modern lines of Azimut, but the depressing remnants of Brno – aka Soviet design in decay.

In any event, the staff could not have been nicer. In an effort to make up for our being disturbed by the "polite men" from the FMS, on our last night there they insisted on giving us free access to the ping-pong table just off the lobby. I reclaimed America's honor (previously disgraced on the fields of Valdai) in four tightly fought games. I will not, however, share the scores, so that Russia can save face. Suffice it to say that the victory was decisive.

We immediately began debating the site of our decisive showdown.

THE FOLLOWING DAY we need to cover some ground. Our next appointment is in Krasnodar, and we decide to make the 900-kilometer hop over two days – in all, about 15-20 hours of driving through fertile agricultural territory, depending on traffic.

Our goal is to hit Taganrog by early in the afternoon, so that we can visit the Chekhov Museum. It requires an early departure, so we slip out of Voronezh before sunrise, about 5:15, with lunches packed by the accommodating hotel staff.

We are now driving almost directly south. As the sun comes up on our port side, we see that the land has become more plains like, with wider, flatter horizons. What rivers we see are wider and slower flowing. We have moved from the taiga (temperate forest) into the steppe, our trip's third ecoregion.

The roads are still smooth and well-serviced, the drivers pushy and dangerous, but we are making good time. Then, at 11:30 AM, with our trip odometer showing 4620 kilometers, we get stopped for the first time by the Russian traffic police.

"What's up, officer?" Mikhail asks through the half-cracked window.

"You were doing 114 kph in a 50 kph zone," says the short, stout defender of Russian justice. "Did you not see the signs?"

Mikhail admits he did not, and follows the officer to his car. I look out the rearview mirror and, given Mikhail's tall, slim frame, the two of them look like a carrot and a beet walking side by side along the wide shoulder.

The officer shows Mikhail a digital photo on his computer of the signs we missed, which both agree are rather small and could be easily missed if, say, one was passing a truck at the time. It is clear from the officer's demeanor that he is going to let us off with just a warning. And the fact that he has pictures of the signs, to show offending motorists, makes it all seem suspiciously like a speed trap. Mikhail mentions that we are doing a book on Russia, and the officer smiles, "Will I be in it?"

Taganrog

Taganrog, a city of about 250,000 souls, lies about 70 kilometers off the main route south to Krasnodar. The singular reason we are making a sidetrip here is because it is the birthplace (on January 17, 1860) of Anton Pavlovich Chekhov. This date is the chief fact that has fixed the city in Russian cultural memory. Well, that and the fact that, in 1825

Tsar Alexander I met his untimely death here – or, as some would say, his *faked* death…

As the legend goes, Alexander had grown tired of ruling, and was suffering from guilt for his complicity in the murder of his father (Tsar Paul I). So he staged his death and became a hermit. More specifically, he became the monk Fyodor Kuzmich and secreted himself off to a monastery, after which his youngest brother, Nicholas I, became tsar. But not before there was a bit of a successional mixup. You see, many would have liked Alexander's brother Constantine (who had officially been the tsarevich) to become tsar, but both Constantine and Nicholas wanted the other to rule. In the end, Nicholas won out (or lost, depending on your perspective). Those who were for Constantine's ascension smelled a rat, and some of them conspired to end the monarchy through feeble organizational meetings disguised as a literary circle. They were found out (betrayed) and became known to history as the Decembrists, five of whom Nicholas had hanged (in Russia's last public execution under the tsars), the rest exiled to Siberia.

Meanwhile, the monk who some believed to be Alexander died in 1864, in Tomsk, and later, in 1984, was made a saint by the Russian Orthodox Church.

Legends aside, history records that Alexander I actually died of the rather common infection known as typhus, after catching a cold while traveling with his sick wife to the South for recuperation. She, meanwhile, died while his body was being transported back to St. Petersburg, where it rests to this day in Peter and Paul Cathedral.

Or does it?

TAGANROG TODAY HAS a rather run down appearance. It could use a bit of love. Yet it also is the first city we have been in that feels southern. The tree-lined streets and relaxed, coastal atmosphere give a hint of what awaits us on the Black Sea. Yet the temperatures are still only in the 40s.

Officially founded by Peter the Great in 1698, Taganrog existed for many centuries before that, and was one of the earliest sites of Greek settlement along the Sea of Azov. Peter made it Russia's first naval base, and it was reputedly the first Russian city built according to a regular street plan.

By the end of the eighteenth century, the city lost its primacy as a naval base, after Crimea was incorporated into the empire, offering significantly better places to moor battleships. By the time Chekhov was born in the 1860s Taganrog's role as Russia's largest southern trad-ing port was being overtaken by the more rapidly growing Odessa and Rostov-on-Don. It was always a trading city and had little industry; by the end of the 1800s there was just a pasta and a tobacco factory, plus as a few smaller concerns. But, thanks in large part to a summer tsarist residence and the large mix of nationalities here, the city had over a dozen foreign consulates up until almost the First World War.

The city was occupied by Germans and White Forces in 1918 and 1919, and by the Nazis in 1941-43. And, in an interesting twist, the city was actually part of the Ukrainian SSR for four years (1920-1924). Even now, it is just a few dozen miles to the Ukrainian border, which probably accounts for the number of military personnel transports we saw in the vicinity.

THERE ARE TWO Chekhov Museums in Taganrog. The main one is housed in the *gymnasium* where he studied for 11 years; the other is in the house where he was born. Of course, we have arrived in town on a Monday, Russia's nationwide Museums Are Closed Day. But in Russia, closed is not so much a fixed state of being as a negotiable reality.

Mikhail has made a few calls, and an amiable, ginger-haired museum guide, Sofie Shchulgina, 24, has come in on her day off to give us a quick tour of the most important exhibits. (A group of about 20 school children is also making the rounds – see what I mean about "closed"?)

The museum is beautifully kept and is the town's main tourist attraction. There are prints of Chekhov's first story ("Komu platit," from *Strekoza*, November 1878), examples of his handwriting; his nine-year-old signature; the desk where he sat; and the highlight: his actual coat, glasses, hat and gloves.

Interesting fact: Chekhov was a great writer and playwright, but he struggled a bit in school, staying back for two grades, the first time for coming up short in math, the second time in Ancient Greek. Some of this can be chalked up to his family's dire economic conditions. When Chekhov was just 16, his father and family fled to Moscow to avoid debtor's prison, and the young Chekhov was left behind to sell off the family's possessions, while hiring himself out as a tutor to pay for his final years of tuition.

Second interesting fact: One of Chekhov's math teachers was the father of Felix Dzerzhinsky, the future founder of the secret police.

AFTER THE TOUR, we meet up with Sofie's friend Julia, an unemployed journalist. They have agreed to lead us to see a strange, dilapidated fishing village, Bogudoniya, that had a long history of being a center for crime in the city. Allegedly, when the Nazis occupied the city they were afraid to go into this area, whose streets resemble the twisted inner chambers of a hornet's nest, and it became a hub of anti-Nazi partisan activity. The houses are literally stacked catterwawl on top of each other, and the ground dips and dives in unpredictable ways, evidence of the many underground fish storage lockers carved out of the earth beneath the homes.

We park on the edge of a rough neighborhood and try to find our way down to the sea in the diminishing light and plummeting temperatures, stumbling down multiple hazardous, rocky paths. Our adventure sets off a cascade of dog alarms throughout the dense neighborhood. We see no human residents.

When we finally emerge on a rocky ledge that leads to the sea, we are surprised to discover a dilapidated Niva jeep wedged between the sea wall and the tide. How it got there is anyone's guess.

It has actually gotten so dark we can't see much at all (making photography all but impossible), but we ramble about on the rocks anyway, using a small flashlight to light our way and keep from breaking our ankles. We see only a battered dingy stranded on its side, washed up against the sea wall. Apparently, due to the catastrophic decline in fish stocks in the Taganrog gulf, very little fishing is done from here any longer. Which leads one to wonder just what is being stored in those underground fish lockers today...

Finally, the cold lashing us from the sea forces us back up the path and we head back into town and our hotel.

Taganrog's Hotel Bristol is a very pleasant, safe, and inexpensive establishment in the heart of the old town, with an extremely helpful desk manager. But the decor of the rooms would give Martha Stewart seizures. The primary color of my room is 1960s Laugh-In orange, and it features a strangely comfortable but eye-jarring chair, a 1970s-style poster hanging over the bed (chubby, smiling baby with the inscription, "no problem"), and a tarantula applique on the bathroom door. Mikhail's room is tastefully done up in an Egyptian theme, with cellophane on the light fixtures to emulate glowing torches.

Chekhov would have loved the place.

The Academy Groceries Built

Our early morning start is fueled by sandwiches and juice supplied by the Hotel Bristol. We had hoped that, by leaving the hotel around 5 AM, we would not only easily make our mid-morning meeting in Krasnodar, but also see fewer aggressive drivers on the roads. Mikhail warned that, in his experience, the drivers in Krasnodar Krai are Russia's worst. Really? There are more aggressive drivers than those who sped around us north of Moscow, west of Yelets, and south of Voronezh?

Apparently so. And, not to partake in vehicular profiling, but our meticulous road-based research revealed that the worst offenders all drive white cars. White BMWs, white KIAs, white Hondas, white Ladas. Usually with blacked out windows.

Somewhere north of Krasnodar, as the sun was just beginning to warm the eastern sky, after yet another white Lada swerved around us with far too little room for error vis-a-vis an oncoming semi, Mikhail captured our shared sentiment perfectly: "Why is Darwin silent?"*

SERGEI GALITSKY (nee Arutunian) has a dream. He wants to turn groceries into football greatness.

Galitsky is "one of the rarest of Russian billionaires," says Aram Fundukian, director of the Krasnodar Football Academy and commercial director of the Krasnodar Football Club (KFC), "because he did not make his money on natural resources." Instead, Galitsky founded the Magnit shopping chain, opening its first red and white convenience store in Krasnodar in 1998, and over the course of a decade and a half built it into Russia's largest national retail chain, with over 11,000 stores, 260,000 employees, and R760 billion in 2014 revenues. We have

---

* Почему Дарвин молчит?

passed many Magnit stores in our travels, and even spotted a massive regional distribution center somewhere in the Black Earth zone that we both can no longer place.

But the Magnit magnate's true passion is football ("he spends 70 percent of his time on business and 30 percent on football," Fundukian says). He wants "every kid to be kicking around a ball in his yard," says Svetlana Kurgina, head of PR at KFC and the Academy. And he wants the majority of the players on KFC to be locally grown, i.e. Russian.

The means toward this end is a gleaming $67 million Football Academy (founded 2008) to house, train, educate, and feed (and train some more) the 278 high-school-aged athletes who have been plucked from KFC's extensive farm system. That system begins with 10 regional centers throughout Krasnodar Krai, where KFC has set up *"manezh"* complexes (covered football pitch, equipment, coach) to give 6-12 year-old kids free, unfettered access to the game. Some 11,000 kids are making use of the facilities, Kurgina says.

When they turn twelve, kids nurtured in the *manezh* system can vie for a spot at the elite Academy. If they succeed, they get free education and housing on the Krasnodar campus, which gives them not just a slim shot at a professional career, but a better shot at higher education, because just like colleges in the US, many institutes in Russia give admission and scholarship preference to proven athletes.

Oak and walnut trees line one side of the Academy's property (formerly an agricultural testing facility), which contains 20 football pitches, workout and classroom facilities, condos, and a student cafeteria where we were treated to a delicious lunch of salmon, baked potatoes, tea and *olady* (a light, tasty pancake).

We can see why some may think the kids here are a little spoiled.

The place has the sleek, futuristic feel of Starfleet Academy, and the "little bulls" (the team mascot is a bull) that roam its grounds are exceedingly polite. Dressed in black and green club gear, they go out of their way to hold doors for us and say hello whenever we pass. But that might just have been because we were being shown around by Kurgina, an attractive twenty-something woman on a campus filled with teenage boys.

Kurgina tells us that chess is a required part of the curriculum, "Because football is the chess of sports," she says, "it is a game of strategy."

And there are the twice-daily practices. The head coach is a Serb, Kurgina explains, and he runs a tight ship. "The coaches are really tough guys," she says, when Mikhail heads off to seek Serbian permission to shoot closer to the action, at the practice we braved countless white Ladas to see. "It can be tough to get them to agree to anything."

But they don't know Mordasov. At first the coaches say he needs to shoot from the sidelines. But he keeps pushing. I chat with Kurgina about football and her long path here (which included a year as an exchange student in Ohio). A few minutes later I turn around and Mikhail has his camera in the face of an injured player, then is all but in the middle of a group scrum. Russia 1, Serbia 0.

Looming over the practice field is the massive KFC stadium, under construction since 2013. Like a huge spaceship, it casts its $280 million shadow over the players, all of whom surely hope to one day board it and play on its forced aeration, artificially-lit lawn before a capacity crowd of 33,000. It is promised to be "one of the most beautiful and functional football-only stadiums in the world."

But, interestingly, it is not on the roster of stadiums where Russia's 2018 World Cup matches will be played. We can't get a straight answer why that might be.

A SUPERMODEL DELIVERS an espresso as I chat with Academy Director Fundukian in his Spartan office. His English is excellent (including the first unaffected use of "dude" I have ever heard from a native Russian speaker). I later learn he agreed to carve 30 minutes out of his busy schedule largely because an American writer was part of our team. He loves speaking English, and loves traveling in the US.

The stadium, which he says will be finished in the spring of 2016, will be "five-star" and includes marble mined from the same quarry that supplied builders of the Coliseum in Rome. "You know rich people, they have to be extraordinary," Fundukian says with a smile, "Because why? You know," he says, mimicking his friend and boss Galitsky, "'I'm building a stadium and I'm bringing the stone from Rome... the Coliseum... do you know the Coliseum? Yeah, same stuff...'"

When I complement the school's facilities, Fundukian smiles, "We're not making money on this, just spending it.

"Eleven thousand kids. We understand that if one percent of them would become a professional athlete, it would be huge success. But, still... that's why we pay attention to the education, because if you play football really good, but you don't study, you are out of here... He [Galitsky] always says that they're not going to be professional athletes, but they have to be good people... this is our job, to make them good people, citizens of their country.

"A lot of people say, 'C'mon guys, stop the bullshit, where are all your players? You talk a lot about your Academy, but where are your players?' Cmon, do your math! We are like five years old... Our players, the oldest is like 17 or 18. Do you know how many are playing in a professional league when they are 17 or 18? Lebron?"

Others, Fundukian says, claim their Academy is "too good for the kids. Because, you know, professional athletes must be raised in bad conditions, in the bad environment, then they will be strong. They will be like tough... and yet you give them everything... In the Soviet Union there was nothing here, nothing there, but they always kept saying 'all the good for our kids,' but they never did that! If you would take our kindergarten, our schools, they are the worst! The offices, where the grownups sit, they are the best. But the kindergartens and schools, they are the worst!"

So Fundukian concludes, "Galitsky says, 'I want to build something good, and I want them to see, there is something good, really good in their life, and they can have it, if they will work hard.' If people don't understand that, it's their problem."

National Unity

Krasnodar was founded as Yekaterinodar, as in "a gift from Catherine" (the Great, that is). In 1792, Catherine granted the Kuban region (roughly between the Kuban River and the Azov Sea) in perpetuity to the Cossacks who were living and serving there. Yekaterinodar was founded as a borderlands military outpost the following year, and about 600 souls called it home. Gradually the settlement became a fortress and then a town. It officially became a city in 1867, and, with the arrival of the railroad in the decades that followed, it was transformed into a thriving metropolitan hub for this rich agricultural region. At times it has even been called the country's "southern capital."

It effectively served that purpose for the Whites during the Civil War years of 1918-20. But when they were defeated and the town fell to the Bolsheviks, it lost its Romanov pedigree. It became the "gift of the Reds": Krasnodar.

Only parts of the city were occupied by the Germans during World War II, and only for six months. Perhaps of greatest moment (and unknown to the outside world at the time), in January 1961, the city was the site of a rare, spontaneous anti-Soviet uprising, a result of Khrushchev's early reforms and a series of unfortunate incidents at a local market.

Krasnodar today, according to an assemblage of recent polls, is at once Russia's most comfortable city, its best place to do business (unemployment is about half a percent), and its most dangerous place to drive.

We have set up camp at a clean, cheap hotel about a 20-minute walk from the city's main drag, Krasnaya Street. The walk takes us through the city's bathroom and kitchen supply, car parts, and car repair district. There is an active car repair shop next to our hotel, making our lobby a comfortable place for repair clients to hang out while their tires are getting changed – a somewhat disturbing arrangement until we understood who all these bored-looking young men were and why they were loitering in the lobby.

Krasnaya, the city's main drag, is a welcoming, prosperous axis, with a wide, well-landscaped central promenade passing through a long stretch of the northern end. The city has thrived in its role as the country's agricultural hub and it also received significant financial spillover from the 2012 Sochi games. Much of that wealth seems to have been plowed into making Krasnaya a commercial hub that boasts loads of coffee shops, a huge indoor mall, monuments, sprawling public squares, shops and restaurants. On weekends and holidays, like today, large parts of the street are closed to traffic.

Today, November 4, is one of Russia's strangest annual holidays: the Day of National Unity.

Ostensibly, it replaces the very Soviet holiday of November 7 – the anniversary of the Bolshevik coup, which few are interested in feting these days. As Tamara Eidelman wrote in *Russian Life*, the government was looking for a way not to lose a national holiday in November (for the workers' sake, ostensibly):

The problem was that nothing else very special had happened in November. Kremlin political strategists had to reach all the way back to 1612, toward the end of the Time of Troubles, when a national uprising, led by the merchant Kuzma Minin and Prince Dmitry Pozharsky, drove the Polish usurpers from the Moscow Kremlin.

This event was deemed to meet all the important criteria. First, November 4 was very close to the date of the previous holiday. The fact that Minin and Pozharsky's feat actually happened in October was a non-issue, since Russia was using the Julian calendar at the time (there were ten days difference between the Julian and Gregorian calendars in 1612). Yet November 4 was chosen despite uncertainty about the exact day the Poles left the Kremlin (some sources cite October 22, which would correspond to November 1). Well, who knows how to make those Old Style/New Style calculations anyway? Close enough.

Second, and most important, the idea of celebrating the expulsion of the Poles fit very nicely with the nationalistic mood being promoted in the country. The first year the holiday was celebrated, nationalists conducted what has become known as the "Russian March," a demonstration of patriotism dominated by anti-immigrant and virulently pro-government organizations. Today, this march is what the Day of National Unity has become best known for – a mass demonstration by young and not-so-young people raising their arms in Nazi salutes and calling for the expulsion of all immigrants.[44]

We begin our day by celebrating at the clearly unavoidable establishment Донатс и кофе (Donuts and Coffee). It has a welcoming natural-wood decor, with lots of plants and large windows. Mikhail, who has never had an American-style donut before, asks for "the most authentic" kind. I wrack my brain for how to say "plain glazed," which is not in fact on offer, and so the young girl behind the counter says she doesn't know about most authentic, but their most popular donut is called "Simpsons," presumably because it is topped with pink frosting and colored sprinkles. Doh.

Mikhail follows the crowd and takes a Simpsons. I buck convention and order a chocolate chocolate glazed and a chocolate covered with peanuts. This is because I have learned the hard way that one donut is never enough and two can make you feel sick. With three between us, all will be right in Krasnodar.

They are actually rather good cake donuts, but the cappuccino is weak and lukewarm, and they only give us a wifi password valid for 40 minutes with each purchase, so we have to work fast on photo and blog editing, ordering multiple additional coffees to keep the lines open.

What won't we suffer in support of our common task?

THE OFFICIALLY SANCTIONED Unity Day demonstration is set for 3 PM at the main square, clear at the other end of Krasnaya, which takes us an hour or two and a lunch break to traverse. It is not a big to-do, yet still there is a police cordon around the square, complete with metal detectors.

The crowd is ultra-unimpresssed, Mikhail says, "as if they could not care less and were only there because they were required to be."

There is a string of short speeches from the stage by various local luminaries, each introduced by an overly enthusiastic announcer, and each trying to outdo the other with their statements of unity and patriotism. The back of the stage is lined by singers dressed in colorful national costume. The general gist of the speeches is this:

We are surrounded by enemies.

We need to unite to defend our interests so that the world will respect us.

Western partners come to us "with nice faces but with evil in their hearts."*

Western nations do not like our success on the international front and cannot reconcile themselves with the fact that Crimea is Russian land.

Russia is great and unified.

By 4 or 4:30, more people are exiting through the metal detectors than entering, so we decide to make our way back up busy Krasnaya, lined as it is with numerous stores and shops filled with the brands, ideas and ethos of Europe and America. Strangely, the shops don't seem to emanate evil or disrespect so much as comfort and acceptance. And of course commercial enticement.

At the broad, beautiful Theater Square on Krasnaya, which has what is reputedly the largest splash fountain in Europe, a huge choir performs patriotic songs to an audience half its size. Meanwhile, the giant indoor mall a few blocks down is buzzing with youth (most dressed in some shade of black) and elders alike. This is clearly the place to be on Unity Day.

We are definitely in the South now. It is November, yet we have been comfortably roaming the city with only t-shirts and light coats. Watching the news in the evening, I catch a report about National Unity Day and its celebration across the country. There is snow in some of the latitudes where we were just a week or two ago (Karelia, Murmansk).

Winter is close on our heels. We need to keep moving south.

---

* С доброй личиной и злым сердцем.

The Journalist

For those curious how to understand the peculiarities of Russia's "free press," I share this opening paragraph to the lead story in the November 2, 2015, issue of *Elektron-TV*, a ten-year-old weekly newspaper in Krymsk, Krasnodar Krai.

> The speech of the head [of municipal education for Krymsk region] was, as always, very long, but also sincere. And if you overlook how resources are being allocated in the district, how the coffers are empty, how humanitarian aid is kept in hidden warehouses (where the majority of medicines that arrived were unusable), how the head is subject to criminal investigations, then when you listen to Anatoly Vladimirovich, it seems as if it would be difficult to find a more honest and truthful person on the face of the earth.

"We don't attack politicians straight on," says Larisa Safronova, the paper's editor, "we let their words speak for themselves. Our people are smart enough to decide things on their own…"

The paper is part of a "holding" that includes a radio and TV station. It was created about a decade ago by the owner of a local electronics store who decided that the best way to advertise and promote his store was to create a local TV station. Cut out the middleman, as it were. Radio and print outlets followed.

The holding is in a storefront office in the city's downtown, which is actually uptown – located as it is on a rise that protected it from the 2012 flood. And this is why we are here, because when Mikhail came here three years ago to cover the flood, the media holding's offices were one of the few places with electricity, so he and many reporters made it their workplace, which was rather generous of *Elektron*.

In fact, the 2012 flood is a dividing line in the town's history.

On July 7, 2012, the Krasnodar region was pelted with 10 inches of rain over 16 hours. Flash flooding resulted and the city of Krymsk – at least those parts that lie along the river, were decimated. Some 150 died, and over 1,000 homes were destroyed, at a cost of upwards of four billion rubles. Subsequent investigations showed that the city's administration knew the waters were rising to dangerous levels the evening before the disaster, but failed to issue a warning.

THE *ELEKTRON* OFFICES are not much to brag about. Dirty windows, cracked tile floors, retail space being used as a reception area, and reporters and staff crammed into small spaces. A small TV studio hides behind a door with a tattered Keep Out sign.

In short, it is a typical regional newspaper office anywhere in the world. As it should be. It's not about appearances, it's about product. And even for the product, actually, appearances are clearly not the main thing. Frankly, the paper is a bit off-putting, full of eye-jarring ads, self-help columns, tightly-spaced text and ads, TV listings, and endless real estate listings in plain text.

But for all that *Elektron* is something of a paper of record, running long interviews and Q&As, or full transcripts of press conferences in which an official, as Safronova put it, often hangs himself with his own words.

Safronova is the paper's brisk talking editor. She has been here since the beginning and is insistent that *Elektron* is an independent paper that does not suffer censorship and has not come under any outside pressure. Somewhat provincial in her views (not really accepting that public breast feeding or handicapped accessibility are important issues), she says she is not wild about the government in power, nor is she particularly taken with most modern Russian journalists, whom she divides into two camps: journalists and "fatty beings with flippers" (it is her own word play on журналисты → жырноласты). Journalists ask tough questions, she says; *zhirnolasty* simply toe the government line. "The old papers are just the same as they used to be," she says. "Only their communist era names have changed."

When Mikhail asks why there are not more independent papers like *Elektron*, Safronova attributes it largely to laziness. People prefer an easier life, she says. They just don't want to do the hard work of journalism; it really has nothing to do with pressure from the top or censorship.

Yet she does note that, at *Elektron*, the younger journalists seem more optimistic than those of her generation. "They don't have the memory of the Soviet era," Safronova says. "We tend to look at things more critically."

But not too critically. She mentions the case of Valery Donskoy, who arrived to work for the holding's radio station just prior to the flood of 2012, and who was instrumental in reporting its effects to the outside world. She says his reporting was sometimes too heavily critical, too negative. "We used to fight, and I would say to him, 'You can only criticize what you love, what you want to improve.' No one needs criticism based in hatred. It leads nowhere…"

AFTER OUR CHAT, we offer to take Safronova to lunch if she will recommend a good place to eat. She agrees, but only if she can interview us over the meal.

The food is good, but the interview is exhausting. Safronova has the habit of asking a question, then not waiting for an answer before piling another one on top of it. As a result, in her article she attributes to me things I clearly would never say (and does not credit Mikhail's invaluable role as an equal partner in the book). Indeed, she seems less interested in hearing about what we have seen and heard on our trip, than in sussing out why an American would be so interested in Russia.

On that score, Safronova concludes in her article that one of the more rational explanations is that I am a spy.

> Paul introduces himself as Pavel and speaks excellent Russian (with a light, pleasant, un-American accent), smiles a lot, is open, and constantly joking. Could he be an American spy? Yes, easily. Today it is easy to suspect any tourist from the US of this, and even more so a journalist, for whom curiosity and endless questions are a fundamental part of their profession.

> Yet I think it is not worth suspecting ill from a person who has spent 20 years, in issue after issue of his magazine, describing for Americans our country, and talking not of bandits and oligarchs, but of great Russian writers and artists, of our history. Perhaps Paul Richardson is one of the few people in America who can be considered a friend of Russia. I want to believe this.[45]

She ends the article noting that, while our trip's blog does not seem to be negatively disposed toward Russia, that danger does lurk… She restates the common Russian trope that outsiders have no right to criticize Russia, no matter how well intentioned… But rather than paraphrase her point, I will, as she says, let her words speak for themselves.

> As we say goodbye, I warned Paul that Russians can themselves criticize their country as much as they like, but if foreigners do this, they should be prepared for our fierce and justifiable indignation. One can only criticize what one loves, only that which you want to change for the better; anything else will be taken as

mockery or spite. You don't need to dissect Russia, its structure, in order to show "you have a metastasis here, and here too." It is our mother, we know all about her ills. Exposure will not heal her… We will not trust her to some foreign doctor, even theoretical recommendations are unnecessary. Our own are already tearing off pieces of her and hiding them somewhere abroad, therefore we are doubly cautious toward foreigners.

Do not be deceived, Paul, by our warm hospitality, our willingness to speak from the depth of our souls. One bad word from your mouth about Russia can instantaneously turn you from a friend into an enemy.[46]

AFTER LUNCH, WE drive around the town a bit, to see how the rebuilding since the flood is going. Mikhail points out where the river channel has been widened and cleaned (brush growing in the river bed exacerbated the flood) and where it has not. We see buildings destroyed by the flood that have yet to be razed, and others that are rebuilt and re-inhabited. I look at the aging structures still standing and wonder silently how much was done to eradicate mold and mildew after the waters receded, or if the ensuing decades will see an epidemic of asthma and other respiratory ailments.

At one point, as we stand by the river, considering photographic vantage points, a middle-aged local approaches us.

"Can I ask what brings you here and what you are photographing?" he asks.

I (being a spy) of course take this as a sign of local suspicion of outsiders, but Mikhail strikes up a conversation and it turns out the man thinks we are here from Moscow or Krasnodar (clearly evidenced by Mikhail's shirt emblazoned with "VERMONT"), surveying the damage for the government. This part of town borders a section of the river that has not been touched, and the man seems to be hoping that we are here to do something about it.

After we leave Krymsk, the flat plains give way to small, wooded hills. We ascend a long crest and then drop down into a wide valley, where we are greeted by sweeping fall views stretching almost to the Black Sea.

Then, suddenly, near the valley floor, there are hillsides filled with vineyards. This is a good sign, because this evening we are staying in the guest cottage of a "garage winery."

The Vintner

We pull to the side of the road by a large school in Anapa. A faded banner extolling Cossack virtues flaps against the wall of the main building. Two boys and their mother trot through the yard with a soccer ball, heading toward the field beyond. To our south and west the sky is beginning to open up in anticipation of a stunning Golden Hour.

Mikhail puts in a call to the vineyard we are staying at this evening. He gets final directions and we head back toward the eastern edge of the valley, where we see the winery's entrance, flanked by a curved wall emblazoned with the words Semigorye ("Seven Hills") Estate. We edge up the long drive, slowing for a flock of geese, admiring the quaint setting with ponds, cottages, and stucco and thatched roof buildings.

As we pull in near the restaurant building, the owner, Gennady Oparin, 54, comes out to greet us. Middle aged, wearing a stylish beret, jeans, and a Ralph Lauren jacket over a fleece vest and red crew neck sweater, he exudes confidence and contentedness. Either he is putting on airs of a twenty-first century Russian country gentleman, or this is in fact what he is. He seems anxious to take us on a tour of his property, but Mikhail, aware of the fading light, insists on an immediate vineyard portrait backed by the now brilliant skies. Oh, and could Oparin please go in and get a bottle of his red wine to pose with?

The light is changing minute by minute, and not for the better. Oparin wants to start telling us the story of his vineyard, but Mikhail needs him to stand quietly and strike just the right pose with the bottle. We can't quite get the tilt and angle right. The sky darkens and a cool breeze is coming up. Mikhail asks Oparin to take off his jacket and vest, leaving just his light red sweater. Oparin obliges and, after five more minutes that seem like fifteen, the shoot is done. Mikhail rushes off to capture more shots of the property and workers, while Oparin shows me around.

BORN AND RAISED in the Urals, Oparin began working in the wine business in the 1990s, importing and trading with five partners, introducing boxed wine to Russia and at one point, he says, selling up to 25 million liters per year. But, as regulations became more onerous, he decided to leave that business, buy some land, and get directly into winemaking. Semigorye Estate was founded 10 years ago and today covers 13 hectares. It includes two restaurants, several cottage accommodations, and a small bottling facility. Recently, he says, they sold off a vineyard parcel to pay for construction and expansion.

Indeed, the property is an assemblage of unfinished construction projects: a long faux adobe wall, a large outbuilding with an impressive barrel and tent roof profile, a second outbuilding cut into the hillside, expansions of production and storage facilities. And, 20 kilometers up the road, Oparin says, they are also building a "Wine Village," where 20 local, small-scale winemakers will unite to show off their production at a tourist type attraction.

At present, however, Oparin and other small winemakers are in a bit of a bind. The law, he says, allows them to create wine for personal use, but not sell it. That right is reserved to larger, factory-scale wine producers. So Oparin crafted a loophole whereby he offers meals, banquets and accommodation at his winery, and a requested amount of his wine is included in the price of said hospitality.

A related reality, Oparin notes, is that the fine for selling wine is "just a little one": 2500 rubles ($40). This can be easily amortized when a bottle of wine is selling for R500. What is more, Oparin adds, one can purchase a "patent" that allows them to operate without a cash register. "Without a cash register, there is no instance of a sale," he smirks, "no basis for opening a case."

"Russians have a saying," Oparin says, "Russian laws are strict, but their execution is not required."

"So you will exploit that?" Mikhail asks.

"Everyone exploits it," Oparin replies. "That is our strength, Russians' that is."

The business is profitable, Oparin says, helped by a very "democratic" tax of just 6 percent.

"What produces the most profit?" Mikhail asks. "The restaurant, the wine, the accommodations?"

"That which produces the most is the satisfaction that we are working and providing unique services for society. This is the greatest profit. Personal satisfaction, satisfaction in quality. We are reinvesting all our money. Money is just a tool for us, something with which to solve problems."

Oparin's hope is that the law will soon be changed and small producers like Semigorye can expand from "garage wine" into small-scale boutique wineries.

The use of the term "garage wine" Oparin borrows from *garagistes*, a movement in France in the 1990s that focused on extremely small lot production and intensive, non-mechanized labor that uses only the grapes on one's own land. But whereas the movement in France was a reaction to traditional Bordeaux wine and its long aging period, for Oparin it seems to be mainly a reaction to the restrictive laws on alcohol production.

OPARIN LEADS US into the dome-shaped restaurant building and to some comfortable couches next to an extinguished stove, beneath a high, vaulted ceiling. An affectionate cat nuzzles our legs as a waitress brings out glasses of Semigorye Estate's 2013 Cabernet Sauvignon.

Yes, a Russian Cabernet.

There is also an unfiltered 2015 Sauvignon Blanc.

The vines, Oparin explains, are mainly from France, but, due to "recent unpleasantries," they are lately being supplemented by grafts from Serbia.

The Cab seems to have been brought up from the basement storage, because it is slightly chilled and in need of warming and resuscitation. But once it has extracted the heat from my palms and been swirled for several minutes, it proves to be a very hearty, well-rounded red wine. No, it does not have the luscious bouquet of a Napa Cabernet, but it is a very respectable wine that easily outdoes $10 or $15 Argentinian or Australian reds.

The Sauvignon Blanc, meanwhile, leaves me unimpressed. It is harsh and uninteresting.

Oparin is largely his own winemaker, though he does admit to having a consultant come in twice a week and help him with the serious laboratory stuff.

I want to tell him he should get some help in to deal with the fruit flies that are buzzing about, interfering with our enjoyment of his fruity Cab, but I hold my tongue out of politeness, hoping that he will notice my demonstrative hand movements.

BEFORE OPARIN CAME along, this area was dominated by three *kolkhozy* (communal farms) that, he says, produced rather respectable wines and were very well off. They went under, Oparin says, not as a direct result of the Gorbachev-era anti-alcohol campaign ("Gorbachev never said anything bad about wine… it was all about hard liquor") or some mass eradication of vineyards, but because of neglect and indirect economic effects: in the early 1980s the government simply stopped making proper investments in the wineries that would have kept production going, and thus the *kolkhozy* never received any direct benefit from the profits they brought the State. Vines that died out were not replaced; the system was assaulted by hidden inflation and the payments crisis; the State squeezed everything it could from the farms; eventually the vineyard operations collapsed in on themselves.

Further negative changes that ensued in the 1990s, Oparin says, can be squarely blamed on American consultants. They came into the Russian market with the evil intent of crippling Russian winemaking.

"It was back in the 1990s, when we lost the war to the Americans, I mean the Third World War. They put in place your CIA agents, who set up our government and dictated what sorts of reforms we needed, what kinds of laws and how to write them. And, it is just my personal opinion, but I think they also said 'What do we need Russian wine for? We have France, California… that's enough.' …They bought up all the breweries, as early as back in 1992… beer, chocolate, vodka, brandy… and they said 'to hell with wine…' "

Later, as we relax with wine and talk expands onto larger political issues, Oparin rattles on at length with stream of consciousness elaborations that include warped perceptions about the Marshall Plan (Soviet involvement was halted because Truman did not know anything about it before FDR died), and the Soviet regime. It was thanks to the Bolsheviks, he says, that the country was transformed from a backward nation of paupers into the one first into the cosmos. "Of course there were defects, but nothing horrific... as to concentration camps, well the US had them too [for the Japanese in WWII], but the victors don't write about them..."

His praise of the Soviet system gone by leads me to ask what sort of worldview Russia has to posit in opposition to that of the West. In reply, he lauds at length American achievements, yet says that "I believe that Russia is the future of the world." What that means exactly, he does not express, instead reviewing Soviet achievements in education, industrialization and the cosmos. Yet near the end of our discussion he does offer a telling summary: "I lived a good part of my life in that [Soviet] era and now have lived through this era. I would not say that we need to return there, but the quality of life in that era was exceptional. Not the living standards, but the quality of life... we lived an active, interesting life in the 1970s... Now nothing remains, everything is destroyed."

WE OVERNIGHT IN an oddly-constructed bungalow (two beds separated by a bathroom whose walls do not stretch to the ceiling, ensuring a noisy wakeup) 40 meters from the restaurant. The setting is picturesque, overlooking a pond, steep hillsides and the fog-covered vineyards.

It is difficult to make anything like a full assessment of this place, with all the construction going on, the fact that we are here in the off season, and the reality that they had a big party yesterday for National

Unity Day. Clearly Oparin is trying to reproduce a bit of quaint French countryside in the heart of Krasnodar Krai, but there is a lack of spit and polish, and a touch of the bizarre.

One of the restaurant bathrooms features a ceramic squat toilet. Downstairs, in the cask and storage area, there are large open vats of grapes that get stirred daily (thus the fruit flies), and both downstairs and up wine is arranged in shelving units with something just short of abandon – different vintages stacked atop one another in bottle pyramids four or five feet high.

Still, the vineyard is in a pretty location, perched on a hillside looking out over a valley that runs down to the Black Sea. Oparin suggests at one point that his venture in Anapa is like what Napa was 20 or 30 years ago. It is a stretch, but there is something interesting about an independent winemaker trying to make something of his piece of land, in a world that may not be quite ready for a Russian Cabernet crafted on a terroir still brimming with Soviet nostalgia.

AFTER A FILLING breakfast prepared by a friendly Dagestani cook (he brags of being able to cook all the major world cuisines – French, Mexican, Georgian, Russian – but serves us eggs sunny side up with hashed potatoes and peppers), we set course for the Black Sea Coast.

The drive takes us through a flat valley of vineyards (and, in Rayevskaya, what appears to be a huge golf course in the making). The vineyards are ripe and rich with fall oranges and yellows.

A bit further on, as we move through some rolling hills dotted with livestock, we come to a very new looking, well-organized facility surrounded by barbed wire. At first I think it is a prison, but it turns out to be a military base. For the next several miles we are surrounded by the facility, passing through a proving ground, a tank testing area and other incomprehensible things. Along the side of the road are signs I easily understand: "No trespassing, we're shooting at things here."

I wonder what the four comrades from FMS would say about this situation and I puzzle why a public road is passing through the middle of a military base.

The Sailor

An hour or so later, we arrive in Novorossiysk, an industrial port that lies on a narrow bay surrounded by steep hills crowned by a thick fog. The slopes would be picturesque, had they not been carved into massive limestone staircases to supply the town's cement plant.

Smoke rises from bayside factories. A few boats ply the harbor, but there is far less traffic than one might expect at this, the largest Russian port on the Black Sea. Russia has invested significant sums to build a naval base that was supposed to be completed here in 2012, but apparently construction is dragging on. Some 80 naval ships are eventually to call this their home port, but we see just one. There are, however, several tankers tied up out in the bay – this port is the busiest oil port on the Black Sea; a major pipeline from the Caspian terminates here.

Yet we have come to this major port not to learn about military or commercial shipping, but private boats. There is not a single one on the water.

We drive to the Yacht Club to meet Andrei Pletnyov, 50.

Pletnyov has a military bearing, belying his status as a member of the naval reserves, and an ironic, jargon-rich storytelling style, often ending his sentences with an accelerating up-lilt, as if cresting a wave before swooping down again to continue his tale.

He is the sort of captain/fixer/mechanic I expect can be found at any boatyard around the globe: a collector of stories, friends and, of course, boats. He has nine going on 10. The longest is 25 feet. "A sailor should never have more boat than he can handle," Pletnyov sagely advises.

We walk over to the *Oryol*, a 25-foot metal hull with a bent propeller and a ripped up, scorched exterior. It looks like it lost a fight with a massive can opener.

"This is what happens when you don't listen to ship owners or ship pilots, when you don't have brains in your head," Pletnyov says. In four months, he claims he'll have the boat repaired better than new.

As we chat, about a dozen young sailors in blue overcoats walk past. They are from the local Ushakov Institute, which trains young sailors. Today they are going to go out in crews of six with an instructor to learn to pilot a 10-meter sailboat.

Pletnyov has been a ship's pilot (*sudovoditel*) for 30 years. It all began in 1976, when he was 9 and his 22-year-old uncle told his mother he should do something, not just loll about. So the uncle took him down to choose a boat, to learn to sail.

He picked out a little red sailing dingy, a two-meter Optimist class boat designed for youth solo sailing. He took to it immediately, and soon won second place in the local Champion of Russia competition. But when they looked him over to be part of the regional team to train for Olympic competition, it was decided his vision was not good enough for competition sailing.

So he left solo sailing and joined up on teams that sailed larger boats. Back then, he says, in order to sail from, say, Novorossiysk down the coast to Gelendzhik, you had to apply a month ahead of time and were carefully monitored by border guards the whole way. He soon got bored with this, because it was too hard to sail anywhere interesting.

So he got involved in mountain climbing, on which there were no such restrictions.

By 1989, things were changing and travel restrictions loosened, so he decided to get back onto the sea, collaborating with a couple of friends to take people out day sailing. They soon found they could earn as much in a day as their parents earned in a month, even after splitting the "salty money" evenly. He has been doing this, plus some boat repair, piloting and general marine yard work, ever since.

WE MOVE INDOORS, to a glass-walled cafe overlooking the harbor. No nautical themes here. The tablecloths have pink flowers and there are silver lamps with pink lampshades. A large flat screen TV hovers over one corner of the bar, and we struggle to get the owner to mute the volume for half an hour so we can hear each other talk over tea.

Outside, the Ushakov sailors tack back and forth in the windy bay. We catch sight of two heads bobbing in the water, a half-dozen yards off shore – apparently extreme weather swimmers.

Crazy people are everywhere.

There is no problem sailing anywhere now, Pletnyov says, particularly for smaller vessels. You just have to keep harbor and other authorities informed of where you are going. Now it is a matter of wanting to keep people safe on the water, rather than penned in behind the Iron Curtain, he says. If you have an AIS (Automatic Identification System), you can even sail through the night. Otherwise, you are supposed to pull into port before dark and communicate your coordinates.

"So why are there not more sailors?" we ask.

"Because for 70 years they [the Soviets] excluded people from the sea," he says.

Add to that the lack of infrastructure. In all of Russia, he says, there are just three good yacht clubs, one in Novorossiysk, where we met, one in Sochi, and one in Balaclava, Crimea (recently annexed to Russia, but not yet recognized internationally as part of Russia).

Without dockside facilities for food, repairs and fuel, private boating will not develop on the Black Sea, Pletnyov says. In fact there are many places along the coast where you can sail for 100 miles without dockside refueling stations. So, he says, some sailors have to drop anchor, walk up to the road with gas canisters, and hitch a ride to the nearest gas station. The problem is no less serious for sailboats, he says, which may not need gas, but their sailors do need fresh water.

It is therefore no surprise to hear Pletnyov say what he would like to change, to make his community, his country, better: "I would like for... every family to have a boat! We have no fewer bodies of water than the Greeks, but whereas on the weekend the Greeks... all go out on the sea... we, for our population of 300,000 have just 300 boats. How is that?"

AFTER OUR CHAT, we drive down the embankment to see some of the monuments lining the shore, and to stroll along the very wide, pleasant pedestrian walkways.

Pletnyov, who has been introducing us all morning as "an American spy and his Russian minder," tells us that the reason the embankment ("expensive real estate") is not built up is because there are the remains of an old nuclear bunker beneath our feet. The echo with Voronezh has me feeling like I am living inside the famous quote normally attributed (wrongly) to Mark Twain: "History does not repeat itself, but it does rhyme."

We look at a monument to all who died on the sea, and at a new work that commemorates the 1920 departure of White Russian forces from Novorossiysk (the Whites held the city for nearly two years in 1918-20). The sculpture is based on the poignant final episode of the

1968 film, *Two Comrades Served*,* starring Vladimir Vysotsky, where the actor's character is fleeing with White forces in Sevastopol, but his horse (perhaps symbolizing Russia) refuses to follow, although he does jump in the water, pointlessly swimming after the departing boat. This crushes Vysotsky's character, who then uses his last bullet on himself, and his lifeless corpse plunges over the side of the boat.

Improbably, as we stand looking at the equine monument, a woman comes trotting by on a horse. It is so out of place on this industrial embankment that we don't know what to think. Mikhail tries to capture her picture, but she turns away.

Elsewhere in the city, I later learn, is the only monument in Russia to Leonid Brezhnev, who fought here against the Nazi occupation. It is a laconic statue and among locals it bears the nickname, "Man walking in the city." I feel almost sad we missed it, as if seeking it out and finding it might have been an adventure unto itself, particularly with Pletnyov's help.

On our way out of the city, we stop at a pharmacy to buy some motion-sickness pills. Mikhail has asked Pletnyov for his recommendations, what with his being a seaman, about what I should take to avoid getting nauseous on the serpentine road between here and Sochi. I have not asked for this, because I know I will be fine. But Mikhail insists, and we drop R80 ($1.20) on Avia-More, which I later learn is a homeopathic drug. Which may be why it made me gag.

---

* *Служили два товарища.*

The Serpentine

A mobile espresso vendor has set up shop on the roadside over-look near the Novorossiysk city sign on the city's southern outskirts. We grab mochas and take in the beautiful panoramic view of the city and bay.

Then we head south and, after Gelendzhik, enter narrow canyons with vineyards and low mountains covered with orange and yellow deciduous trees. Shortly thereafter, the serpentine begins. The last 100 kilometers will be some of the hardest of our trip.

The two-lane road is like a 60-mile version of California's Highway One, only with ridiculously stupid Russian drivers and loads of smoke-belching semis thrown into the mix. Still, the driving is not so much harrowing as tedious. It takes about four hours and I drive much of it. On the last stretch, we switch and I nod off for about 20 minutes. Later, Mikhail reports that I was murmuring in my sleep: "Kukisvumchorr… Azimut… Kukisvumchorr… Azimut…"

I half believe him.

We arrive in Sochi at 6:12 PM with 5,651 kilometers on the trip odometer.

Google Maps says the distance between Kirkenes and Sochi is 4,539 kilometers and we should have been able to drive it non-stop in 59 hours. Needless to say, we have made numerous stops and did it in something more like 615 hours.

Zemfira's "Ne Otpuskay" is roaring through the car speakers.

We drop into a 2.5 kilometer tunnel, one of the new roads built for the Olympics, and then pop up in the middle of downtown Sochi. It feels exotic and almost Mediterranean, driving through the warm streets at twilight with the windows down. We find a pleasant restaurant right on the harbor, and order up a pizza. It is only our second pizza since the monster-pie in Norway, now 26 days ago.

We are not done with traveling, of course, but we have reached our final city. It is warm enough for shirtsleeves, and the pie is beyond delicious.

Life is good.

And then I get dragged off to an hour-long, 30-on-one interrogation by a local English language class, where the young students want to know everything from what it was like to visit the Soviet Union in 1981, to who my favorite authors and bands are, to how I have stayed married to the same woman for longer than they have been alive.

It turned out to be just the first in a series of ham-fisted attempts by my traveling companion to soften me up in anticipation of our final grudge match…

Above Sochi

Today's goal was to turn up the heat on the American.

Why do I say this?

Because it was made rather clear at the outset of this journey that said American has no evidence of inner ear fluids and thus is likely to suffer from motion sickness if he is (a) required to sit in the back seat of a car or be a passenger on serpentine or bumpy roads, (b) set afloat on a maritime vessel, (c) led to any sort of high ledge or precipitous lookout.

In spite of this, said American's Russian travel partner set up meetings in one day that involved (1) a visit to the world's longest (439 meter) suspension pedestrian bridge (which spans a 207-meter, vertiginously deep canyon) and (2) a forty-minute drive in a top-heavy UAZ through a boulder field that etches a steep, bone-jarring path up a mountain.

But I am getting ahead of myself.

Late in the morning, we drive up the new, multi-lane, Olympics-financed highway toward the ski resort town of Krasnaya Polyana. Partway there, we pull off onto the older, two-lane road that threads up through the valley, then turn off onto an unmarked, pockmarked cement road that goes nearly straight up the side of a mountain, through tiny settlements with stunning views, past little boys selling persimmons by the side of the road.

We are heading up to the Skypark, an adventure tourism attraction built by a New Zealand company to terrify Russians (and the occasional foreigner). The point is not actually to visit the park, but to meet Nikolai Polyakov, who for 16 years has been developing an adventure tourism business with his wife and partner, Inna Didenko. Today's theme is family businesses. And crazy people.

Polyakov and Didenko have been hired by Skypark to expand its range of offerings, because apparently the 69- and 207-meter bungee jumps and the death-defying free-fall swing across the abyss are, well, rather "special interest." So they are looking to branch out into things like Via Ferrata (tethered rock climbing) and canyoning.

Polyakov is a fireplug of a guy, about 5' 6" and 150 pounds of pure muscle. He loves the region's rich outdoor offerings, and has been investigating, arranging and managing group tours here since the late 1990s, when he wrote his degree on developing extreme tourism in the Sochi area.

He has worked for the Ministry for Emergency Situations, spent 10 years climbing mountains, and, in the build-up to the Olympics, guided surveyors and geologists, helping them do their work around the region's difficult terrain.

Now, aside from his work at Skypark, he is back to setting up special adventure tours, mainly for Russians (foreign clients are just 10 percent of his business in summer, 30 percent in winter). It means spending a lot of time with maps, looking for and investigating the best routes tailored to visitors' special needs, so that they can achieve things they could not do on their own. And Polyakov appears to know his stuff. "We have had up to 250 people in the mountains at one time and in over 16 years of work we have never had an emergency situation. We always get good feedback. It's all about preparation."

Their goal, Polyakov says, is to be a balanced company. "Growth is not the be all and end all," he says. "We want to be in several regions: here, Crimea and Abkhazia." Uncontrolled growth, he says, would probably mean he would end up spending all his time at a desk, and that's not what he wants.

"This is work that makes me happy," he says. "The main thing is balance… that is what helps me create possibilities for others."

MIKHAIL WANTS TO take Polyakov's picture at the other end of the 439-meter Skybridge. Okay, I say, I'm game. It's just a bridge, right? Sure, it spans a gaping chasm, but it is surely well-engineered and does not look at all scary from here (200 feet away, downslope).

We lope up into the large lounge area and then out onto the platform that leads to the bridge. So far so good.

There is some commotion near the bridge entrance. A couple is getting ready to launch on the SochiSwing, which is where they tie you into a harness, whose bungees are anchored about halfway across the bridge, and then they pull the floor out from under you, so that you go swinging off 170 meters over the abyss in a half-kilometer-wide arc. Fun, right?

I begin to make my way down the stairs to the bridge and start inching across, being careful not to look down or alarm anyone about the distressful situation we are all in. I look at the strangely calm

Russians passing me in either direction. They don't seem to be the least bit worried about their predicament, quite the opposite, in fact. Some are not even holding onto the railing, which I am grasping firmly in my white-knuckles.

I get about 20 feet across the bridge (Mikhail swears later it was only about five feet, but he is prone to wild exaggerations, like all Russians) and decide that will be plenty far, thank you very much. This bridge is rocking and gyrating in ways I am pretty sure a suspension bridge should not. And yet, strangely, I seem to be the only one who recognizes the precarious nature of the situation.

I slink back up to the platform, heading for the comfort of coffee and a couch. On my way up the stairs, the couple in the swing drops into the abyss. Predictably, they scream. I marvel at the amazing diversity of the human species.

As I sit in the lounge, safely distant from the ledge, I watch the comings and goings of the crowd. Most are far younger than me, and yet there is a small minority who I can immediately recognize as fellow travelers. They walk through the lounge confidently, as if there is no question that of course they will traverse the narrow metal bridge. But, then, about three feet from the edge they pause. They pull their hand from their partner's grasp and slow down, circling around and away, in order to watch the death-defying action from a safer distance. Some time later, while they wait for their partner to return ("Oh, you go on without me, honey, I'll be just fine here. I'll get a coffee or something.") they join me on the couches and we share a knowing smile that speaks multitudes: "We are the sane ones."

The Soap Makers

This is not a road.

At best it is an assemblage of rocks, gravel, and boulders that have gathered in anticipation of the next glacier. In the very distant, unknowable future they have the potential of forming a very rough goat path.

But it is not even the inkling of a road. And it is certainly not something humans should attempt to traverse by motor vehicle, particularly one that is basically a loaf of bread on wheels.

"Буханка" (Breadloaf) is the popular nickname for the vehicle we are riding in, the UAZ-452. It is also sometimes called a Таблетка or Пилюля (Tablet or Pill), because it is often used as a medical vehicle. Strangely, none of the nicknames connote an ability to cling to mountainsides or keep from tipping over on steep, rocky terrain (for instance, "Mountain Goat" would be reassuring). But certainly they are durable 4x4s. They have been in continuous production since 1965, a feat unmatched by any other Russian vehicle.

Still, none of this offers much comfort as we climb the boulder field to visit our second family business of the day.

"How often do you have to change the tires?" I yell, for some reason feeling a need to make conversation with the driver, who is but a Gaussian blur to my left.

"Once per season," he shouts back (the ride may be bumpy, but at least it is also loud), and then proceeds to rattle off some incomprehensible, slang-filled praise of the vehicle's prowess while swerving around boulders the size of corpses.

Forty minutes of gut twisting, spine crunching travel later (distance covered: four km), we pull into the village of Medoveyevka, on the top of a mountain in the middle of the Caucasian Nature Preserve. There are at most a dozen houses here, but one stands out. It is a beautiful three- or four-story lodge that features modern construction, welcoming lighting, and whimsical design touches. It looks as supremely out of place here as Versace in Vermont.

I have just one thought: "How did they get it up the mountain?"

INSIDE, LICENSE PLATES hang from the wood-shingled walls, and wide oak flooring gives the lodge a warm, inviting feel. Pendant lamps accent the wide bar, and a selection of craft beers line the back wall, alongside large jars of homemade tea and selected liquors.

Yet we are not here because of the lodge. Not in the main, anyway.

We settle in behind a wooden table, order tea and chat with Kristina Suderevskaya, who seven years ago turned her back on a Moscow career in banking and fled with her husband Dima to these mountains outside Sochi.

To make soap.

"We were living in Moscow," Suderevskaya says, "and someone gave me a gift of homemade soap. I tried it, and, well, I could not sleep after that." Soon after the couple's first child was born, they decided to flee the megalopolis, move to an "ecologically clean" area of the country, and set up their soap making enterprise.

That was seven years ago, before the 2008 economic crisis. The lodge has only been open for a year. "My husband and I started with the soap making," Suderevskaya says, "and then our friend wanted to do something here, and he said, 'Let's open a pub with good food.'" So they built OLD Boys, which is a pub, a restaurant featuring natural food products, and a B&B with four cozy guest rooms.

Yet, Suderevskaya says, building the lodge was very expensive, as everything had to be brought up the mountain.

You don't say?

BEFORE SUDEREVSKAYA AND her husband arrived, before the Soviet Union collapsed, Medoveyevka was home to a thriving *kolkhoz*. There was even a time, Suderevskaya says, when there were more residents in Medoveyevka than Krasnaya Polyana, the booming ski resort recently transformed into an Olympic Village – the Tahoe of the Caucasus.

Just 50 Medoveyevka residents remained when they moved in, and their family's business has started to have a positive economic effect on the village, Suderevskaya says. Others are creating related businesses, including hotels. Some who were partners have become competitors, she smiles.

While the isolation is the attraction for visitors, and a selling point for the soaps (and creams), which use local herbs and bank on the association of the mountains with purity, it makes hiring staff a challenge.

In all, about eight people work in the soap making side of their business, and the same in the lodge/pub side of things.

"It is hard to get people to come up here to work," Suderevskaya says. "Nothing is close by and the sort of people who have the right attitude and insight, the people you would like to hire, are the same people who are going to leave earliest to start out on their own. Plus it is difficult to get people to live in the village and the villagers, they really don't want to work for us… You have to understand, a village by its nature is a closed society."

So what motivates them? "We are restless sorts," Suderevskaya smiles. "We need to do something." The business, she admits, is not highly profitable, and they reinvest everything they can to make it sustainable for the long term. "I feel a responsibility toward the staff we have hired," she says. "Our success is dependent upon whether we can create a structure that can work without our constant involvement, something that will not collapse in our absence." She says they feel they have achieved that sort of self-sustenance in the soap making business (kpsoap.ru), but it is still a ways off with the lodge and pub.

"Perhaps," Suderevskaya says, "this is because soap making has very exacting requirements in its production process. It demands good planning and process control." With the pub and B&B, she says, "it is very important that the collective work like a family. We can't have problems occurring that keep them from being good hosts, like bickering amongst themselves or being in a bad mood."

Around 5 PM, the pub starts to fill up with about a dozen patrons, likely back from day-hikes in the area, from trips to local waterfalls, to circuits that take in the statue of Prometheus or the beautiful lookout tower. It is a lively crowd. We enjoy Caucasian style burgers (with sulunguna cheese and spicy Caucasian sauce with cilantro), followed by a sampling of exotic preserves the family is adding to their product line.

Later, after dragging the whole family out into the woods for a portrait in the fading light, we are again sitting in the pub, waiting for the UAZ to return so it can ferry us down over the floe of boulders to Kukisvumchorr.

The pub is humming by now, largely thanks to Suderevskaya's family and extended family, when a fellow named Alexei stops in to share the first taste of this year's wine, which he has harvested and bottled on his small acreage in Anapa. He has brought in one bottle each of his white and red wines, both marked with the date November 1, 2015 – six days ago. Alexei makes about 200 bottles a year and calls his red wine Cabernet Anapa.

It is a nice, mellow Cab without much in the way of floral bouquets or nose, but very smooth and mild. Alexei is proud to proclaim that the wine contains nothing but grapes. No water. No additives. Just grapes and a bottle. He says he took up the hobby because he loves wine but just can't drink what they sell in stores, what with all the stuff those wineries put in their bottles.

His organic ethos brings to mind Suderevskaya's response when we asked her what she would like to change about her business.

"I want," she says, "to find people who will to be invested in this work because they want it to be done right, people who, in the process, will bring new ideas to the business…"

The Outlier

Technically, the city of Sochi (or Greater Sochi as it is sometimes called) stretches for 145 kilometers along the Black Sea coast. The towns hugging the coast along the serpentine are called microdistricts of the city as a whole, which gathers together about 400,000 residents.

Also technically, the region became part of the Russian empire in 1829, yet it took about 30 or 40 years for the tsar's troops to subdue and/or eradicate the local Circassian (and Abkhaz and Ubykh) population. The area began to be settled by outsiders in the late 1860s, and its first resort was planted here just over a century ago, in 1909. Throughout the Soviet era, it grew in significance as a southern vacation destination, increasing the local population from around 13,000 after the Revolution to nearly 300,000 by the late 1970s.

But the real turning point for Sochi came on July 4, 2007. On that day it was announced that Sochi had beaten out Salzburg, Austria and Pyeongchang, South Korea, and would, in less than seven years, host

Russia's first-ever Winter Olympic Games. Russia committed to spending over $12 billion on the effort, but actual expenditures have been estimated at over $50 billion, making it the most expensive games ever.

To say that the city was transformed by the 2014 games would be an understatement of Olympian proportions. Seven years of round the clock construction turned this sleepy Black Sea town of resorts and natural wonders into a world-class sports megalopolis with broad freeways, gleaming shopping zones, a massive Olympic Park, and a world-class ski resort in Krasnaya Polyana, just a 30-minute drive up into the mountains.

The park in Adler, a district about 20 minutes from downtown Sochi, is a sprawling monument to Olympic excess. It has wide, impressive plazas that echo Stalinist monumentalism and open onto the broad reaches of the Black Sea. An ample boardwalk lines the waterfront, protected in places by huge boulder breakwaters (the seas can surge a dozen feet here during storms). The crashing and recession of the waves across the round, smooth pebble beach releases an eerie murmur that sounds suspiciously like applause.

Getting into the park's center is a bit of a challenge, as someone has gone overboard with protective fencing. One reason for this could be the Formula One track that now sits in the middle of the park, filling the subtropical air with the roar of hyper-tuned engines and the squeal of fattened tires (audible until at least 11 PM some nights). It is one part of Russia's answer to "what do you do with Olympic facilities after the games are gone?" Until at least 2020, Sochi will host Formula One Grand Prix races. Other parts of the answer: the large open-air Fisht Stadium is a training center for the Russian national football squad and will host matches in the 2018 World Cup; Adler Speed Skating Arena has been turned into a tennis center and was the site of the finals for this year's FedCup; the Bolshoy Ice Dome is home ice for the Sochi Hockey Club. And that is why we are here.

CONVENTIONAL WISDOM WOULD give at least three reasons we should not be meeting with Sochi Hockey Club's PR Director Kseniya Tsukareva, 28.

First, Sochi is not a place people should be playing hockey. It is a subtropical city of beaches, palm trees and outdoor cafes. Football or tennis? Of course. Hockey? Don't be ridiculous.

Second, Tsukareva is female, and sports management is a heavily male-dominated arena. Russian sports perhaps more so.

Third, Tsukareva is a Ukrainian war refugee.

This is clearly an Outlier situation: Tsukareva has gotten where she is – against all odds – not by trusting in convention, but by force of will and hard work. And a little bit of luck.

Tsukareva has been involved in hockey since 2009, when she was employed as PR director in an effort to create a hockey club in another non-hockey town – the southern Ukrainian city of Donetsk. Their objective was to build a vertically-integrated operation, from youth players to pros, that would eventually build the team up to the Kontinental Hockey League (KHL) level, the top tier in the post-Soviet space.

They expected their effort to take 10 years. Yet within three, they had qualified the team for the KHL – no mean achievement. Then, two years later, war came pounding.

Ukraine has always been linguistically and culturally split between the Ukrainian-speaking, agricultural West and the Russian-speaking, industrial East. But in March of 2014, soon after Russia's annexation of Crimea, anti-Kiev separatists, funded and supported by Moscow, began military actions to take over the southeastern part of the country known as the Donbass (Donetsk and Luhansk Oblasts), declaring the Luhansk and Donbass People's Republics and occupying government buildings by force.

In the spring of 2014, Tsukareva remembers. "Everyone thought it [the war] would be over in a few days," she says, "then in a few weeks." But it dragged on.

Late in the spring, the team's hockey arena was destroyed by the fighting. It was, Tsukareva says, "a symbol of everything we were trying to create," and it was demolished beyond saving. She fell into a funk, then a depression. Finally, in July, she and her husband, who worked as a spokesperson for the club, decided to leave the team.

Her husband started making calls to KHL teams, but of course everyone already had the personnel they needed. Then, by chance, they heard that a team was being started up in Sochi. A lucky call to just the right person at just the right time, and a door opened. Her husband was offered a job.

Driving directly east from war-torn Donetsk to Russia's Krasnodar Krai was not an option, so the couple drove in their tiny compact car via a long, circuitous route north and then east. "We were one of the last cars to get out of the city," Tsukareva recalls.

Tall and dark-haired, with a ready smile and open manner, Tsukareva exudes optimism and grit. "When we first arrived here," she says. "They said they did not need me. But I didn't have another job, so I said I would just show up and work for free, and help out." Yet it didn't even take a day for her to realize that the team – created largely at the instigation of hockey legend Pavel Bure, which helped secure access to the Bolshoy Stadium – had no idea what it would take to get into the KHL. The team needed Tsukareva as much as she needed them. By early September, both she and her husband were on staff.

Of course, creating a team was one thing, filling a 12,000 seat arena another altogether, to say nothing of setting up all the required marketing, sales, back office systems and sponsorship deals. By the end of the first year of operations, there were financial difficulties and other snafus, and a new general manager was hired – a former major general in the police. He cleaned house, clearing out the excess staff who had seen the club as an easy meal ticket.

"A hockey club is an expensive pleasure," Tsukareva notes. "When we got started, everyone naturally assumed it was a Putin project, and that one sponsor would follow another and we would be swimming in *babki*" [money]. But reality has been quite different.

Tsukareva recalls how she was once stopped in Sochi for speeding and the cop asked what she did for a living. "I said I worked with the hockey club," she says. To which the cop replied, "So what are you driving a crappy little car like this for?" She replied frankly, "Because I am not a hockey player!"

The club is now in its second year and Tsukareva says she is optimistic that by the end of their third season, their financial troubles will be behind them, that they will have lined up the sponsors without which any professional sports team is doomed. Attendance is averaging about 5,200 fans per home game – "the atmosphere of a match really depends on the number of fans," she notes, "even a good match can be boring if there are not enough fans," and the team is rising in the rankings. In its first year it finished in 13th place and made it into the playoffs (as eighth seed among eight teams, that meant it had to face off against top-ranked CSKA, to whom they lost 0-4). In its second year it finished in fourth place, but again lost in the first round of the playoffs (0-4 to Dinamo Moscow).

Meanwhile, the team runs a tight budget. "Unlike in the NHL," Tsukareva says, "in Russia the business and sports side of things don't mix. Sport is Number 1… and the two sides don't really talk to each other." This is a legacy of the Soviet era, when clubs were all state-owned.

That raises one of the biggest issues Tsukareva feels Russian hockey must grapple with if it is going to be viable long term: "The price of players has gone up, but the clubs don't yet know how to earn more money to pay them." Thus, they need to find a way to change the mind-set of fans, so that they will be willing to pay ticket prices comparable to what they are in the US – e.g. $1,000 for Stanley Cup tickets. At present, tickets are R200-600 ($3-10), and it costs a family of four just R2,000 ($35) to attend a match (including meals and transport). That may not seem like much, but an average monthly salary in the region is just R35-40,000 ($600-700).

Needless to say, there is a lot on the plate of the Deputy General Director for Marketing and Public Relations at Sochi Hockey Club. Tsukareva says she has to have her fingers in everything, from verifying how ticket sellers are working to the quality of food on sale, because the quality of every little thing reflects back on the fan's whole experience.

And, given that there is no budget for her department ("Any start-up should invest 30-40 percent of its budget in PR and marketing. I have zero to one percent," she grins), it requires a bit of thinking outside the box.

"My mom is my control fan," she reveals. "After a recent match, I asked her how the food was, and she said, 'Oh, I was going to get some-thing to eat, but the line was too long and I didn't want to wait.' So, we need to work on that."

The End

This is how it ends.

Prior to our final interview, with Kseniya Tsukareva, Mikhail set up his tripod along the rocky shore and we took a picture of us standing in the Black Sea, to be counterposed with our selfie taken almost a month prior, up on the banks of the Barents Sea (which we were only brave enough to dip our hands into).

After that interview, we drove into Sochi and had a big final feast, at a very nice Georgian restaurant in the center, then strolled around the port and downtown, trying to walk off our excessive consumption of *khachapuri*.

As the light was fading, we drove back to our hotel in Adler, the comfortable Azimut Sochi hotel, a complex so huge that its restaurant is a separate building, 200 meters away.

As fate would have it, right next to the hotel was a basketball court, and the concierge was kind enough to rustle up a basketball. Mikhail and I thus decided that hoops would be the decisive US vs. Russia match of this trip. If you recall, Russia won at billiards, the US at ping-pong, so basketball was to be our rubber match.

We warm up a bit, and I feel pretty confident about the situation, watching Mikhail's layup form, yet I am wary about my shoes. I brought along just one pair of shoes for this trip. They are good for hiking and street walking, but they do not belong on a basketball court. So I declare there will be no one-on-one. Instead, I will teach him how to play Horse.

Mikhail is not happy, but he learns the game and we play it out, with America winning by a letter, maybe two.

This is where a sound mind, reasoned diplomacy, and good judgment would have left things. But, as I believe I have noted previously, Mikhail can be persistent, and he is not satisfied. "Horse is not basketball," he insists, "we need to play one-on-one." He, I should note, is wearing sneakers.

Stupidly, I give in.

"Okay, one game to five," I say.

I'll just take it easy, I tell myself. No heroics… The problem is, what Mikhail lacks in form, he more than makes up for in tenacity. And height. He's got two or five inches on me. And, let's face it, the pride of two nations is at stake.

The score stands tied at 1-1. I rebound and take the ball around the free-throw line. Then I throw a head fake and lurch around Mikhail, opening a clear lane to the hoop. But my left foot lands strangely and I feel something give way. Or rip open. Or apart. I drop the ball and limp off in excruciating pain, trying to walk it off. It does not help. This is not just a sprain. I have ripped something in my heel, perhaps my Achilles.

Game over.

I hobble to the restaurant, angry for having given in.

I will, in fact, hobble and limp all the way home, looking a bit like Kevin Spacey in *The Usual Suspects*, which, being the paranoiac I have become, has me worried it will make me look suspicious. But in fact the only trouble I have (other than the long, painful walks through endless airport corridors) on the way home is in JFK airport, when the 100 percent natural soap I have purchased in the mountains outside Sochi is flagged by TSA scanners, requiring my entire suitcase to be unpacked in a very public area and wiped down with those strange swabs.

I limp for about ten days and cannot walk without pain for about a month.

But I figure I got off easy. After just one day's rest, Mikhail (again with his saintly wife Nadya in the passenger seat) had to drive Kukisvumchorr back through the Black Sea Coast serpentine, then north to Moscow, to return it to the Volkswagen dealership that kindly lent him to us. It was a three-day, 1,800 kilometer drive, and it means that Mikhail effectively drove the entire Spine route twice (having driven Kukisvumchorr from Moscow to Murmansk at the outset).

But if there are scars and crosses to bear at the end of the trip, they are more than compensated for by our adventures of the past five weeks.

IT WOULD BE folly to attempt to draw some sort of grand or broad conclusions from this trip. Instead, the trip was filled with many small conclusions (or epiphanies) along the way, all of them shared in the pages above.

After all, we did not set out down Russia's "Spine" to arrive at Great Truths, but to get a feel for the breadth and depth of the Russian landscape, to ease into the places where people live, rather than dropping in by train or plane. In the end, we covered over 6,000 kilometers in 30 days (I wish we had had 50); we conducted in-depth interviews with 43 "heroes" in 22 cities and towns; we passed through three geographic zones (tundra, taiga, steppe) and visited five seas (Barents, White, Baltic, Azov, Black), innumerable lakes and forests, and were only stopped three times by traffic police – all without fines or incidents; we ate at least a dozen bowls of borshch, most of it reasonably good.

Our goal was to talk to people behind the headlines who are *doing* things, striving to make a better life for themselves and their world, people who prove that Russia is not all about Putin, vodka, *matryoshkas*, oligarchs and spies. We sought to see the people and places that tourists do not, and then take others there through our storytelling.

While ours was not a random sample, the people we spoke with from Nikel to Sochi nonetheless comprised a broad sampling of Russians who differed widely by age, occupation, location, and socioeconomic status.

Any stereotypes we might have begun the trip with were quickly obliterated. We met few barriers or hindrances. The people we became acquainted with were friendly, helpful, generous, and happy to share the stories of their lives. And most of the people we met were optimistic and imperturbable. They are the sort of restless, striving people who make things happen in any country. They are studiously applying the best experience from around the world to their undertakings, while adapting them to local, Russian needs. They generally have little interest in or patience with politics or politicians. They are tirelessly building the country that Russia is and will become.

We feel privileged that our "heroes" gave so generously of their time and showed us the world through their eyes. I can only hope that this book, indeed this entire project, adequately conveys the reality our heroes live in, and will in some small measure bring this book's readers in closer touch with Russia, its people, and its changing place in our world.

Endnotes

1. Clifton, Gallup, 21 April 2015.
2. *The Guardian*, 2 October 2015.
3. Granovsky, *Populyarnaya Mekhanika*, 5 February 2009.
4. Witte and Harcave, 196.
5. Richard, 17.
6. Willett, 133.
7. Ibid.
8. Ibid.
9. Vladimov, 355-6.
10. "Russia to Crack Down..." Marinelog.com, 11 July, 2011.
11. Solzhenitsyn, 6.
12. Haney, xviii, quoting Nechaev.
13. Bernshtam.
14. Bulatov.
15. Ekshtut.
16. ibid.
17. Applebaum, 67.
18. Applebaum, 70.
19. Vereykina.
20. Stroilov.
21. Kelly, 495.
22. UNESCO, 136-7.
23. Rankin, *Moscow Times*, 31 August 2012.
24. "Education Trends," UNESCO, 136-7.
25. Yoder.
26. Vernadsky, 20.
27. Ibid, 22.
28. Solzhenitsyn, 5.
29. Arkhipov and Meyer, Bloomberg, 13 May 2015.
30. Epple, Grozovsky, Apteka, *Moscow Times*, 16 April 2015.
31. Arkhipov and Meyer.
32. Epple, Grozovsky, Apteka.

33. Arkhipov and Meyer.

34. Sologub, 1915.

35. Lieven, 141-3.

36. King, 45.

37. Freeze, 339-344, in Kaiser, 1994.

38. "Социальное самочувствие," VTsIOM 2010; "Образ православного верующего," Carnegie 2012.

39. "Свято-Троицкий храм," Website of the Oryol Metropolia.

40. Yarovykh, *Orlovskaya Sreda Plus*, 2012.

41. Ibid.

42. Sapyrkina, "Authentic Stories of the War," 2010.

43. White, 31-55.

44. Eidelman, *Russian Life*, November/December 2016.

45. Safronova, *Elektron TV*, 16-22 November 2015.

46. Ibid.

Select Bibliography

Applebaum, Anne. *Gulag: A History*. New York: Anchor Books, 2004.

Arkhipov, Ilya, and Henry Meyer. "In Putin's Russia, Universal Health Care Is for All Who Pay." Bloomberg News, May 13, 2015. http://www.bloomberg.com/news/articles/2015-05-13/in-russia-universal-health-care-is-for-all-who-can-afford-it.

Bernshtam, Tatyana. "Поморы. Формирование группы и система хозяйства." (monograph), 1978.

Bulatov, V.N. *Русский Север: учеб. пособие для студ. высш. учеб. заведений*. Moscow: Gaudeamus, 2006.

Chizhova, Lyubov. "Russian Medics Take On 'Destructive' Health-Care Reform." Radio Free Liberty/Radio Free Europe, November 4, 2014. http://www.rferl.org/content/russia-health-care-reform/26674311.html.

Chuev, Feliks Ivanovich, Vyacheslav Mikhaylovich Molotov, and Albert Resis. *Molotov Remembers: Inside Kremlin Politics: Conversations with Felix Chuev*. Chicago: I.R. Dee, 1993.

Clifton, Jon. "Russia Receives Lowest Approval in World; U.S. Highest." Gallup, April 21, 2015. http://www.gallup.com/poll/182795/russia-receives-lowest-approval-world-highest.aspx.

Conquest, Robert, and Rogers D. Spotswood Collection. *The Great Terror: A Reassessment.* New York: Oxford University Press, 1990.

"Education Trends in Perspective." UNESCO, 2005. http://www.uis.unesco.org/Library/Documents/wei05_en.pdf.

Eidelman, Tamara. "Russian Calendar." *Russian Life*, November/December 2015: 23.

Ekshtut, Semyon. "Tuber or Not Tuber." *Russian Life*, September/October 2000: 28–31.

Epple, Nicole, Boris Grozovsky, and Pavel Aptekar. "Russian Health Care Is Dying a Slow Death." *The Moscow Times*, April 16, 2015. http://www.themoscowtimes.com/opinion/article/russian-health-care-is-dying-a-slow-death/519253.html.

Gogol, Nikolai Vasilyevich, Richard Pevear, and Larissa Volokhonsky. *Dead Souls.* New York: Vintage Books, 1997.

Goldstein, Darra. *A Taste of Russia: A Cookbook of Russian Hospitality.* 3rd ed. Montpelier, VT: Russian Information Services, 2012.

Granovsky, Yuri. "На пороге преисподней: Кольская сверхглубокая скважина." *Populyarnaya Mekhanika*, February 5, 2009. http://www.popmech.ru/science/8792-na-poroge-preispodney-kolskaya-sverkhglubokaya-skvazhina/.

Haney, Jack V., ed. *Long, Long Tales from the Russian North.* Jackson: University Press of Mississippi, 2013.

Hazzard Cross, Samuel, and Olgerd P. Sherbowitz-Wetzor, trans. *The Russian Primary Chronicle: Laurentian Text.* Cambridge, MA: Mediaeval Academy of America, 1953.

Heat Moon, William Least. *Blue Highways: A Journey into America.* 1st Back Bay. Boston: Back Bay Books, 1999.

Kaiser, Daniel H., and Gary Marker, eds. *Reinterpreting Russian History: Readings, 860-1860's.* New York: Oxford University Press, 1994.

Kasack, Wolfgang, Wolfgang Kasack, and Rebecca Atack. *Dictionary of Russian Literature Since 1917.* New York: Columbia University Press, 1988.

Kelly, Catriona. *Children's World: Growing up in Russia*, 1890-1991. New Haven [Conn.] ; London: Yale University Press, 2007.

King, Charles. *The Ghost of Freedom: A History of the Caucasus.* Oxford; New York: Oxford University Press, 2008.

Kolskaya Enciklopedia 1 1. Sankt-Peterburg: Inst. Sotsologii, 2008.

Kuzmin, Victor. "Big Western Beer Brewers in Decline on Russia's Market." *Russia Behind the Headlines*, October 21, 2013. http://rbth.com/business/2013/10/21/big_western_beer_brewers_in_decline_on_russias_market_30991.html.

Noack, Rick. "How Different Are Russians and Americans, Anyway?" *Washington Post*, December 7, 2014. https://www.washingtonpost.com/news/worldviews/wp/2014/12/07/how-different-are-russians-and-americans-anyway/.

Pidot, Justin. "Forbidden Data: Wyoming Just Criminalized Citizen Science." Slate.com, May 11, 2015. http://www.slate.com/articles/health_and_science/science/2015/05/wyoming_law_against_data_collection_protecting_ranchers_by_ignoring_the.html.

Rankin, Jennifer. "Education Reform Inching Forward." *The Moscow Times*, August 31, 2012. http://www.themoscowtimes.com/news/article/education-reform-inching-forward/467381.html.

Riasanovsky, Nicholas V. *A History of Russia*. 6th ed. New York: Oxford University Press, 2000.

Richard, Carl J. *When the United States Invaded Russia: Woodrow Wilson's Siberian Disaster*. Lanham: Rowman & Littlefield Publishers, Inc, 2013.

Riha, Thomas. *Readings in Russian Civilization*. Second. Vol. I. University of Chicago Press, 1969.

"Russia to Crack Down on Vessel Safety After River Cruise Tragedy." Marinelog.com, July 11, 2011. http://bit.ly/2011ship-medved

Safronova, Larisa. "Зачем им хребет." *Elektron TV*. November 16, 2015.

Sapyrkina, Maria. "Не верилось, что немцы могут захватить город…," December 3, 2010. http://www.world-war.ru/ne-verilos-chto-nemcy-mogut-zaxvatit-gorod/.

Sologub, Fyodor. *The Little Demon*. Translated by John Cournos. New York: Alfred A. Knopf, 1915.

Solzhenitsyn, Aleksandr Isaevich, and Yermolai Solzhenitsyn. *"The Russian Question" at the End of the Twentieth Century*. 1st ed. New York: Farrar, Straus and Giroux, 1995.

Stroilov, Pavel. "Revealed: The Kremlin Files Which Prove That Nato Never Betrayed Russia." *The Spectator*, September 6, 2014. http://new.spectator.co.uk/2014/09/russias-nato-myth/.

Vereykina, Elizaveta. "Rampaging Pseudoscience Turning Russia into 'Medieval State' — Q&A." *The Moscow Times*, September 8, 2015. http://www.themoscowtimes.com/news/article/rampaging-pseudoscience-turning-russia-into-medieval-state--qa/529301.html.

Vernadsky, George. *A History of Russia*. 6. rev. ed., 7. print. Yale Paperbound 43. New Haven: Yale Univ. Press, 1975.

Vladimov, Georgi. *Three Minutes' Silence*. London ; New York: Quartet Books, 1985.

White, Stephen. *Russia Goes Dry: Alcohol, State and Society*. Cambridge ; New York, NY, USA: Cambridge University Press, 1996.

Willett, Robert L. *Russian Sideshow: America's Undeclared War, 1918-1920*. 1st ed. Washington, D.C: Brassey's, 2003.

Witte, Sergei, and Sidney Harcave. *The Memoirs of Count Witte*. Armonk, N.Y: M.E. Sharpe, 1990.

Yarovykh, Kira. "Загадка разорения усыпальницы Ермоловых." *Orlovskaya Sreda Plus*. December 19, 2012. http://orelsreda.ru/zagadka-razoreniya-usy-pal-nitsy-ermolovy-h/.

Yoder, Audra Jo. "Making Tea Russian: The Samovar and Russian National Identity, 1832-1901." Miami University Masters Thesis Essay, 2009. http://rave.ohiolink.edu/etdc/view?acc_num=miami1240596270.

"В Смольном заинтересовались деятельностью атамана общества «ИРБИС» Андрея Полякова." St. Petersburg City Administration Official Site, n.d. http://gov.spb.ru/gov/otrasl/c_zakonnost/news/55482/.

"Образ православного верующего в современной России." Accessed February 20, 2016. http://carnegie.ru/events/?fa=3725.

"Свято-Троицкий храм г. Орла." Website of the Oryol Metropolia. Accessed February 21, 2016. http://www.orel-eparhia.ru/objects/deaneries/orel/svyattroic.

"Социальное самочувствие россиян и экономические реалии: непересекающиеся пространства?" VTsIOM Website, October 28, 2014. http://wciom.ru/index.php?id=268&uid=13365.

"Счетная палата раскритиковала реформу системы здравоохранения." Лента.ру, April 14, 2015. http://lenta.ru/news/2015/04/14/medicine/.

Acknowledgements

First and foremost, a heartfelt thank you to my traveling partner, the fine photographer, producer, driver and connoisseur of *melnitsas*, Mikhail Mordasov. Thanks for latching onto this crazy idea and for becoming a dear friend in the process. And to the amazing Nadya Grebennikova, for her trenchant commentary, excellent translations, and driving much of our route with (her husband) Mikhail to get Kukisvumchorr where he needed to be.

At the risk of neglecting to list some of the many people who helped us along the way, our trip owes a great debt to each of the following individuals for reasons only they and we can appreciate: Valery Alekseyev, Maria Antonova, Mary Ann Allin, Bob Barrett, Alexei Bayer, Elena Bobrova, Tatyana Bogomazova, Kristina Brazhnikova, Dmitry Chembartsev, Anna Chervyakova, Marcy De La Mare, Elena Dobrynina, Brian Erwin, Nora Favorov, Nicky Gardner, Darra Goldstein, Alexandr Gontar, Lisa Hayden, Charles Heberle, Anatoly Kargopolov, Sergey Karpov, Brendan Kiernan, Yulia Korchagina, Becky Kraemer, Robert Krattli, Annie Lucas, Ksenia Luchenko, Peter Morley, Thomas Nilsen, Mark Oettinger, Sofie Perelygina, Oleg Poltevsky, Monika Raab, Victoria Savchenko, Veronika Seliverstova, Anna Sergeeva, Eileen Shine, Daria Suboch, Sharon Tennison, Rick Walker, Laura Williams, Aigul Yangalina, Andrei Zelenov, Olga Zvyagina.

A special thanks is also due the nearly 400 backers who stepped in and backed our project when it was just an idea, pledging on Kickstarter to our crowdfunding campaign and then following our posts and progress along the way. These individuals are listed in *The Spine of Russia* coffee table book which is the journey's primary product, and for which this armchair travel book is a companion book. They are also listed on the project's website.

Last but far from least, I wish to thank my beautiful wife, Stephanie Ratmeyer, and my two ever-patient children, Sarah and Christopher. Thank you all for your tireless support – never sufficiently acknowledged but always appreciated – and for enduring countless discussions about itineraries and packing lists.

About the Author

Paul Richardson is a journalist and publisher.

Raised in southern California, he went to college and graduate school in Iowa and Indiana, respectively. He now makes his home in Montpelier, the capital of Vermont.

In 1990, after two years living and working in Soviet Moscow, Richardson founded a niche publishing company focused on all things Russian. Today the company publishes *Russian Life*, a bimonthly magazine on Russian culture, history, travel and life, as well as books, maps and calendars, and the literary journal *Chtenia*.

In his spare time, Richardson can usually be found running Vermont's roads, photographing its beautiful landscapes, or enjoying a dark cup of coffee (extra room for cream, please) or a hoppy IPA with friends.